Economics, Economists, and Expectations

The concept of rational expectations has played a hugely important role in economics over the years.

Dealing with the origins and development of modern approaches to expectations in micro- and macroeconomics, this book makes use of primary sources and previously unpublished material from such figures as Hicks, Hawtrey, and Hart. The accounts of the "founding fathers" of the models themselves are also presented here for the first time. The authors trace the development of different approaches to expectations from the likes of Hayek, Morgenstern, and Coase right up to more modern theorists such as Friedman, Patinkin, Phelps, and Lucas.

The startling conclusion that there was *no* "Rational Expectations Revolution" is articulated, supported, and defended with impressive clarity and authority. A necessity for economists across the world, this book will deserve its place upon many an academic bookshelf.

Warren Young is Associate Professor of Economics at Bar Ilan University, Israel. **Robert Leeson** is Associate Professor of Economics at Murdoch University, Australia. **William Darity Jnr.** is Cary C. Boshamer Professor of Economics and Sociology at the University of North Carolina, Chapel Hill, USA. Another of his books, *Boundaries of Clan and Color* is also published by Routledge.

Routledge studies in the history of economics

1 **Economics as Literature**
Willie Henderson

2 **Socialism and Marginalism in Economics 1870–1930**
Edited by Ian Steedman

3 **Hayek's Political Economy**
The socio-economics of order
Steve Fleetwood

4 **On the Origins of Classical Economics**
Distribution and value from William Petty to Adam Smith
Tony Aspromourgos

5 **The Economics of Joan Robinson**
Edited by Maria Cristina Marcuzzo, Luigi Pasinetti and Alesandro Roncaglia

6 **The Evolutionist Economics of Léon Walras**
Albert Jolink

7 **Keynes and the 'Classics'**
A study in language, epistemology and mistaken identities
Michel Verdon

8 **The History of Game Theory, Vol. 1**
From the beginnings to 1945
Robert W. Dimand and Mary Ann Dimand

9 **The Economics of W. S. Jevons**
Sandra Peart

10 **Gandhi's Economic Thought**
Ajit K. Dasgupta

11 **Equilibrium and Economic Theory**
Edited by Giovanni Caravale

12 **Austrian Economics in Debate**
Edited by Willem Keizer, Bert Tieben and Rudy van Zijp

13 **Ancient Economic Thought**
Edited by B.B. Price

14 **The Political Economy of Social Credit and Guild Socialism**
Frances Hutchinson and Brian Burkitt

15 **Economic Careers**
Economics and economists in Britain 1930–1970
Keith Tribe

16 **Understanding 'Classical' Economics**
Studies in the long-period theory
Heinz Kurz and Neri Salvadori

17 **History of Environmental Economic Thought**
E. Kula

18 **Economic Thought in Communist and Post-Communist Europe**
Edited by Hans-Jürgen Wagener

19 **Studies in the History of French Political Economy**
From Bodin to Walras
Edited by Gilbert Faccarello

20 **The Economics of John Rae**
Edited by O.F. Hamouda, C. Lee and D. Mair

21 **Keynes and the Neoclassical Synthesis**
Einsteinian versus Newtonian macroeconomics
Teodoro Dario Togati

22 **Historical Perspectives on Macroeconomics**
Sixty years after the 'General Theory'
Edited by Philippe Fontaine and Albert Jolink

23 **The Founding of Institutional Economics**
The leisure class and sovereignty
Edited by Warren J. Samuels

24 **Evolution of Austrian Economics**
From Menger to Lachmann
Sandye Gloria

25 **Marx's Concept of Money: the God of Commodities**
Anitra Nelson

26 **The Economics of James Steuart**
Edited by Ramón Tortajada

27 **The Development of Economics in Europe since 1945**
Edited by A.W. Bob Coats

28 **The Canon in the History of Economics**
Critical essays
Edited by Michalis Psalidopoulos

29 **Money and Growth**
Selected papers of Allyn Abbott Young
Edited by Perry G. Mehrling and Roger J. Sandilands

30 The Social Economics of Jean-Baptiste Say
Markets and virtue
Evelyn L. Forget

31 The Foundations of Laissez-Faire
The economics of Pierre de Boisguilbert
Gilbert Faccarello

32 John Ruskin's Political Economy
Willie Henderson

33 Contributions to the History of Economic Thought
Essays in honour of R.D.C. Black
Edited by Antoin E. Murphy and Renee Prendergast

34 Towards an Unknown Marx
A commentary on the manuscripts of 1861–63
Enrique Dussel

35 Economics and Interdisciplinary Exchange
Edited by Guido Erreygers

36 Economics as the Art of Thought
Essays in memory of G.L.S. Shackle
Edited by Stephen F. Frowen and Peter Earl

37 The Decline of Ricardian Economics
Politics and economics in post-Ricardian theory
Susan Pashkoff

38 Piero Sraffa
His life, thought and cultural heritage
Alessandro Roncaglia

39 Equilibrium and Disequilibrium in Economic Theory
The Marshall–Walras divide
Michel de Vroey

40 The German Historical School
The historical and ethical approach to economics
Edited by Yuichi Shionoya

41 Reflections on the Classical Canon in Economics
Essays in honor of Samuel Hollander
Edited by Sandra Peart and Evelyn Forget

42 Piero Sraffa's Political Economy
A centenary estimate
Edited by Terenzio Cozzi and Roberto Marchionatti

43 The Contribution of Joseph Schumpeter to Economics
Economic development and institutional change
Richard Arena and Cecile Dangel

44 On the Development of Long-run Neo-Classical Theory
Tom Kompas

45 **F.A. Hayek as a Political Economist**
Economic analysis and values
Edited by Jack Birner, Pierre Garrouste and Thierry Aimar

46 **Pareto, Economics and Society**
The mechanical analogy
Michael McLure

47 **The Cambridge Controversies in Capital Theory**
A study in the logic of theory development
Jack Birner

48 **Economics Broadly Considered**
Essays in honor of Warren J. Samuels
Edited by Steven G. Medema, Jeff Biddle and John B. Davis

49 **Physicians and Political Economy**
Six studies of the work of doctor-economists
Edited by Peter Groenewegen

50 **The Spread of Political Economy and the Professionalisation of Economists**
Economic societies in Europe, America and Japan in the nineteenth century
Massimo Augello and Marco Guidi

51 **Historians of Economics and Economic Thought**
The construction of disciplinary memory
Steven G. Medema and Warren J. Samuels

52 **Competing Economic Theories**
Essays in memory of Giovanni Caravale
Sergio Nisticò and Domenico Tosato

53 **Economic Thought and Policy in Less Developed Europe**
The 19th century
Edited by Michalis Psalidopoulos and Maria-Eugenia Almedia Mata

54 **Family Fictions and Family Facts**
Harriet Martineau, Adolphe Quetelet and the population question in England 1798–1859
Brian Cooper

55 **Eighteenth-Century Economics**
Peter Groenewegen

56 **The Rise of Political Economy in the Scottish Enlightenment**
Edited by Tatsuya Sakamoto and Hideo Tanaka

57 **Classics and Moderns in Economics Volume I**
Essays on nineteenth and twentieth century economic thought
Peter Groenewegen

58 **Classics and Moderns in Economics Volume II**
Essays on nineteenth and twentieth century economic thought
Peter Groenewegen

59 **Marshall's Evolutionary Economics**
Tiziano Raffaelli

60 **Money, Time and Rationality in Max Weber**
Austrian connections
Stephen D. Parsons

61 **Classical Macroeconomics**
Some modern variations and distortions
James C.W. Ahiakpor

62 **The Historical School of Economics in England and Japan**
Tamotsu Nishizawa

63 **Classical Economics and Modern Theory**
Studies in long-period analysis
Heinz D. Kurz and Neri Salvadori

64 **A Bibliography of Female Economic Thought to 1940**
Kirsten K. Madden, Janet A. Sietz and Michele Pujol

65 **Economics, Economists, and Expectations**
Microfoundations to macroapplications
Warren Young, Robert Leeson and William Darity Jnr.

66 **The Political Economy of Public Finance in Britain, 1767–1873**
Tukuo Dome

Economics, Economists, and Expectations

Microfoundations to macroapplications

Warren Young, Robert Leeson, and William Darity Jnr.

Routledge
Taylor & Francis Group
LONDON AND NEW YORK

First published 2004
by Routledge
2 Park Square, Milton Park, Abingdon, Oxfordshire OX14 4RN
Simultaneously published in the USA and Canada
by Routledge
711 Third Avenue, New York, NY 10017
First issued in paperback 2012
Routledge is an imprint of the Taylor & Francis Group

Typeset in Times by Wearset Ltd, Boldon, Tyne and Wear

British Library Cataloguing in Publication Data
A catalogue record for this book is available from the British Library

Library of Congress Cataloging in Publication Data
A catalog record for this book has been requested

ISBN 978-0-415-08515-1 (Hardback)
ISBN 978-0-415-64732-8 (Paperback)

Contents

Preface

In his centenary address to the Royal Economic Society in November 1990, Sir Alec Cairncross said that "of all kinds of human behavior, the forming of expectations seems to me particularly rich in irrational elements" (1991: 9). Over three decades after the initiation of the "Rational Expectations Revolution" in macroeconomics most economists who teach and utilize the rational expectations approach would probably question this. For was not the "Gordian knot" – as Simon called it in his 1978 Nobel lecture (1979: 505) – of modeling expectations formation in economic models "cut" by Muth's description of expectations as "the same as the predictions of the relevant economic theory" (1961: 316). And was not this "revolution" brought about through the "rediscovery" and application – by Lucas and others – of the rational expectations approach as it "first" appeared in Muth's "overlooked" 1961 paper, thereby bringing it into the mainstream of economics in the 1970s and 1980s?

The fact that most economists would accept these statements – which reflect the conventional account of the origin and development of rational expectations – illustrates one of the main problems in modern economics. This consists of a distinct lack of knowledge and interest among many in the economics profession, especially concerning questions of the type "what, when, where, why, and how" regarding the origins and development of the core concepts they teach and utilize daily. Our concern with "what, when, where, why, and how" with respect to the origins of the concept of rational expectations is not merely to set the historical record straight, although that is important. Rather, a reconstruction of the development of rational expectations facilitates a close inspection of the issues at stake in economic theory and practice. Looking backward is far from solely a question of documenting who was first, i.e. who was the originator, but the motives of the researchers for pursuing this line of work, the intellectual problems identified by those who promoted the development of rational expectations and those who resisted its development, the issues that have been forgotten, and the promising paths taken as well as the promising paths that were forsaken. As is well known, there are two fundamental types of expectations formation: exogenous and endogenous.

The former encompasses expectations based upon survey data collected from consumers or producers, or are derived from exogenous data, such as short- and long-run rate of return differentials. Spontaneous shifts regarding optimistic or pessimistic expectations ("animal spirits") are also considered exogenous. Endogenous expectations formation, based upon what has been called "model consistent theory", is inherently part of the economic model itself. Among these are adaptive, rational, implicit, and quasi-rational expectations. This book focuses upon endogenous expectations formation with special reference to the development of rational and implicit expectations.

In fact, as we will try to show, there are at least three approaches researchers have taken regarding rational expectations. There are those who see it as an economic *axiom* and an applicable basis for *both* micro- and macroeconomic expectations formation, albeit not *directly* testable; others accept the possibility of its applicability and testability at the microeconomic level, but doubt its applicability at the macroeconomic level; and finally there are those who *reject a priori* its applicability at both micro- and macroeconomic levels. Rational expectations was essentially a "solution in search of a problem". The problem emanated from the breakdown of large-scale Keynesian macroeconometric models and their predictive failure as gauged by turning point errors, due to their inability to adequately deal with inflation and inflationary expectations. Indeed, at the time, better short-run and turning point forecasts were obtained from statistical approaches, such as Box-Jenkins ARIMA models. Rational expectations came to the rescue of macroeconomics and especially macroeconometrics in the form of, as Frank Hahn once put it, "3 equation log-linear models". More substantively, there was no presumption that anything like rational expectations was relevant to aggregative or macroeconomic analysis at that time. It was not until after the belief became pervasive that macroeconomics required microfoundations of the neoclassical optimizing variety that RE became the cornerstone technique for specification of expectations within macro models, that is to say, aggregative relationships had to be built up from individual optimization.

Now, in the specification of the typical macroeconometric model what was usually practiced was a pseudo-aggregation where the postulated behavior of a single "representative agent" was generalized to all to construct the consumption, investment, or money demand function. Real world heterogeneity of economic actors was eschewed in favor of the simplifying assumption that everyone is basically the same. This practice extends readily to the use of RE as a basis for modeling expectations. All economic actors usually are assumed to share the same structural model as a machine for generating expectations that are consistent with the model; consequently they all hold an identical rational expectations of whatever variable must be forecast for them to reach an optimal decision, whether it be the inflation rate, the rate of growth of the money supply, or the term structure of interest rates. The possibility that there are a multiplicity of models from which expectations are formed, does not enter into standard macroeconometric practice. Nor does the possibility that individuals may find it necessary to anticipate the actions of other actors who are simultaneously seeking to anticipate their behavior enter into standard macroeconometric practice either. Of course, the latter slice of reality generally renders the construction of a mathematical (and model consistent) expectation intractable (see, e.g. Frydman, 1982).

In Chapter 1, after a brief survey of the contributions of Hayek (1928), we go on to discuss the attack by Morgenstern (1935) on the early Hayek–Hicks approach to expectations (1933). In the second section of this chapter we go on to present the unpublished exchange between Hicks and Hawtrey in 1939 over the nature of expectations and Hick's notion of "detailed forecasts" and the "elasticity of expectations". The third section of this chapter deals with the previously overlooked relationship between game theory and RE as seen in the work of von Neumann (1928) and von Neumann and Morgenstern (1944) and that of Nash (1950), and Simon's critique of this approach. The fourth section focuses on what we maintain are the actual bases for the development of the RE approach at the microeconomic level. These involve the expectational problems thrown up by the "Cobweb Theorem", and how they were handled by Buchanan (1939) and others, such as Coase and Fowler (1935a, 1935b, 1937), Goodwin (1947), Hooton (1950) and Newman (1951), and in the overlooked work of Samuelson (1957) and Lindahl (1957) on price expectations and inflation.

Chapter 2 outlines the treatment of entrepreneur's and firm's expectations by Fisher (1896) and Knight (1921), and presents Hart's "research agenda" (1949) in detail, based upon his work from 1937 onwards. It also presents the approach of Modigliani (1949) and the link between this and later expectations research programs. Chapter 3 then focuses upon the various expectations research projects in the US and UK during the 1950s and 1960s and shows how they formed the context within which the RE approach on the microeconomic level of Muth and Mills developed. In this connection the work of Machlup, Nerlove, Lovell and Hirsch, Simon and Modigliani, and others in the US and Richardson in the UK will be surveyed and the relationship between the work of some of these key personalities in the treatment of expectations and the approaches of Muth and Mills will be established and explained. This will be done by utilizing both published material and correspondence from Muth and Mills and those who influenced them and their work – including Nerlove, Lovell, and Simon and Modigliani, among others. This chapter also deals with the impact of the Public Finance and Money Workshops at the University of Chicago and the contributions of Laidler, Meiselman, Holmes, and Bailey to the application of expectations.

Chapter 4 deals with the work of Muth and Mills from 1954 onwards and compares their pathbreaking approaches to that of Tinbergen, who is shown to be a precursor of Mills, rather than Muth. This chapter also surveys Muth's previously overlooked 1957 lectures at Chicago on "dynamics and uncertainty". Chapter 5 deals with what could be considered the most enigmatic part of the RE story at the microeconomic level, that is the presentation of Muth and Mill's paper on rational and implicit expectations at the December 1959 Washington meeting of the Econometric Society and the reactions of those economists who were present or were influenced by these papers before the "RE revolution in macroeconomics" even took place. In addition, this chapter focuses on the aftermath of the 1959 contributions of Muth and Mills, that is the application of RE in microeconomics in the period 1959–69 and the microeconometric testing of rational and implicit expectations and its outcome.

Chapter 6 surveys the work of Patinkin and its relationship to RE in the context of the "Chicago approaches" to expectations of Knight and Stigler, among others. Chapter 7 focuses upon expectations in the context of the "monetarist counter-revolution" in macroeoconomics, and the application of adaptive and rational expectations by Friedman, Phillips, and Lucas. In the "overview and conclusions", we describe some alternatives and extensions to RE in closed and open economy models, as suggested by Muth himself and Nerlove such as the "errors in variables model" and "quasi-rational" expectations, in the closed economy, and "theories consistent expectations" in the open economy case, as developed by Goldberg and Frydman.

Acknowledgments

The authors wish to thank all those whose correspondence is cited in this work for their assistance in our attempt to put together the story of modern "expectational economics". Special thanks must go to: John Muth, Edwin Mills, Mark Nerlove, Mike Lovell, Edmund Phelps, David Laidler, Albert Hart, and Herbert Simon. Mark McGillivray also greatly assisted our efforts to get the Muth–Mills–Tinbergen story straight.

Many thanks are also due to Alan Jarvis and Rob Langham at Routledge for bearing with a decade-long project, which has only now come to fruition.

We also wish to thank Duke University Press for permission to use material already published by Warren Young and William Darity Jr., "The early history of rational and implicit expectations" in *History of Political Economy*, Volume 33, No. 4, pp. 773–813, 2001.

Abbreviations

AER	*American Economic Review*
EJ	*Economic Journal*
JASA	*Journal of the American Statistical Association*
JEL	*Journal of Economic Literature*
JPE	*Journal of Political Economy*
QJE	*Quarterly Journal of Economics*
RES	*Review of Economic Studies*

Introduction

It is commonly asserted that the monetarist anti-Keynesian counter-revolution introduced adaptive expectations into macroeconomics (via the "natural" rate of unemployment model) and that its sequel, the New Classical anti-Keynesian counter-revolution, performed a similar cleansing task with the introduction of "rational" expectations. Having claimed the linguistic high ground ("natural" and "rational") for these counter-revolutions the textbook writers have followed suit with this assertion.

The conventional chronology is that (a) Milton Friedman's 1967 AEA Presidential Address transformed macroeconomics by focusing on the neglect of expectations in the Keynesian Phillips curve and (b) John Muth's 1961 paper was neglected prior to the new classical counter-revolution in the mid-1970s. Muth, it was asserted, may have had a few precursors, but after Friedman it was Robert Lucas (1976) who further thrust expectations onto center stage.

Moreover, even the writers of textbooks on the history of economic theory and "comprehensive" studies of rational expectations have succumbed to this tempting counter-revolutionary assertion (see for example, Landreth and Colander 1994; Blaug 1997; Niehans 1990; Redman 1992; Pesaran 1987; Hamouda and Rowley 1988).

The following chapters demonstrate that prior to the monetarist and new classical counter-revolutions, the problem of expectations was at the forefront of economic inquiry both in the US and elsewhere. Expectations had received extensive treatment by members of the "Stockholm School", such as Myrdal, Lundberg, and Lindhal; by Dutch economists such as Tinbergen; by English economists, such as Pigou, Robertson, Hawtrey, Keynes, Harrod, Hicks, and Shackle; and also by economists of Austrian origin, such as Hayek and Morgenstern, among others (see Chapter 1).

The monetarist counter-revolution took one of the variables (inflationary expectations) that macroeconomists had hitherto believed to be important and burdened it with the entire force of equilibrating adjustment. Thus policy makers could safely double unemployment and move the economy out along a short-run Phillips curve. The resulting divergence of approximately 0.5 percent between actual and expected inflation would adjust the entire macroeconomy back to the natural rate of unemployment. The new classical counter-revolution took the same variable (inflationary expectations) and asserted that monetarists had understated the anti-mainstream case: disinflation could be costless. The empirical evidence for either proposition was – and is – non-existent. The assertion that inflationary expectations had been neglected by the economics mainstream is also, as we shall demonstrate below, entirely without foundation.

This monistic preoccupation with expectations has not proven fruitful. The cost of disinflation in the United Kingdom in the 1970s and 1980s, for example, was much greater than anticipated by the expectations counter-revolutionaries. With respect to a central policy implication of new classical macroeconomics, Robert Lucas confessed that "Monetary shocks just aren't that important. That's the view I have been driven to. There's no question that's a retreat in my view" (cited by Cassidy 1996: 55). Also, Thomas Sargent's (1993: 21–2, 28) essays on *Bounded Rationality in Macroeconomics* involved a self-conscious "retreat from rational expectations". It is time to reassess the role that expectations played in mainstream economics before being usurped by these counter-revolutionaries.

It is also time to acknowledge that A.W.H. Phillips, the author of the original curve that was the object of so much counter-revolutionary derision, played a pioneering role in the analysis of expectations (adaptive expectations in particular) and also developed a version of what became known as the Lucas critique years before Lucas (see Chapter 7 below).

Muth presented his famous paper at the 1959 Econometric Society meeting. A decade earlier there had been an important development at the December 1949 AEA meeting. In the intervening decade three projects and conferences addressed the role of expectations: the Research Project on Business Expectations and Planning at the Bureau of Economic Research of the University of Illinois (1949–52), the 1954 Federal Reserve task force groups on expectations and statistics and the 1955 Carnegie Tech conference (see Chapter 3 below).

Even before the 1949 AEA meetings, there were important integrating works on expectations by Pigou (1927), Hayek (1928, 1937), Tinbergen (1932, 1934), Hicks (1933), Kaldor (1933–34), Coase and Fowler (1935a, 1935b, 1937), Morgenstern (1935), Lindhal (1939), Buchanan (1939), von Neumann and Morgenstern (1944), Marschak (1946), Machlup (1942a), and Hurwicz (1946).

Between 1949–59, there was a veritable explosion of work further integrating expectations into economics: Eisner (1958), Ferber (1953, 1955, 1958), Modigliani and Sauerlender (1955), Friend and Bronfenbrenner (1950, 1955), Marschak (1950), Nash (1950), Mills (1954–55), Hahn (1952), Richardson (1953, 1956, 1959, 1964), Machlup (1952), Samuelson (1957), Lindahl (1957), Grunberg and Modigliani (1954), Modigliani and Weingartner (1958), Hurwicz (1950, 1951), Bossons and Modigliani (1960), and others.

The decade from 1959–69, that is, what we call "the missing decade", is replete with *seminal* works on rational and implicit expectations on the microeconomic and microeconometric levels (Mills 1961, 1962; Nerlove 1961a, 1961b; Negishi 1964; Radner 1967, 1968; Hirsch and Lovell 1969), but most of these studies, which influenced those who brought rational expectations into macroeconomics, have been forgotten or overlooked (see Chapter 5 below).

Lionel Robbins (1976: 39) referred to "the extraordinary provincialism in time of much contemporary professional literature". This provincialism has not merely impoverished economic thought but has contributed to inadequate policy outcomes. An unmistakable conclusion that emerges from the "monistic expectations" episode is that we must pay more attention to the dynamics of our own subject (Leeson 2000a).

1 From Hayek to Vernon Smith

Prices, the cobweb, and game theory

Hayek, Hicks, Kaldor, and Morgenstern

In the decade between 1928 and 1937, Hayek developed an approach to expectations which still stands as one of the most original – albeit controversial – aspects of his overall approach to economic analysis. Much has been written about Hayek and Hayekian economics, and also about *general* aspects of his treatment of expectations, and it is not our intention to survey this material here. What has *not* been surveyed, however, are the *specific* characteristics of his treatment of expectations which highlight the originality of his approach, that is the distinction he made between *level* of expectation, the way in which he distinguished between *types* of foresight and the *link* he made between equilibrium, foresight, and expectations (Hayek 1928; 1933). For example in *Monetary Theory and the Trade Cycle* (1933) (originally published in German in 1928) Hayek asserted that given a large number of independent producers with individual views regarding future price, then their errors of pessimism and optimism would cancel each other out thus producing equilibrium output. While this somewhat "impossible result" was later criticized by, among others, Rosenstein-Rodan (1936) and Coase and Fowler (1937: 73), Hayek was perhaps the first to differentiate in this and subsequent work (Hayek 1935) between the individual agent (micro) and the aggregate (macro) aspects of expectations. For example, in an overlooked paper published in 1935 in *Nationalokonomisk Tidskrift*, Hayek distinguished between equilibrium and foresight regarding "complete" economic systems as against "certain" prices, such as interest.

In his now classic 1937 paper "Economics and knowledge", Hayek went even further by establishing a connection between what he called "correct foresight" and equilibrium, treating the former as "the defining characteristic of a state of equilibrium" and distinguishing it from the case of "perfect foresight". Moreover, Hayek provided a framework for what could be considered an "expectational equilibrium" by asserting that equilibrium existed *only* during the period when expectations *were* correct (1937: 36, 41–2). Furthermore, Hayek delineated an additional category, which he termed "relevant foresight", asserting that for a state of equilibrium to be maintained, expectations needed "to be correct only on those points which are relevant for the decisions of the individuals" (1937: 2). Finally, Hayek focused on the role of expectations as *primus inter pares* with regard to equilibrium analysis and the problem of "constancy of data". He said that in order to "include changes which occur periodically or perhaps even changes which proceed at a constant rate" the only way of defining "constancy" was with reference to expectations" (47–8). But, as in the other focal points of his treatment of economics, Hayek's approach to expectations was overshadowed by that of Keynes, and thus, even though it was taken over and synthesized by Hicks (1933, 1939a) into a Walrasian general equilibrium framework, as will be seen below, it remains until today a somewhat overlooked aspect of his contribution to economics.

Hicks, Kaldor, and Morgenstern

As in Hayek's case, the general treatment of expectations put forward by Hicks in *Value and Capital* (1939a) [below *V&C*] is well known and will not be repeated here. What has *not* received attention, however, is the *specific* approach to expectations he proposed in his 1933 paper "Gleichgewicht und Konjunktur" ("Equilibrium and the trade cycle" (Hicks 1980)), its relationship to Hayek (1928) *and* Tinbergen (1932), and Morgenstern's (1935) overlooked critique of it on the one hand, and his *unpublished* debate in correspondence with Hawtrey over his 1939 *V&C* treatment of expectations, on the other hand.

In his 1933 paper among other things Hicks focused on the link between equilibrium and expectations. Indeed, to get around the " 'famous fiction' of the Stationary State" as characterized in the general equilibrium system, Hicks pointed to the work of Knight (1921), Hayek (1928) *and* Tinbergen (1932) in which account *was* taken, in the production processes they described, "of the influence of future (expected) as well as current prices" on behavior. Moreover, according to Hicks, by "confining attention to stationary equilibrium, we can set future prices and present prices equal to one another, and so make the equilibrium determinate". He went on to say, "however, the economic data vary, there will always be a set of prices which, if it is *foreseen* [our emphasis], can be carried through without supplies and demands ever becoming unequal to one another and so without expectations ever being mistaken. The condition for equilibrium, in this widest sense, is Perfect Foresight. Disequilibrium is the Disappointment of Expectations" (1933 [1980], 525–6).

In his own seminal *RES* paper entitled "A classificatory note on the determinateness of equilibrium", Kaldor (1933–34) also dealt with Hicks' 1933 treatment of expectations and especially the linkage between foresight, anticipations, equilibrium, stability, and "static" as against "dynamic" analysis. Kaldor identified what he took to be the two basic and "implicit" assumptions of "static analysis" as "all independent variables remain constant through time" and "all individuals expect the prices actually ruling to remain in force permanently: no price changes are anticipated" (1933–34: 123). To this he added in a footnote, referring to Hicks' 1933 paper

> Just because the dependence of equilibrium on anticipations is not always clearly realised, this assumption is hardly ever expressly stated although it is inherent in any type of static analysis which aims at demonstrating the tendency towards equilibrium independently of the degree of foresight. The only alternative assumption consistent with the degree of abstractness necessary for the generalisations of pure theory would be the assumption of *complete foresight* [italics in original]: that everybody foresees correctly the future course of prices. In this latter case, however, there is no need to assume constancy of the independent variables in order to show the determinateness of equilibrium: and consequently this latter assumption can be more conveniently adopted as the basis of a "dynamic" as distinct from a "static" type of analysis.

Kaldor concluded that "instability in the real world then appears as the result of *wrong* [italics in original] expectations (1933–34: 136) and added in a footnote to this, again referring to Hicks' 1933 paper

> Whether in any actual case anticipations will be in the right direction or not will depend partly on the nature of the change and partly on the efficiency of the institutions of the market whose function it is to anticipate future price movements. Given the forecasting ability of a speculative market, anticipations of future price-changes are as a general rule much more likely to prove correct when they are due to localised causes than when they are of a more general "monetary" character.

Now, the passages cited above have been referred to by a number of economists, as has Morgenstern's (1928) earlier critique of "predictability in economics". What is much less known, however, is the severe criticism leveled by Morgenstern (1935, [1963]) at the position advocated by Hicks (1933) regarding equilibrium, foresight, and expectations. For, in an article entitled "Perfect foresight and economic equilibrium" originally published in 1935 in the *same* journal (*ZFN* – in German) Morgenstern not only took issue with the position Hicks advocated, but asserted that it was completely mistaken!

In his critique, Morgenstern not only asserted that "full" and "perfect" foresight were synonymous, but he employed both terms, as he put it "in the essentially more exact sense of *limitlessness*" (1935, [1963]: 45). According to him, "full", "perfect", or as he defined the case "unlimited" foresight involved an "insoluble paradox" characterized by "*an endless chain of reciprocally conjectural reactions and counter-reactions*" (Keynes' beauty contest metaphor) and claimed that "*this chain can never be broken by an act of knowledge but always only through an arbitrary act – a resolution*". Morgenstern concluded therefore, that "*Unlimited foresight and economic equilibrium are thus irreconcilable with one another*" [Morgenstern's emphasis] (1935, [1963]: 47). Morgenstern went on to say in regard, as he put it to "the famous Walrasian formulation that the equilibrium takes place 'par tatonnement'", i.e. "the determination of prices by Walras through the 'prix crie' and its successive improvements through the differing bids of buyers" that "*successive adjustments are likewise irreconcilable with perfect foresight*" (52) [Morgenstern's emphasis]. He then dealt with the issue of "rational economic behavior" and what was involved if individuals acted rationally. In this regard, Morgenstern noted that "rationality" in this context posited "that the economic subjects themselves perceive the connections and dependencies – that they really see through the relationship to a certain degree" (53–4). Once again, in Morgenstern's view, individually perfect foresight in this context would "assume that all individuals in the case have perfect knowledge – indeed uniformly perfect knowledge", once again leading to the "completely insoluble paradox" in regard to "perfect foresight" and equilibrium (54).

In order to get around the problem, Morgenstern distinguished between perfect foresight and what he called perfect "*purely theoretical* knowledge of relationships" that is "perfect knowledge of a completed theory of equilibrium" assuming "that the theory of equilibrium already *exists* in complete form" and that "this complete science would be recognized uniformly by all economic subjects and understood equally well by all" (54–5). In other words, according to Morgenstern "a group of economic subjects can, consequently, have a perfect knowledge of the science, but they need not have greatly different knowledge of the future than men have today. These individuals are distinguished only by deeper insight into the relationships which arise from the arrangement of the data. But they may err in their assumptions about the data; optimism and pessimism can be expressed" (55).

Morgenstern then proceeded to state what can be said to be the *strong* form of the rational expectations hypothesis (REH). As he put it "with perfect foresight . . . there is *identity* between *foresight* and *the expectation of the future*" [Morgenstern's emphasis]. He went on to explain this as follows (58):

> If I know quite clearly that in three days a specified price will be at a specified level, then my *knowledge* is precisely the same as my *expectation* of the occurrence of this event. Had I expected another price, I should not have had certain, perfect foresight. In such an economy too, all factors of sentiment etc. would be eliminated. In the case of imperfect foresight, some other price is conceivable, for I cannot eliminate factors of disturbance from my expectation.

Having *rejected* the notion of perfect foresight, Morgenstern concluded that "*Expectation depends, thus, only to a limited degree on foresight*" (59) and that "it follows that the assumption of 'perfect' foresight is to be cut out from economic theory" (64).

However, while Morgenstern *rejected* the notion of perfect foresight and its link with equilibrium, he still maintained, as cited above, that there *was* a linkage between expectation and foresight. Thus, at the end of his 1935 paper, when talking about areas for "broader investigation", Morgenstern proposed that it "proceed in a direction such that there are always ... expectations about the future and that these ... are bound up with a certain degree of foresight" which also "assumes a certain minimum amount of insight into economic relationships" (65). To obtain what he called "some picture of the relevance of the element of expectation" therefore, Morgenstern said that this would "require a new technique" and cited "a fruitful example of the introduction of the element of expectation" as being "illustrated by the special theory of duopoly" (66). In other words, as early as 1935 Morgenstern was advocating the introduction of expectations into economic analysis via a framework similar to the game – theoretic one he was to propose and publish with von Neumann a decade later, but more about this below.

Hicks, Hawtrey, Pigou, and Keynes

The early reactions to Hicks' *V&C* (1939a) in general and Hawtrey's 1939 review of it have already been dealt with (Young 1991) and this material will not be repeated. What has *not* been dealt with in detail up to now, however, is the *unpublished* exchange between Hicks and Hawtrey over the nature of foresight and expectations, and what can be seen as Pigou's "early expectations augmented Phillips curve". In addition, while the relationship between Keynes' treatment of uncertainty and expectations in the *Treatise on Probability*, as against the *General Theory*, has been dealt with by many authors, the main issues deserve to be recalled here.

Hawtrey had taken issue with the *V&C* approach to "detailed forecasts" and expectations and challenged what Hicks called "perhaps the most important proposition in economic dynamics" that is his notion of the "elasticity of expectations" (Hawtrey 1939a: 310–11; Young 1991: 300–1). Attached to a letter from Hicks to Hawtrey dated 15 August 1939 can be found his "Notes on Hawtrey's review of 'Value and Capital'". With regard to Hawtrey's critique of Hicks' *assumed* need for *detailed* "forecasts of input, output, prices, and rates of interest" by both "traders and consumers" in order to "regulate their actions" (Hawtrey 1939a: 310). Hicks replied:

> This is of course a very crucial matter. I believe that the objections raised here at some length are largely answered on pp. 125–6 of the

> book [*V&C*] and by the reviewer himself on p. 310. There are two issues: the assumption of price-expectations rather than expectations of the "state of the market"; and the assumption of detailed expectations at all. On the first issue, I quite agree that it would have been better to assume "state of the market" expectations, but this meant assuming imperfect competition throughout, and I couldn't see any way of getting to grips with my main problems if I assumed imperfect competition. But here I quite admit that my solution is a *pis aller*; still I hope the deficiency may be rectified some day to some extent.
>
> On the other issue I feel on stronger ground. I do not of course suppose that a person who sets up a boot factory has to have some particular expectation of the state of the market in (say) three years' time. Still this is a thing which will affect the profitability of his enterprise; so he has to make (implicitly) some assumption about it, even if that assumption is nothing more than a vague expectation of the continuance of something like his present conditions. However, he won't always assume that; and even if he does, he will hold to these stationary expectations with more or less confidence in different cases, and these differences in confidence will make a difference to his policy. The whole point of my analysis is to get something general enough to include all these cases; and of course to include (as it does include) the ordinary cases as well.
>
> *The reader is perfectly at liberty to assume expected prices equal to current prices* [our emphasis]. If he does so, he gets a special case of my more general construction. But it is not actually a very much simpler special case, because it is only in special circumstances that stationary expectations mean stationary plans (inputs and outputs constant over time) . . . We really have to be more general in order to get to the unity underlying this diversity.

Interestingly enough, this is quite similar to what Keynes wrote on conventions utilized in the face of untractable uncertainty and on the undue weight given to day-to-day fluctuations in business profits (1936: 148). Keynes went on to say (1936: 154) that he did not think undue weight should be given to day-to-day fluctuations in business profits "which are obviously of an ephemeral and nonsignificant character".

According to his "Reply to notes on the review of 'Value and Capital'" found in his papers (Hawtrey 1939b), Hawtrey replied as follows:

> You say that to assume "state of the market" expectations would have meant "assuming imperfect competition throughout". I do not think this is so, unless you regard the existence of goodwill or of the selling power of the individual trader as itself implying imperfect competition. But to my mind the trader's selling power is such an essential part of the economic mechanism that it cannot be disregarded. The

> primary motive of enterprise is the expectation that the product contemplated can be sold at a remunerative price. That expectation may be based on the actual expansion of demand felt by an existing concern, or a new concern may be started to serve a new or expanding community or to put a new product on the market. The reward expected is demand at a remunerative price, but apart from being remunerative the price itself does not enter explicitly into the trader's calculations. He is quite prepared to assume that, if his costs change, those of his competitors will change similarly, and that no very violent change in the volume of demand will result. There is of course a risk of a big change of costs (e.g. a serious scarcity of raw material) or of a collapse of demand, which would upset all his calculations. But traders are not deterred by these hazards. If you want to form a picture of the trader's expectations, you will put in the foreground his hope of a steady stream of sales at a price which will yield a normal margin over the cost of producing in the most up-to-date manner prevailing in the industry. This hope will be modified by the possibility of various contingencies, favourable and unfavourable, but few if any of these will have even an approximate *date* suggested for them. By attributing dates to a series of contingencies extended into the remote future, you are not giving the theory greater generality, but only divorcing it completely from the facts.

Finally, Hawtrey concluded that he did not think "traders to make detailed estimates for every week a thousand weeks ahead".

Pigou's early expectations augmented Phillips curve

Pigou sought to bring business cycle theories to "the test of fact" (1927: 23–4, 34–5, 120, 192–3) and while warning against inferring causation from simple correlation, presented a curve (Curve 11) displaying British unemployment and prices for an almost identical period (and sub-periods) from which Phillips (2000 [1958]) derived his curve. Chart 16 (Pigou 1927: 194) showed a "very close" correspondence between unemployment (inverted) and the rate of change of prices; in "close accord" with Fisher's results for the United States.

Inflationary expectations and animal spirits, in part, drove Pigou's system. Keynes (1936: 154, 161) wrote of the market being "subject to waves of optimistic and pessimistic sentiment ... the outcome of the mass psychology of a large number of ignorant individuals ... animal spirits". Pigou had earlier written of the "fluctuating character of the demand for labour" caused by business confidence: the "tendency towards optimism in the conception which businessmen entertain of the prospects of investment ... the judgments which people form are biased by their feelings ... optimism and pessimism have a strange power of diffusing themselves among people assembled, as businessmen often are, in close proximity ... a quasi-hypnotic system of mutual suggestion"; "if a seed of optimism or of pessimism is planted in any year, and if no new cause intervenes, the seed will multiply continuously". Links between businessmen "act as conducting rods along which error of optimism or pessimism, once generated, propagates itself ... By their joint action they exert a powerful influence, in favour of action in droves" (1927: 79, 114–15, 117, 81–2; 1912: 469).

Movements in prices that are "not merely imperfectly but also unequally foreseen ... augment the amplitude of industrial fluctuations". The expectations of price movements, which business people and the suppliers of labor (and the providers of capital) bring to the negotiation of contracts, are "unequal in a particular way". In periods of rising prices, business people expect a larger further rise in prices than those they negotiate with. In Pigou's "Expectations augmented Phillips curve" these optimistic and pessimistic errors set up cumulative and reinforcing (not always self-correcting) reactions: "this mutual stimulation of errors and price movements may continue in a vicious spiral, until it is checked by some interference from outside". This could be the "detonation which accompanies the discovery of a given mass of optimistic error" (1927: 163–5, 188, 86; 1912: 453–66; 1933: 235–7). Pigou advised the Macmillan Committee that a "cumulative downward movement ... carries the seeds of its own worsening". The mechanism by which this happened was the tendency to "hoard money" in periods of high unemployment (cited by Casson 1983: 51).

There seem to be two major differences between Pigou's model and current textbook versions of this model. First, Pigou (1933: 251) argued that "accelerationism" would increase the "natural-rate" of unemployment: "This kind of policy, however, through adverse reactions on the accumulation and retention at home of capital, is liable, if pressed beyond a point, to defeat itself, and has in fact, as a deliberate policy never been advocated". Second, Pigou (1927: 163–5, 188, 296) advocated policies which would speed recovery: "How much creation or transfer [of demand] is socially desirable depends, in each individual case, on all the surrounding conditions being taken into account, on a balancing at the margin of gain against cost; but the presumption in favour of some creation or transfer beyond what comes about 'naturally' is very strong ... The practical importance of this analysis is very great". Without conjuring up the image that Keynes would later colorfully use, Pigou (1933: 38, 250; 1927: 30–1) argued that "stationary state" perceptions "afford no argument, of course, against the State temporarily adopting these devices as 'remedies' for unemployment in times of exceptional depression. For here it is not their long-run, but their short-run, consequences that are significant". In this stationary state, "real causes of varying expectations could not, by definition exist ... [in] a state of steady self-repeating movements ... rational beings would be bound to realise that this was happening, and so could not fall into error". Pigou contrasted this state with reality: "In the actual world both sorts of causes are present".

In view of the role that inflationary expectations played in the demise of Keynesian economics, it is interesting to report that Keynes (1936: 9, 142) was willing to accept money illusion as the basis of his rebuttal of a labor supply being a function of the real wage; but Keynes deemed to be unsuccessful "Professor Pigou's expedient of supposing that the prospective change in the value of money is foreseen by any one set of people but not foreseen by another". Pigou (1933: 100) stated that money wages, not real wages, were the subject of wage bargains: "In a monetary economy decisions to change the real rate of wages cannot be taken in a direct way". He also advised the Macmillan Committee that inflation would only work if wage earners were "bamboozled" (cited by Casson 1983: 52).

Keynes on uncertainty and expectations in the Treatise on Probability vs. the General Theory

One of the recent controversies that has emerged as students of Keynes have looked at him wearing his hat as philosopher is the relationship between *A Treatise on Probability* and *The General Theory*. The extremes in the debate are perhaps best represented in the works of O'Donnell (1989) and Bateman (1987, 1993). While O'Donnell argues that there is deep continuity between the fundamental issues of concern to Keynes in *A Treatise*, Bateman argues that the theory of probability advanced in *A Treatise* had been discarded long ago by the time Keynes came to write *The General Theory* and, moreover, the route to Keynes' views on uncertainty in *The General Theory* was grounded in policy issues dating from the period of his debate with the Treasury, circa 1929 and thereafter.

Indeed, Bateman (1993) has taken the position that Keynes' attention to subjective uncertainty in *The General Theory*, particularly in Chapter 12, constituted a reversal of his previously dismissive attitude toward the role of "business confidence" as an exogenous actor on economic processes. The period in which Keynes dismissed the importance of "business confidence" altogether encompassed the years 1930 through 1933, again well past the period in which his attention was drawn to the arguments of *A Treatise*.

Without addressing the matter of Keynes' personal intellectual transition between the writing of *A Treatise* – which apparently was composed as early as 1914, some seven years before its publication – and the writing of *The General Theory*, Allin Cottrell (1993) has argued that there is no necessity for maintaining a linkage between the two works. In short, for Cottrell, the view of decision making under uncertainty presented in *The General Theory* does not require the argument of *A Treatise on Probability* as an analytical prop.

Keynes himself did aver to a linkage between the two works at one and only one point in *The General Theory*. When he observed that "It would be foolish, in forming our expectations, to attach great weight to matters which are very uncertain" (Keynes 1936: 148). In the accompanying footnote (Keynes 1936: 148, n. 6) he goes on to say "By 'very uncertain' I do not mean the same thing as 'very improbable'. Cf. my *Treatise on Probability*, chap. 6, on 'The Weight of Arguments.'" Cottrell, given the nature of his analysis of *A Treatise*, presumably would find it ironic that the portion of the work on probability that Keynes would invoke in *The General Theory* concerns Keynes' concept of "weight".

Cottrell (1993) makes the following central points: First, Cottrell argues that Keynes' attempt to develop a logical theory of probability, ostensibly as a more *general* alternative to the conventional frequentist approach, was not successful. Concomitantly, it has had little or no impact on subsequent developments in probability theory. Therefore, *A Treatise* would provide a very weak reed for Keynes to lean upon in developing his analysis in *The General Theory*. Second, Frank Ramsey's (1931) critique of *A Treatise* identified fundamental difficulties with Keynes' logical theory of probability. Keynes' concern in *A Treatise* was with what he called knowledge obtained "indirectly" via argument, knowledge, or belief arrived at, in Keynes' terms, rationally – under conditions of incomplete information. An argument provided the support for a proposition, which might be the claim that the likelihood of such and such an event taking place at a future date is such and such a numerical measure or is qualitatively high or low. As Cottrell (1993: 27) puts it, the conclusion drawn from the premises can be assigned "some degree of rational credibility . . . bounded by the values 0 and 1" but that degree of rational credibility "is not always measurable, either in practice or in principle".

Keynes identified two components to a proposition, a subjective and an objective component. The former involved the process of the selection of the "premises of *our* argument"; the latter involved "the purely logical relations between the propositions which embody our direct knowledge and the propositions about which we seek indirect knowledge" (Keynes 1971: 4). At this stage, Keynes appeared to be treating the rules of logic, the rules that carry the seeker of indirect knowledge from the premises to the conclusions, as fixed, definite, and unchanging. Cottrell (1993: 27, emphasis in original) refers to "a Platonistic element here" observing that "These probability relations subsist in a kind of logical space and are 'perceived' via the faculty of intuition. If opinions differ *on the same evidence* somebody's perception must be faulty."

Now Keynes (1971: 18) was not wholly consistent about the objectivity of the probabilities so derived even in the pages of *A Treatise*; elsewhere in the text we find him acknowledging that a certain relativism could enter into the process of moving from premises to conclusions: "We cannot speak of knowledge absolutely – only of knowledge of a particular person. Other parts of knowledge – knowledge of the axioms of logic, for example

– may seem more objective. But we must admit, I think, that this too is relative to the constitution of the human mind, and that the constitution of the human mind may vary in some degree from man to man." Unless it is possible to determine which human's mind has the strongest constitution – and Keynes frequently seemed inclined to believe that his own possessed the strongest constitution – then subjectivism enters not only into the process of selection of the relevant premises but also in the process of derivation of the conclusion. Nevertheless, Keynes' position in *A Treatise* proceeds as if, once the premises of an argument are chosen, the conclusion is incontrovertible given proper application of the rules of logic.

Game theory, "outguessing", and rational expectations

Building on earlier work (e.g. von Neumann 1928; Morgenstern 1928, 1935) by the beginning of 1943, von Neumann and Morgenstern (1944: v) had formalized the "new technique" of analyzing economic problems Morgenstern had mentioned in his 1935 paper (66). In 1944 they published perhaps one of the most influential books of the twentieth century. In *Theory of Games and Economic Behavior*, Morgenstern, for his part, had advanced the connection between expectation and foresight he proposed (1935 [1963]: 59ff.) linking it with the notion of "complete" and "perfect" information and rational behavior (von Neumann and Morgenstern 1944: 30, 112ff.).

While having originally given it a favorable review when first published (Simon 1945), by 1957, Simon had come to criticize game theory on the basis of its "unrealistic assumptions of virtual omniscience and unlimited computational power" (Simon 1957: 202). In later critiques (Simon 1976, 1978a, 1978b, 1979), Simon focused on the limitations of the ability of game theory to deal with the problems thrown up by imperfect competition and oligopoly, the adoption of unique and universally accepted criterion of rationality and especially the "outguessing problem". Indeed, in his Nobel lecture (1979: 505–6) Simon asserted that

> Game theory addresses itself to the "outguessing" problem that arises whenever an economic factor takes into account the possible reactions to his own decisions of the other actors. To my mind, the main product of the very elegant apparatus of game theory has been to demonstrate quite clearly that it is virtually impossible to define an unambiguous criterion of rationality for this class of situations.

In his collected papers (Simon 1982), when discussing "the possibility of public prediction", his own paper on the topic (Simon 1954) and its relationship to that of Grunberg and Modigliani (1954) and Muth (1961), Simon wrote "in both the Grunberg-Modigliani article and my own, the 'outguessing' problem is traced back to Frank Knight (1921). Neither article mentions *The Theory of Games* (von Neumann and Morgenstern 1944) as relevant, an omission that by retrospect surprises me" (1982: 405). Now, whether or not one agrees with Simon's critique of the efficacy of game theory, his observation regarding the relationship between game theory and rational expectations is very important. In fact, in recent correspondence (1991–92) Simon has asserted that RE is *implicit* in game theory, reinforcing the assertion he made in 1957, that is of the "assumption of omniscience" of game theory and the implications of the types of uncertainty assumed regarding "random events that have a joint probability distribution" and "the future behavior of another player" (1957: 203). Player A would need to know the decision-making rule used by player B or at least know, in a precise way, the strategy being used by player B. That is to say Player A would then be able to forecast the reaction of player B, aside from sheer randomness in the plays made by player B. Player A would understand fully the basis for the systematic actions taken by player B.

But, in his review essay on *The Theory of Games* published in the April 1946 issue of the *JPE*, Marschak had *already* recognized the *expectational implications* of their approach. For, as he put it, if the game player "knew the distribution p(s) of the future situation s, he would choose x [individual's action] so as to maximize the long-run gain [g] E(g) = F(x, p). This determines x and also the long-run gain itself, $Max_xF(x, p)$" (1946: 109). Moreover, in an article published in the April 1950 issue of *Econometrica* entitled "Rational behavior, uncertain prospects, and measurable utility" – whose results were "inspired" by von Neumann and Morgenstern's work – Marschak (1950: 112–13) also dealt with rationality among *all* economic agents (consumers, firms, and government) under the assumption of what he called *complete* information as inherent in game theory. Marschak (1950: 113) defined *complete* information as the situation in which the agent "thinks he knows certain relevant probability distributions" and where "a special case of complete information is that of *certainty*" [Marschak's emphasis] in which "all probabilities have values 0 or 1".

Interestingly enough, in his classic paper entitled "The Bargaining Problem" published in the same issue of *Econometrica*, Nash said that with regard to the problem of a "bargaining, bilateral monopoly" which could "also be regarded as non zero-sum two-person game" (1950: 155) the "solution should consist of *rational* [Nash's emphasis] expectations of gain by the two bargainers, these expectations should be realizable by an appropriate agreement between the two. Hence, there should be an available anticipation which gives each the amount of satisfaction he should expect to get. It is reasonable to assume that the two, being rational, would simply agree to that anticipation, or to an equivalent one" (1950: 158). Now, while the type of expectations Nash was talking about here is not RE *explicitly* in its *modern* form, it *does* show that the notion is *implicit* in *both* the types of games that von Neumann and Morgenstern (1944, 1947) and Nash (1950) were dealing with.

Indeed, Smith *et al.* (1991 [1988]: 356–7) made the distinction between "rational expectations in the sense of Muth (REM)" and "rational expectations in the sense of Nash (REN)". According to them, Nash "defined the concept less restrictively" and "REN implies only that expectations are sustained (or reinforced) by outcomes that in turn support the predictions of some theory". In an important note to this (1991 [1988]: 357, n. 5) they added: "When testing REM using field survey data, investigators assume implicitly that observed prices are randomly distributed about some equilibrium theoretical price. It should be emphasized that unless this assumption is satisfied, these investigators are testing REN". Smith and his co-authors also reported (1991 [1988]: 368) that

> Our results ... support the view that expectations *are adaptive* and the adaptation over time is to REM *equilibrium outcomes* [their emphasis] ... Real people in any environment usually do not come off the stops with common expectations; they usually do not solve problems of maximization over time by ex ante reasoning and backward induction, nor is this irrational when there is sufficient reason to believe that expectations are common. What we can learn from the particular experiments reported here is that a common dividend, and common knowledge thereof is sufficient to induce common expectations. *As we interpret it this is due to agent uncertainty about the behavior of others* [our emphasis]. With experience, and its lessons in trial-and-error learning, expectations tend ultimately to converge and yield an REM equilibrium.

Schotter (1992: 106–10) attempted to explain why the Nash equilibrium approach and what he called "the Rational Expectations Equilibrium" that "forms a Nash Equilibrium in beliefs and actions", that is to say Smith's "REN", was not dealt with by von Neumann and Morgenstern in their 1944 book. According to Schotter (1992: 106).

> In fact, it is quite remarkable that the Nash equilibrium concept was not defined nor its existence proven in *The Theory* [*of Games and Economic Behavior*] since at least Morgenstern was well aware of Cournot's work. I suspect the main reason for this omission is that both von Neumann and Morgenstern were looking for a way to break the circularity of the "I think he thinks that I think" logic of strategically interdependent situations. They wanted to provide a way for players to behave that was independent of their expectation of what their opponent intended to do.

Furthermore, Schotter maintained (1992: 107) that the Nash approach and its refinements are essentially "inconsistent with the world view expressed in *The Theory*", and went on to say: "For Morgenstern, indeterminacy was not something to run from but rather to embrace. The world is uncertain and social situations interesting only because they contain indeterminacies that many physical situations do not". He continued (1992: 109–10)

> Since Morgenstern's study of strategic interaction was stimulated by his interest in the problem of perfect foresight and prediction, the recent work on rational expectations equilibria was a welcome event. This concept, in some sense, solves the problem that motivated Morgenstern's interest. Morgenstern's prediction problem is solved by Muth, Lucas and others by assuming that all agents in the economy make their predictions using the same model of their situation ... *At the equilibrium* (Schotter's emphasis) the circularity of beliefs is settled and Morgenstern's original problem disappears. Still, the Austrian in Morgenstern would not have tolerated such a simplistic view of the world ... Beyond this, Morgenstern would probably have trouble agreeing with the assumption that all agents adhere to the same theory of the economy, a theory describing the objectively correct model of the economy. In fact, Morgenstern (1935) had already anticipated the rational expectations common-model solution in economics and rejected it since economics even now is not yet a science for which we have a commonly accepted correct theory.

Schotter concluded (1992: 110)

> My feeling is that Morgenstern would have been more inclined to think of the agents in the world as adhering simultaneously to many theories and to think, in truly Austrian fashion, that many subjectively correct models of the real world exist, reality being determined, in part, by the different subjective models that people use ... Hence, while in some sense the theory of rational expectations equilibrium would have been a very welcome event for Morgenstern since it dealt with precisely the problem that first aroused his interest in game theory, its treatment in the profession might ultimately have left him dissatisfied.

More recently, Schmidt (2002: 61) has even made the distinction between Morgenstern's approach and that of Hayek, linking Hayek's idea of the equilibrating tendency (1937) to Nash's (1950) limited information approach to evolutionary game theory.

The cobweb: price expectations, firms, and futures markets

Until Muth's pathbreaking work (1959a, 1959b, 1961) the treatment of expectations as manifest in what Kaldor called "the cobweb theorem" (1933–34: 134–5) presented considerable difficulties to the economic analyst. Indeed, over the three decades from its introduction by Moore (1929) and Tinbergen (1930), the approach to expectations in "cobweb models" brought about a *divergence* between the "prediction of the cobweb theory" and "that of the firms" (Muth 1961: 331); something which Muth's *RE* approach *reconciled.* But many earlier writers had been just as critical as Muth of the efficacy of the cobweb and its treatment of expectations and information. For example, Coase and Fowler (1935a, 1935b, 1937) dealt with the situation where, if economic agents (in their case, farmers) *did forecast and also learn from experience*, then they would tend "to produce equilibrium output assuming demand and supply conditions to remain unchanged". However, Coase and Fowler asserted that if these agents "acted in the way postulated by the 'cobweb theorem', fluctuations would occur even under these static conditions" (1935b: 427). They went on (1937: 79) to say that if economic agents [farmers] learn from experience and therefore corrected their errors, they would "tend to be more accurate in their forecasts" so that the time period taken for reaching equilibrium output would be in part, functionally related to the rate at which they learnt from their experience, but that this "would appear to be a problem lying rather within the province of the psychologist than that of the economist". Interestingly enough, Coase and Fowler concluded (1937: 80–1) that their investigation regarding the *non-applicability* of the "cobweb theorem" to the agricultural market they studied also supported Rosenstein-Rodan's (1936) view that "As long as no unique correlation between changes in actual prices and anticipations can be shown – and it is most improbable that it ever will be shown – anticipations of future prices must be considered as independent variables determining the demand in the same way as actual ('real') prices".

Buchanan (1939) for his part, showed that the cobweb theorem brought about a situation where "losses will inevitably exceed profits" and that it had validity *only* if economic agents were *not* rational. As he put it, "on the special assumption that there is always a group of new producers willing to rush in and dissipate their capitals with each swing of the cycle, the theorem may perhaps be valid". He went on to say that "for those empirically established fluctuations in output and price it is doubtful if the cobweb theorem provides a logically acceptable explanation" and concluded that "the inviolable assumption that people never learn from experience, no matter how protracted, is at least debatable" (81). In other words, according to Buchanan (1939: 74, 81) *given* that *rational* behavior implied profit *maximization* and that the "cobweb" implied behavior that was *not* rational, *rational* economic agents *would not* act according to the "cobweb theorem" and its expectational structure. Simply put, in Buchanan's view, *rational* agents *would* exhibit *rational* expectations since they *would* "learn from experience" (74). It is not surprising, therefore, that Robert Clower for one, maintained that *RE* is implicit in Buchanan's somewhat overlooked paper; albeit a paper cited by none other than Muth himself! (1961: 317).

But does learning lead to rational expectations? Consider two different types of misinformation with respect to the model that serves as the machine from which expectations are formed. First consider a circumstance in which an agent has a properly specified model of the process of concern, like the cobweb, but does not know the correct values of the parameters of the model. Second, consider a circumstance in which an agent has an incorrectly specified model of the process of concern (either irrelevant variables are included in the model or relevant variables have been omitted). In neither case will the finding, period by period, that predictions depart from actual outcomes insure that the agent will uncover the true structure of the model. After all, as long as the agent believes that the parameters of the model are valid or that the model is properly specified, then all errors must be due to purely random effects. Even the discovery that errors might be serially correlated would not give the agent any precise guidance about how to revise the model; without such a discovery the agent would remain convinced that forecasts are based upon the true model of the process.

Despite the critiques of the "cobweb theorem" mentioned above, only a decade or so later, both Goodwin (1947) and Hooton (1950) seemingly resurrected the approach. For example, in the July 1947 issue of *Econometrica*, Goodwin maintained that it was "inherently quite unlikely that all producers would have the same expectations" (1947: 192) and went on to praise the "cobweb theorem" not only as "an example of the fruitfulness of the restrictive assumptions of partial analysis but as "probably the most successful attempt at dynamics" (1947: 204).

In his critique of the cobweb, Muth not only took issue with the first point but went on to specifically cite Goodwin's praise of the cobweb in the context of focusing on the importance of the effect of RE (1961: 330). With regard to the possibility of the similarity of producers expectations, Muth said that if true, RE meant that "expectations in different markets and systems would not have to be treated in completely different ways". In other words, *all rational* economic agents would hold rational expectations. Muth also used the cobweb as an *empirical "benchmark"* against which to gauge the efficacy of his approach. This was in order to provide, as he put it, "the only real test ... whether theories involving rationality explain observed phenomena any better than alternative theories" (1961: 330).

Hooton (1950) for his part, sought to "dynamize" what he considered to be the "static" approach of the *original* cobweb model by including "risk" in his own treatment of the "cobweb theorem" (1950: 69). However, as Newman (1951: 334) put it in his comment on Hooton, this constituted an attempt to "dust off" the approach in order to demonstrate "the minor importance of the cobweb theorem for economics". In fact, Hooton actually *overlooked* the *original* English language literature regarding the cobweb as manifest in Moore (1929), Kaldor (1933–34), Rosenstein-Rodan (1934), and Coase and Fowler (1935a, 1935b, 1937); and *mistakenly* asserted (1950: 69) that the "theoretical interpretation had received only scanty attention in the English language" until Ezekiel (1938). This issue aside, however, as Newman (1951: 341) concluded in his critique of Hooten's approach:

> it seems necessary to point out that the assumptions of the cobweb theorem are so unrealistic as to bring into question its usefulness. For instance, the producers are supposed to act on an assumption (that of constant-price expectations) which is falsified as soon as they act on it, and this disappointment is supposed to have no effect on their future behaviour! Such considerations seem to put out of court any large future developments of the cobweb cycle. Its past successes have been to explain, partially, commodity cycles, and to have focused attention on problems of the stability of equilibrium ... As to its future use, may the author put in a plea for the great merits of drawing cobweb cycles as a new form of solitaire for economists, imprisoned in their studies on wet afternoons?

Interestingly enough, in a footnote to his concluding remarks, Newman said (1951: 341, n. 2) that the assumption mentioned above regarding constant price expectations was "analogous to the assumption, made by Cournot and Bertrand, that duopolists do not learn from experience", something which von Neumann and Morgenstern's game-theoretic approach to the "duopoly problem", based as it was upon *complete* information *and rational* expectations was able to overcome (1944: 13, 30 and sections 61.2–61.6).

In a somewhat overlooked, albeit very insightful paper published in 1957, entitled "Intertemporal price equilibrium: a prologue to the theory of speculation", Samuelson proposed a simple model based upon certainty and perfect foresight to explain the nature of and convergence to equilibrium in a "futures" or "forward" market. He said that if "the future behavior of prices" is "fully foreseen", then "there is only one equilibrium pattern that can prevail". He then asked "why must the presently quoted futures price ... always be exactly equal to the current price which will then prevail?". His answer was that "if it did not, arbitragers could make money by buying cheap and selling dear". He went on to say "under conditions of certainty, the equilibrium pattern would result virtually instantaneously". He concluded that "under conditions of perfect foresight the future literally exists in the present and a perfect futures market gives us to a dramatic representation of this fact" (1957: 192–4). In Samuelson's 1957 model, as in Muth's, price expectations are the prediction of the model itself.

In 1965, Samuelson returned to the price expectations "enigma", as he put it (1965: 41). In his paper "Proof that properly anticipated prices fluctuate randomly", published in *Industrial Management Review*, "by positing a rather general stochastic model of price change", Samuelson deduced "a fairly sweeping theorem in which next-period's price differences are shown to be uncorrelated with (if not completely independent of) previous period's price differences" (1965: 42). In essence, his 1965 model "defining behavior of a futures price" (1965: 43–4) is an extension of his earlier 1957 model. But, in the conclusion to his 1965 paper, Samuelson raised a number of pertinent methodological questions regarding the "representative individual" and his expectations; some still remain unanswered (1965: 48–9).

Another important – albeit overlooked paper – was also published in 1957 by Erik Lindahl, in which he proposed a method of attaining "full employment without inflation". In his paper, Lindahl distinguished between profit and income inflation, and analyzed the process by which "the public tries to adjust itself to ... inflation" (1957: 29–30). He said (1957: 30–1) "a policy declaration favouring a mild and advantageous inflation will have consequences that conflict with the objectives of such a programme ... A condition for the successful execution of such a policy would be that it is kept *secret*, the public being given the idea that the rise in prices is fortuitous and will not be repeated ... If inflation is used in the future as a policy measure, it must be assumed that both the authorities and the public will be aware of the fact". Lindahl's models of perfect and imperfect foresight had been developed from 1929 onwards, and were brought together in his seminal, albeit almost forgotten book *Studies in the Theory of Money and Capital* (1939). As he wrote in his preface (1939: 10) "if perfect foresight is assumed, the dynamic problem can evidently be handled in a manner quite parallel to the Walrasian scheme. I believe that this approach is not entirely unrealistic, since people actually do anticipate correctly much of what takes place". It is not surprising, therefore, that his book had the blessing of his British mentor, John Hicks (1939: 12).

2 The Hart Research Agenda

Information, anticipation, and the firm

At about the same time Muth's RE paper was published in 1961, two other articles appeared regarding the role of information and expectations in economics. Stigler's 1961 *JPE* paper on the economics of information is well known and will not be discussed here. The other paper by Malmgren entitled "Information, expectations and the theory of the firm" published in the August 1961 issue of *QJE* deserves attention because of the linkage the author made between the types of information available to and the expectations of the firm. Now, Malmgren cited Knight (1921) as the source for his own approach to foresight and risk and Hayek (1937: 36) as the source for the notion of what he called "expectational equilibrium" (1961: 403, 405). While Hayek himself had said (1937: 33–4) that Knight (1921) had stimulated work on foresight and risk, Hayek added "a more complete survey of the process by which the significance of anticipations was gradually introduced into economic analysis would probably have to begin with Professor Irving Fisher's *Appreciation and Interest* (1896)".

According to Malmgren (1961: 408–9) there are three possibilities regarding the "state of information in which a firm's decision is taken": *perfect*, *complete*, and *incomplete*. The characteristics of each can be briefly described as follows: "*Perfect information*", in Malmgren's view (1961: 408–9) "is quite impossible" since not only does it imply "omniscience", but cannot occur due to "an environment which is not always predictable" facing the firm. "*Complete information*", on the other hand, can be distinguished from the first "state of information", since as he put it "we can still think of *complete information*, where everyone at least thinks he knows what everyone else knows, even though they may all turn out to be wrong in some degree, when the various plans mature". According to Malmgren "*incomplete information* is the usual state of affairs, when each firm decides on the basis of a limited amount of information relative to the total amount dispersed throughout the economy".

Now, if information is economically valuable in the sense that it contributes to the prospect of achieving profits, then it would pay someone to find ways to collect it and to provide it to users. Rivalry among data collectors/disseminators should lead to a diminution in the cost of obtaining information. Information cost should not prove to be a persistent barrier to the formation of "correct" expectations. Knowledge of which data is relevant, or seemingly relevant, and how it is to be interpreted is the contentious matter. In principle rivalry among forecasters should lead to a similar outcome – a winnowing out of those approaches and prognosticators that are less effective – leaving only the most accurate predictors. However, if interpretation involves the "outguessing" or "beauty contest" problem, if it involves learning, and if it involves the prospect, stressed by Keynes (1936), that there is little or no information available today regardless of the cost of procuring it that is relevant to the forecast, e.g. profitability of an enterprise a year from now or five years hence, then market competition will not lead to a consistent capacity to form correct expectations.

In other words, for the firm to ensure *optimal* use of information in expectations formation, this would involve it using *all possible available information*; that is the firm would have rational expectations. As Malmgren noted (1961: 410), various approaches as to "how expectations are formed and plans made", and exactly how information was evaluated by firms, was dealt with by many authors before his own efforts and those of his contemporaries, and it is to these that we now turn.

Now, it is "public information" that two divergent branches of the economics profession emanated from the Graduate School of Industrial Administration (GSIA) of the Carnegie Institute of Technology in the 1950s and 1960s (Sheffrin 1983: 1). Both branches – Rational Expectations and bounded rationality – proved fertile, as will be seen in Chapter 3. Both bounded rationality and the rational expectations approach shared a "common ancestry" prior to the period at Carnegie Tech. Aspects of both approaches can be found in the research project on "Expectations and Business Fluctuations" based at the University of Illinois. Albert Hart (1949) wrote what was in effect a research agenda for the project, which was interrupted due to a mass departure from Illinois, as will be dealt with in Chapter 3 below.

Hart on anticipations and the firm

The early work of Hart on anticipations and the firm (1937–48) is crucial for an understanding of the expectations story. Rather than giving a cursory survey of his work based upon secondary sources, below we present Hart's *own* detailed previously *unpublished* "chronological account" of his "role in expectational economics". This is based upon an interview and correspondence with Hart in which he outlined his "recollections about development of expectational economics in a chronological sequence" (Hart 1991).

As an undergraduate at Harvard, Hart was taught economic theory by Taussig. After graduating summa cum laude from Harvard, Hart was awarded a European traveling fellowship for 1930/31, and Taussig gave him introductions to Haberler, Hayek, and Morgenstern in Vienna. Hart attended their "trio-seminar", devoted that year to Fisher's *Theory of Interest*, which had just been published, and also went to their courses on international economics, money, and price theory, which he said "were eye-openers". As Hart recalled

> Hayek had been invited to lecture on cycle theory at LSE in early 1931. He insisted on writing in English rather than getting a German text translated, and brought me in to straighten up his English in what turned into *Prices and Production* [1931]. Between Austro/German semesters, I naturally visited LSE, where I found tacked to a bulletin board a cable to me from the University of Chicago, offering me a fellowship for 1931/32 – which I hastily wired to accept.

He continued

> I found that Hayek's lectures had already been given, and that Lionel Robbins was rushing the book into print. But whereas the version I had helped on had two parts (the first starting a Schumpeterian inflationary upswing from a full-employment equilibrium, the second starting from a stabilized depression), the second part had somehow disappeared [I got a chance, on a visit to Freiburg in the 1970's, to ask Hayek about this disappearance, and Hayek told me he had been dissatisfied with his second part and was unwilling to hold up publication while he struggled with it].

Hart went on to say

> It was my afterthoughts about the Hayek book in early 1931 that started me on the expectational-economics track. I found I couldn't decide whether I agreed with his mysteriously-vanished second part until I figure out whether the expectations of the entrepreneurs in his capital-goods section and consumer-goods sector were mutually consistent, and how the *surprises* implied by his theory were distributed.

Between Autumn 1931 and 1934, Hart undertook graduate work at the University of Chicago, and studied with Knight, Schultz, Viner, and Yntema – who also made up his PhD dissertation committee. He took price theory with Viner, statistics with Yntema, and a number of courses with Knight. When walking Knight home after a late class, Hart recalled, he mentioned to Knight that he was reading *Risk, Uncertainty and Profit*, to which, as Hart remembered, Knight replied "I don't recommend it". Hart was also appointed a teaching assistant and taught, along with Mints and Simons, undergraduate courses on money and price theory.

The academic year 1932/33 was an important one for economics graduate students at Chicago, for as Hart recalled:

> This was the year when Kenneth Boulding came to study at Chicago, on a traveling fellowship, and changed the whole flavor of economics-graduate student life at the university. I had been inveigled by Eric Lundberg (who had been at Chicago as a graduate student through the summer of 1932) and by Fritz Machlup (who was at Northwestern University – to teach a 1932 summer course) into setting up a cooperative graduate student seminar. When this seminar opened in the autumn, Boulding instantly became its king-pin. This graduate-student cooperative was a really distinguished group. I remember saying to myself once during a meeting, "It just shows how easily you can build up delusions of grandeur. But it seems to me that I am seeing as many really good economists in this one roomful as were working in the United States during the 1920's!" Not such a delusion though! For the seminar included besides Boulding: Bronfenbrenner, Carlson, Friedman, Lange, Lerner, Stigler and Wallis, and several others who may not have achieved celebrity but performed in the same league ... I'm not sure which ones were present the day I had this thought; but most members attended steadily. Particularly memorable was an occasion when Friedman served up a handsome set of micro-economic formulas – just before they were published by Hicks and Allen. The only faculty members invited were Knight and Simons, who came regularly. I was there in my student capacity, not as (very junior) faculty.

In the preface to the 1951 reprint of his monograph *Anticipations, Uncertainty and Dynamic Planning* (1940b) Hart dealt with the evolution of his dissertation topic. As Hart wrote "this monograph ... was a revision of the parts of the dissertation dealing most specifically with the firm" (1940b: vi–vii), with "various offshots" of the work, as Hart called them, appearing during 1936–37 (Hart 1936, 1937a, 1937b).

Hart went on with his chronological account as follows:

> Late in the winter quarter of 1934, the department chairman ... told me I was being granted two quarters of leave-with-pay for study abroad in 1934–35. Being aware that Sweden was the great center of expectational economics, I decided to head for Stockholm, and took a course in Swedish language in the spring quarter.

In 1934/35 Hart had to change his plans, as he recalled

> because Jacob Viner offered me a summer job at the U.S. Treasury, as a member of his six-man "freshman team of the brain trust".

He went on

> Lacking the time to get further with the Swedish language ... I dropped the idea of Stockholm, and instead headed for London, where Hayek was now in residence as full-time professor at LSE ... I attended lectures by Hicks, out of which grew the expectational dynamics that presently appeared in his *Value and Capital* ... There is no doubt that this Hicks work was a masterpiece in my general area.

Hart then stressed the following points [his emphasis]

> But one of my central themes is the importance of *flexibility* (a strategy of acting so as to keep options open and benefit from information not yet available) which is missing in Hicks. And I found it unnecessary to think of the fruits of investment as "discounted for uncertainty" as well as for futurity. This Knight/Hicks notion (used to "explain profit") is today still regrettably popular in investment literature. Knight himself, in my time in Chicago, told his students that very likely "pure" profit would be found by proper measurement to be *negative* in the real world – in which case we would have to say that self-selection for the role of entrepreneur makes dominant the psychological types who revel in risk!

The academic year 1935/36 saw Hart complete and submit his PhD dissertation entitled "Anticipations, business planning and the cycle" for examination. As he recalled

> Frank Knight gave me a very hard time in the late stages of revision. He started with the position that what I said was all wrong, and later shifted to the position that it was all too obvious to be worth saying ... At Chicago in those days, the final oral exam on subjects was held at the same session with the dissertation defense. Frank Knight asked me quite a few searching questions on price theory, on which my answers gave little satisfaction either to the examining committee or to myself. Finally he said, "Well, what *do* you know?" Everybody laughed, and we went on to very painless questioning about the dissertation.

Hart continued on to say

> It was really generous of Knight to give me such an easy ride at the very end. I had managed to conceal from myself the extent to which the dissertation was a direct attack on Knight's own work. In *Risk, Uncertainty and Profit*, Knight made out that what was interesting about uncertainty was that it "explained" the otherwise inexplicable phenomenon of (residual net) profit. But I was saying that uncertainty

> is interesting because it requires *building flexibility into investment decisions* [Hart's emphasis]. This conflict was underlined by the tactless title which I gave presently to my article in the memorial volume for Henry Schultz, which I called "Risk, Uncertainty, and the Unprofitability of Compounding Probabilities".

While Hart's remarks focus on Knight's approach to uncertainty as a rationalization for the existence of profits, much more needs to be said. Knightian uncertainty due to its subjectivist rejection of the general applicability of the frequestist approach to probability in the formation of expectations often is taken as similar to Keynes' views on uncertainty. Knight's famous distinction (1921: 19–20) between "risk" as "a quantity susceptible of measurement" and "uncertainty" as "non-quantitative" certainly leads to the suggestion that the latter resembles Keynes' notion (1936: 152) of the type of uncertainty that envelops business decisions: "our existing knowledge does not provide a sufficient basis for a calculated mathematical expectation".

But unlike Keynes (and Hart) who ultimately argued that human beings coped with uncertainty through the adoption of conventions (rules of thumb), Knight argued that the market system afforded a mechanism for managing uncertainty. That mechanism was insurance; even "uncertain" events, in Knight's sense could be insured against. As he put it (1921: 250) "the insurance principle can be applied even in the almost complete absence of scientific data for the computation of rates".

What limits the efficacy of this solution to the problem of uncertainty, for Knight, was not the measurability versus non-measurability of prospects in the future. Knight wrote (1921: 251): "The fact which limits the application of the insurance principle to business risks generally is not therefore their inherent uniqueness alone". The decisive limitation on the insurance principle for Knight (1921: 251) was the "moral hazard" problem, that is to say, the potential that the provision of insurance would lead the insured to undertake actions that would bring about the even protected against to collect on their policy. Organizational reform and so on would not overcome this limitation; to mitigate the moral hazard problem would require nothing less than a "a revolutionary transformation in human nature itself" (Knight 1921: 253; also see LeRoy and Singell 1987).

Hart was a Knight student but not a Knight disciple, despite his obvious affection for his teacher, he did not follow Knight down the road of the insurance principle when he took up the question of uncertainty and expectational economics, although his views on uncertainty were as distant from rational expectations as those of Knight.

After being awarded his PhD, in 1936/37 Hart visited Berkeley but returned to Chicago and "began to reshape" his dissertation into the monograph that "eventually appeared in 1940 (as a supplement to the *Journal of Business*)". The next year 1937/38 found Hart as project director of the Twentieth Century Fund in New York, having been placed there by Jacob Viner, and after completing his work there returned to Chicago. Early in 1939, Hart joined the faculty at Iowa State at Ames, and in October 1940, he engaged in a debate with Shackle in the pages of the *RES* on "the nature of the inducement to invest" and the role of uncertainty and expectations in the process (Hart 1940b; Shackle 1940a, 1940b).

After wartime service at the US Treasury and the Committee for Economic Development, Hart took a position at Columbia University. In "Model Building and Fiscal Policy" Hart (1945: 532, 549) complained that recent model-systems were "in some respects seriously misleading . . . with all improvements, such systems cannot bring us as near the threshold of policy recommendations as their sponsors seem to think". The idea that economists could "ask our model-system what would happen under different policies" was a "pipedream". At this stage of his thinking, Hart focused on "the imperfection of foresight" and the static nature of the models to derive his conclusion that such an approach was "incapable of guiding policy in this way". Within three years, his thinking had apparently expanded to include the implausibility of "invariance" (later associated with Lucas and Sargent) and the idea that it was essential to model forward-looking expectations on the grounds that backward looking models "wastes evidence". This predates Muth's argument (1961: 315) that the rational expectations hypothesis involves the belief that "the economy does not generally waste information".

In 1948 he published his important textbook *Money, Debt and Economic Activity* which contained expectational analysis. As Hart recalled

> Having taught "Money and banking" for several years at Chicago, I naturally felt (as early as the mid-1930's) the quasi-instinctive impulse of the ambitious teacher to seek to develop a worth-while textbook. Hick's "Suggestion for Simplifying the Theory of Money", whose initial presentation I had heard at LSE, had booted me out of the American money-velocity approach. My favorite idea that in the face of uncertainty a decision-maker wants to keep options open led me on into the view that a strong cash position "reduces the linkage of risks". My work at the Treasury in 1934 and with the Twentieth Century Fund in 1937/38 (both times under the influence of Viner) gave me special qualifications for analyzing debt structures. And I had not forgotten the Hayekian "cycle" problems which had led me into the problems of expectations in the first place.

Hart's book was published in 1948 and actually went into a fourth edition in 1969, but as he said "to an undue extent I let this book become the primary vehicle for ideas which should have been more fully worked out in articles and book reviews". Having introduced the "principle of linkage of risks" in his book, Hart came to realize that "this procedure failed to reach economists interested in the 'probability approach' to decisions under uncertainty, except as they might happen to be assigned to teach monetary courses". In fact, as Hart noted, in his 1948 book "expectational analysis came to the fore", when not only did he introduce his "linkage of risks" principle but when he dealt at chapter length in detail with "anticipations and surprises" (1948: Chapter 9).

The Hart Research Agenda

Hart's "research agenda" was presented at the December 1948 meeting of the American Economic Association in a joint session with the Econometric Society on "Liquidity and Uncertainty". Marschak and Hart presented papers with Friedman and Modigliani, among others, as discussants. Knight attended the conference, where his report was delivered at the business meeting.

Now, in his book *Risk Uncertainty and Profit*, Knight (1921: 197, 237–8, 259) explained that "chief among the simplifications of reality prerequisite to the achievement of perfect competition is, as has been emphasized all along, the assumption of practical omniscience on the part of every member of the competitive system". Knight continued: "the fundamental uncertainties of economic life are the errors in predicting the future and in making present adjustment to fit future conditions ... At the bottom of the uncertainty problem in economics is the forward looking character of the economic process itself ... It goes without saying that rational conduct strives to reduce to a minimum the uncertainties involved in adapting ends to means". His work on uncertainty was referred to in Marschak's paper "The role of liquidity under complete and incomplete information" (1949: 184). But it was Hart's paper "Assets, liquidity and investment", which outlined a research agenda based on the same premise from which Lucas (1976: 25) and Sargent and Wallace (1976: 172) began: the implausibility of the implicit assumption of "invariance" with respect to estimation patterns when the economic environment changes.

In the *AER* papers and proceedings issue of May 1949, Hart and Marschak published their papers, with Friedman, Goodwin, Modigliani, and Tobin taking part in the "discussion" that followed. Hart dealt with the role of knowledge, plans and expectations in investment theory, while Marschak dealt with the "role of liquidity under complete and incomplete information. In his paper Hart presented (1949: 171), as he put it then, "the questions which investment theory has to ask of such an investigation as that now being launched at the University of Illinois" and went on to propose a research program which focused on "some areas of ignorance" in this field (1949: 174–7). Among other questions, Hart asked (1949: 175–6) "How do firms accept estimates at second hand, and how do they formulate ... estimates at home? Are estimation procedures ... slow changing or are they subject to frequent impulsive changes in response to waves of opinion? How far can we trace changes in businessmen's estimation patterns to definite actions or utterances by government officials . . . ?" In order to conduct the research needed to answer these and related questions, Hart (1949: 177) proposed that "the remedy lies in building up teams which include both economists and specialists in 'attitude studies' . . . and will be the procedure in the University of Illinois study".

Hart (1949: 178) explained that "the theory of fluctuations" was "probably the main place to apply a theory of investment in the firm". In his section on "Suggestions for macroeconomic models of business fluctuations", Hart (1949: 180) argued that "we must formulate our models so as to give explicit recognition to plans and estimates. There has long been a tendency to shy away from plans and estimates on the grounds that they are "not observable". If estimates rely on experience of "observables", and plans rest on estimates, why not "dynamicize" our economic equations simply by setting up models where past observables (prices, outputs, etc.) enter the determination of present observables? The objection to this simplification should be overwhelming. First, it wastes evidence, since estimates and plans are in fact observable if we adopt correct procedures. Second, and more important, it can yield correct results only if estimation patterns are invariant relative to the economic changes we wish to study. But this invariance is implausible – both in the light of scattered evidence on estimation procedures and in the light of the well known failure of "lagged" relationships to stand up in the next period".

Invariance also figured in other areas of Hart's argument (1949: 180–1). For example, one of the "major advantages" of "explicit formulation in terms of plans and expectations", was that models could be used which gave "explicit recognition to uncertainty". Previously, there had been a "strong tendency among theorists to push uncertainty under the rug". This was unfortunate because "several phenomena which are of key importance for fluctuations cannot be adequately explained without explicit recognition of uncertainty". Uncertainty was not invariant over the course of the business cycle, indeed: "changes in degree and type of uncertainty also bear importantly on fluctuations". Likewise, the political climate was not invariant: "the effect of politics on business, again, must take hold largely through its influence on the uncertainty attached to business estimates". Hart's conclusion was that "there is no substitute for a pattern of dynamic analysis which takes the forward-looking thinking of businessmen into account and seeks its simplification in observed patterns of such thinking rather than in its neglect".

But Hart's research agenda also called for an empirical investigation into these areas. In addition to exploiting "underutilized knowledge", Hart proposed that economists collaborate with other social scientists to formulate fieldwork questionnaires: "attitude studies" to be conducted at the University of Illinois. The purpose was to acquire "facts about the firm" so as to facilitate "affected theorizing". Hart drew up a catalog of questions where "we urgently need more and better fact-finding". These questions involved the investigation of the relationship between the external environment and estimation patterns: "How far can we trace changes in businessmen's estimation patterns to definite actions or utterances by government officials, trade associations, business leaders, politicians?" (1949: 174–7).

Hart's paper is interesting in that it contained ideas that flourished into two very distinct approaches to economics. The debate was in part about the appropriate starting point for economic analysis. The rational expectations approach sought to place macroeconomics on respectable neoclassical microeconomic foundations; the bounded rationality approach sought to discover respectable microfoundations for microeconomics. It also provided some stimulus to the method of economic research that came to be dominant postwar period. For example on 8 November 1948, Friedman wrote to Don Patinkin that he had been "trying to write some kind of logical methodology on the general methodological problem you raise" (cited by Leeson 1998 [2003]: 444). On 29 December 1948, when discussing Hart's paper Friedman took issue with Hart (1949: 198–9) and said that he did not believe that [Hart's] Agenda for research is useful. In particular I venture to predict that few really useful results will be obtained by his implied proposal to fill in the areas of ignorance ... by asking questions of businessmen ... It seems to me that as yet we do not know what phenomenon Hart wishes to see explained, and that it is therefore premature to seek explanations. When we are in a position to seek explanations, we should do so in the objective data determining the phenomena and describing past reactions to similar phenomena, not in what selective people think". He concluded

> I doubt that any reasonably simple answers to many of Hart's questions exist; or that if the answers exist, businessmen know them; or if they do know the answers, they will give them in response to questioning. In work of this kind, it is important to remember that homo sapiens is distinguished from other animals more by his ability to rationalize than by his ability to reason.

Now, in his *Methodology of Positive Economics* Friedman (1953: 30–1) drew "Some implications for economic issues". Friedman's interest and method was informed by his concern about the direction of economics: "The abstract methodological issues we have been discussing have a direct bearing on the perennial criticisms of 'orthodox' economic theory as 'unrealistic' as well as on the attempts that have been made to reformulate theory to meet this charge". One of these criticisms that his proposed method was designed to overcome was the view that economics "rested on outmoded psychology and must be reconstructed in line which with each new development in psychology ... A particularly clear example is furnished by the recent criticisms of the maximization-of-returns hypothesis on the grounds that businessmen do not and indeed cannot behave as the theory 'assumes' they do. The evidence cited to support this assertion is generally taken either from the answers given by businessmen to questions about the factors affecting their decisions ... or from descriptive studies of the decision-making activities of individual firms".

In the footnote attached to this material Friedman made it clear that he had gained methodological inspiration from his interaction with Hart's research agenda. Citing his reply to Hart, Friedman (1953: 31, n. 22) concluded that "descriptive studies of the decision-making activities of individual firms" were described as "almost entirely useless as a means of *testing* the validity of economic hypothesis" [emphasis in text]. Herbert Simon (1959: 254, n. 3) indicated that in turn he too had been "negatively" inspired by Friedman's methodology: "as an example of what passes for empirical 'evidence' in this literature, I cite pages 22–3 of Friedman's *Essays Positive Economics* which will amaze anyone brought up in the empirical tradition of psychology and sociology, although it has apparently elicited little adverse comment among economists".

Friedman (1949: 198) issued a disclaimer with respect to Hart's research agenda: "the proof of the pudding is in the eating". Modigliani – who had been recommended by Hart to lead the Illinois project – supported Hart's proposed research program and the questions it raised, but also found inspiration in Friedman's criticisms. Indeed, with some prescience, Modigliani said (1949: 202) "there hardly is a rational theory of deriving expectations current data". He continued on to say "indeed the economists own experience has not been too encouraging in this respect. On these types of problems the prospective investigation might help supply the needed factual background and to enable us to test the possible relevance of the psychological factors in the business cycle". He went on:

> even in those cases where the theory of rational behavior exists or can be elaborated, we frequently suspect that actual behavior follows a different pattern and that this pattern is not necessarily an erratic one. This pattern may be simply irrational (e.g. due to custom or prejudice) or it may be rational, or close to it, though in a sense not fitting our postulates of rationality. For instance, the cost of making the best decision, both psychological and material, is hardly taken into account in our theorizing, though it may in fact be a very important factor in explaining rules of thumb and non-optimal decisions. In this field then the inquiry should help to check our theoretical schemes against reality, indicate systematic biases and help perhaps to construct more useful schemes of analysis. Finally, it may suggest profitable lines for further development of the theory of rational behavior under the institutional setup that effectively confronts the decision makers.

Specifically, in Modiglianis' view, Hart's paper provided "a very useful conceptual framework from which to organize the University of Illinois projects on factors governing investment decisions". Finally, Modigliani concluded (1949: 203) that

> the inquiry we are undertaking, as well as a number of similar investigations which are being carried out from many sides, may well fail to produce any definite results, or perhaps even any valuable insight. Yet I feel that the a priori skepticism that is well represented by Professor Friedman's remarks ... should not deter us from trying. The considerable number of research projects which are already proceeding or are getting under way in this and closely related fields indicates that we are not the only ones who feel that this method of approach is worth trying ... By co-ordinating our intellectual resources we should be able to make our work far more productive and we might really succeed in disappointing the pessimistic expectations of Professor Friedman. And I know that Professor Friedman himself would ask for nothing better.

Friedman's "pessimistic expectations" thus contributed to the momentum of the bounded rationality literature. What then, were the "considerable number of research projects" which were "already proceeding" or "getting under way" on expectational economics "and closely related fields" that Modigliani mentioned? How did the Illinois project that he led come into being, and for that matter, what was its outcome and what were its results? It is to this that we now turn our attention.

3 Expectations research projects

From Illinois to Carnegie Tech

In his autobiography, Herbert Simon (1991: 250) summed up his ongoing critique of RE by saying how ironic it was that both his own theory of "bounded rationality and RE", although totally "antithetical" were developed in the same institution – the Carnegie Tech Graduate School of Industrial Administration. Now, the Carnegie Tech research project was a *direct* "spin-off" of the Illinois expectations research project, as will be seen below. Between 1949, when the Illinois project was first discussed at the American Economic Association meetings by Hart, Modigliani, and Friedman, as noted above, and 1959, when Muth and Mills first gave their respective RE papers at the December 1959 meeting of the Econometric Society, there were a number of important expectations research projects conducted on a "formal" and "informal" basis in both the US and UK.

"Formal" projects were *specifically established* at universities and other institutions to study the role of expectations, while "informal" projects consisted of academics and graduate students who dealt with expectations in the context of *individual* research programs or in small groups.

Formal large-scale projects were conducted at the University of Illinois and later at Carnegie Tech, among other institutions, while there were more informal and small-scale projects at Oxford and Birmingham Universities in the UK and at Northwestern and Johns Hopkins in the US. In addition, a number of institutions and organizations collected, analyzed, and published data on consumer, producer, and investment expectations and intentions, such as the Survey Research Center at Michigan and the NBER at Columbia in the academic sector; the Federal Reserve Consultant Committee, National Industrial Conference Board, US Department of Commerce, and Consumer's Union in the public sector; and McGraw-Hill and Dun and Bradstreet in the private sector. In this chapter, we will deal with what we think were the most important formal and informal projects, committees, and conferences involved in the developmental period of expectational economics, and also deal with the interaction between these projects and the personalities involved.

Programs, committees, and conferences: from Illinois to Carnegie Tech

In August 1954, the "Subcommittee on Economic Statistics" of the Congressional "Joint Committee on the Economic Report" persuaded the Chairman and the Board of Governors of the US Federal Reserve System to establish five "task groups" on expectations and statistics. The object of these groups was to provide "an evaluation of available statistical information in the fields of savings, business inventories, and business and consumer expectations" to serve as "a basis for improvement of both public and private statistical programs in these areas over the years ahead" (McChesney Martin 1954). Among economists in the "savings statistics" group were Raymond Goldsmith of the NBER, who served as chairman, and Simon Kuznets of Johns Hopkins and the NBER. The "consumer expectations" group was chaired by Arthur Smithies of Harvard and included Guy Orcutt of Harvard and James Tobin of Yale. The "inventory statistics" group includes Moses Abramovitz of Stanford and the NBER and Ruth Mack of the NBER. The "plant and equipment expenditure expectations" group included Irwin Friend of Pennsylvania. Finally, the "general business expectations" group included Albert Hart of Columbia University. Hart was the "primary author" of the chapters in the Committee report dealing with "present knowledge of business expectations" (Chapter II) and "open questions and agenda for the study of expectations" (Chapter VII). As Hart later recalled "the work of this committee led our chairman to persuade his private research agency (the National Industrial Conference Board) to introduce its quarterly survey of capital appropriations. This was launched in 1955 and is still running on the same basis in 1991".

Albert Hart played an important role at the start of the Illinois research project on expectations. In an interview (Hart 1991), Hart recalled that

> at the time when Adlai Stevenson ... was governor of Illinois, a major effort was made to bring economics at the University of Illinois out of its long standing mediocrity. Under the leadership of Howard Bowen (who was brought over from Iowa to be Dean of Business) a splash of really excellent appointments brought the Department of Economics up suddenly to a standing among the best five U.S. universities. One aspect of this "splash" was the establishment of a center for research in the expectational field. When Bowen consulted me about the directorship of this center, I recommended Franco Modigliani whom I had placed somewhat earlier as a postdoctoral fellow with T.W. Schultz at the University of Chicago.

Hart continued

> Modigliani brought into this research center a number of excellent young economists ... But presently the atmosphere at Illinois turned sour ... the survivors of the traditional mediocre department staged a successful counter-revolution and made life impossible for the new batch of distinguished new members of the department. Modigliani was one of the early ones to leave Illinois. Since I had long been on good terms with Lee Bach (then Dean at Carnegie Tech) I recommended Modigliani for a vacancy there (this was the last time I "placed" him in a new job. I had no part in his moves to Northwestern and then to MIT) ... He brought some people with him, and recruited some new young people of high quality.

In a letter to one of the authors, Modigliani wrote (16 September 1991)

> I became interested in problems of expectations in 1949 when I became the Principal Investigator in a project entitled "Research Project on Business Expectations and Planning" initiated at the Bureau of Economic Research of the University of Illinois. It was financed together with the N.O.R.C. of the University of Chicago, primarily from a grant by the Merrill Foundation ... The project lasted from 1949 to 1952, but many of the ideas that were inspired by that research have been used in papers which have appeared throughout my career and that of others. It dealt broadly with the role of expectations in business planning and their use for economic forecasting.
>
> The main results of the project were brought together and summarized in a monograph "The Role of Anticipations and Plans in Economic Behavior and their use in Economic Analysis and Forecasting" co-authored with K.J. Cohen, and published in 1961 by the Bureau of Economics and Business Research of the University of Illinois.

He went on to say

> Several people worked with me, of whom two have since reached wide recognition. One is Robert Ferber, a distinguished statistician who died a few years ago; his contributions to the project and to the role of expectations are listed in the bibliography of the monograph cited above. The other, Robert Eisner is covered only partly in the same bibliography ... My own published contributions are listed in the bibliography of the monograph.
>
> The project ended in 1952, when I left the University of Illinois. However, the ideas generated by the project have played a role in much of my subsequent work. One well-known extension was a paper with Emil Grunberg (1954) which supposedly provided the foundation

> for the theory of macro-rational expectations of Lucas and Sargent. The collaboration with Grunberg was fostered first by the fact that we had known each other before meeting at [Carnegie] Tech, as we both worked at the Institute of World Affairs of the New School for Social Research. We both developed an interest in the effect of forecasts on changing behavior. I showed him some examples of what I had worked out, and we decided to pursue the matter more formally. Our work made a great step forward when Herbert Simon suggested that our results could be generalized by means of Brower's Fixed Point Theorem. Similarly, one of the ideas central to the project, namely the importance of smoothing production in the face of erratic and systematic (seasonal) changes in sales has inspired my work on the Life Cycle Hypothesis of Savings, where what is being smoothed is Consumption by means of Saving.

Among the most important individual and group research projects involved in the Illinois research program that eventually reached the publication stage were: "The predictability of social events" (Grunberg and Modigliani 1954); "Economic expectations and plans of firms in relation to short-term forecasting" (Modigliani and Sauerlender 1955); "Forecasting uses of anticipatory data on investment and sales" (Modigliani and Weingartner 1958, 1959); "The source of regressiveness in surveys of businessmen's short-run expectations" (Bossons and Modigliani 1960); "Expectations, plans and capital expenditures: a synthesis of ex post and ex ante data" (Eisner 1958); "Measuring the accuracy and structure of businessmen's expectations" (Ferber 1953); "The stability of consumer expectations" (Ferber 1955) and "The accuracy and structure of industry expectations in relation to those of individual firms" (Ferber 1958); "Business investment programs and their realization" and "Plant and equipment programs and their realization" (Friend and Bronfenbrenner 1950, 1955); and "The role of anticipations and plans in economic behavior and their use in economic analysis and forecasting" (Modigliani and Cohen 1961).

Despite their focus upon empirical questions, nevertheless, the expectations researchers were self-consciously attempting to formulate a "theoretical structure" to accommodate their insights. James Savage's "expected utility" hypothesis (Friedman and Savage 1952) was the starting point for their analysis of "rational behavior". This consisted of two postulates. First, "that the information available to the agent concerning an uncertain event – such as the value of an unknown parameter – can be represented by a "subjective" probability distribution". The second postulate was that "the agent act as though he was endeavoring to maximize the expected value of his utility". The theory was then elaborated to include the relationship between "expectations" and forecasting without "a satisfactory theory which explains the underlying mechanism ... We believe that both the stated plan and actual behavior are caused by some common mechanism. This proposition holds with even greater force for the relation between anticipations and the behavior of the environment. The observed regularity does not per se throw any light on the nature of this underlying common mechanism" (Modigliani and Cohen 1961: 9, 28, 84).

Now, the Illinois project on "Expectations and Business Fluctuations" was designed to address the question: "Can expectations independently be a source of instability in an economy?" In the introduction to his *Collected Papers*, Modigliani (1980: xx) emphasized "the impact of that research on my professional development". The Life Cycle model, for which he was awarded the Nobel Prize, "was partly inspired by the analysis undertaken during the course of that project". As noted above, Modigliani (1995: 147–50), was recruited by Howard Bowen, the Dean of the College of Commerce of University of Illinois, to head the expectations research project. But, Modigliani also recalled that there was an old guard at Illinois who "felt passe, inferior" to the new recruits. The new guard included Don Patinkin, Everett Hagen, Dorothy Brady, Robert Eisner, Margaret Reid, and Leonid Hurwicz. There were ideological divisions within the faculty between "self-styled free marketeers and Keynesians". Indeed, Bowen was regarded as "anti-business". Editorials in various Chicago newspapers complained that basic teaching now favored deficit spending and government controls rather than free enterprise. The old guard was finally victorious and Bowen, together with Modigliani and Hurwicz and the others resigned from the University. Modigliani complained to the University President that the victorious group were "interested not in Scholarship but in personal power [and] in the gratification of their vindictive impulses". Their victory was "the peace of death" (Solberg and Tomlinson 1997: 55, 73, 66, 80). Thus a remarkable group of economists with a remarkable research project was broken up.

In 1944, Hurwicz taught Patinkin at Chicago. During their joint time (1946–48) at the Cowles Commission, Hurwicz "tutored" Patinkin (1981: 9, 15) in mathematical statistics and in "clarifying the properties of homogenous functions". The New Classical economists describe the Natural Rate hypothesis as "the homogeneity of degree zero of supply with respect to prices and expected prices". They added to this the rational expectations hypothesis to derive the policy ineffectiveness proposition, as will be seen below (Sargent and Wallace 1976: 174–5). In an *Econometrica* essay on "Theory of the Firm and of Investment", Hurwicz (1946: 109, 133) sought to provide "a general theory of entrepreneurial behavior" in part to resolve "some of the most fundamental controversies in the theory of economic fluctuations". Citing Knight's *Risk Uncertainty and Profit* (1921), Hurwitz (1946: 120, 131, 133) titled a section "Risk, uncertainty, rational expectations". He also stressed that "just how expectations are actually formed is one of the most important questions and it can be answered by appeal to empirical evidence".

In a 1949 NBER "Conference on Business Cycles" Hurwicz (1951: 417) emphasized that "while government is attempting to carry out the policy, a good deal of freedom will be left to the individual units (consumers, entrepreneurs, labor unions, banks, etc.). Such a unit is primarily motivated by its own objectives (individual utility maximization) and its decisions are based to a considerable extent on the expectation of future actions of the government. More precisely, the *public* i.e. the aggregate of the individual units, follows a rule of behavior dependent on the (subjective) information available to it" [emphasis in original]. Hurwicz (1951: 419) stressed that "in particular, there is nothing obvious about the effectiveness of the 'automatic stabilizer' as a class, once the possible changes in expectations are taken into account".

In "Prediction for policy purpose" Hurwicz (1950: 278) also emphasized that "one of the most important cases of need for prediction under changed structure is that of certain types of economic policies. There are cases where structural changes are not due to policy decisions (e.g. spontaneous changes in taste); nor do all policies imply structural change; some only improve manipulation of ... non-structural policies. But when a change is to be made between two policies implying the respective structural changes ... one cannot decide between them (no matter what the policy objective) without knowing just how they will affect certain variables".

Modigliani left for Carnegie Tech, which he found to be "an ideal place for working together ... that was before any of the people associated with Chicago were there, except Alan Meltzer" (Klamer 1984: 119). Lucas recalled that during his time at Carnegie (1963–74), prior to his return to Chicago, there "was a kind of Chicago faction and a non-Chicago faction" (Klamer 1984: 33). Nevertheless, the tensions at Carnegie were obviously productive academically, unlike those at Illinois.

The 1954, the *Journal Political Economy* published "The predictability of social events" by Modigliani and his Carnegie colleague Emil Grunberg. Modigliani specifically described his own contribution to the paper as "an outgrowth of the research on 'Expectations and Business Fluctuations' ". The final footnote describes a future research agenda: "the argument of this paper suggests that the agents' reactions may create difficulties for the formulation and execution of policy. The problem raised by this relationship between public prediction and policy do not belong within the scope of the present paper" (Grunberg and Modigliani 1954: 465, n. 2, 478, n. 45). It was this question that Lucas addressed (Klamer 1984: 125).

In October 1955, the Committee on Business Enterprise Research of the US Social Science Research Council sponsored a conference on "Expectations, Uncertainty and Business Behavior" which was held at the Carnegie Institute of Technology. While the proceedings of the conference were only published three years later (Bowman 1958), the conference was *crucial* in the development of expectational economics. Among the participants in the conference were: Boulding, Eisner, Friend, Hart, Katona, Mack, Georgescu-Roegen, Koopmans, Modigliani, Simon, and Theil. Shackle also had a paper read on his behalf. The crucial importance of this conference has been recognized by Hart, who in an interview (Hart 1991) maintained that "the layout of the conference went a long way to establish Carnegie Tech as the new center for expectational research". Among the papers presented at the conference was one by Modigliani and Cohen on "The significance and uses of ex ante data" (1958 [1955]); a fuller and more rigorous exposition of which appeared later (that is Modigliani and Cohen 1961). Another important paper presented was by Simon entitled "The role of expectations in an adaptive or behavioristic model" (Simon 1958 [1955]). With regard to the latter paper, Albert Hart maintained as late as 1991 that

> This difficult but rewarding paper has apparently not yet been fully digested by expectational economists [including myself!]. His [Simon's] distinction between programmed and unprogrammed decision-making seems very fundamental; and its implications as to the urgency of avoiding time consuming reorientation would seem to have much to do with the danger of being swamped with possibly relevant but difficult data.

Interestingly enough, the problem of data collection and its usefulness in expectational economics, as Hart termed it, also concerned Modigliani and Cohen. Indeed, at the end of their 1961 monograph – which was based on their 1955 conference paper (1958 [1955]: 9) – they stated (1961: 152)

> In concluding our analysis, we should like to point out one somewhat paradoxical implication to which it leads. The position we have taken throughout … is that the usefulness of *ex ante* data stems primarily from our inadequate present knowledge, at least from a quantitative viewpoint, of the factors controlling many relevant aspects of economic behavior. For forecasting purposes, such data help us as a substitute for missing knowledge; for analytical purposes, they should help us to acquire the missing knowledge by throwing light on the intervening links in the process by which *ex post* data generate other *ex post* data. This being the case, if through the collection and analysis of anticipatory data we should someday in fact succeed in acquiring the missing knowledge, continual compilation of such data may well become unnecessary from an analytical point of view – although it may still be justified as an efficient forecasting device.

In her introduction to the volume that dealt with the conference, Bowman also stressed the importance of the papers by Simon on the one hand, and Modigliani and Cohen on the other, the links between the two, and the influence of Simon's "insights" (Bowman 1958: 3–7). As she put it (1958: 3)

> It is hardly surprising that some of his basic concepts were picked up by discussants from different backgrounds and provide unifying links among many papers. The reader can easily reconstruct these links if he keeps Simon's paper in mind when reading the others.

Bowman went on to present points from Hart's comments on Simon's paper and noted that in his discussion, Hart "summarizes an underlying theme of much of the paper by Modigliani and Cohen" and that this "indicates the underlying links between that paper and Simon's analysis" (1958: 7). Interestingly enough, in her own discussion of the Modigliani and Cohen paper, Bowman wrote (1958: 8) that "revisions" of it "have been extensive".

The linkage between the Modigliani–Cohen and Simon papers noted by Bowman is another illustration of the Illinois–Carnegie Tech connection described by Hart. For if the object of the 1955 Carnegie Tech conference was to "salvage for the profession" the results of the Illinois expectations project, then it succeeded. After the conference Carnegie Tech became the focal point for expectations research in the US.

One somewhat overlooked, albeit interesting example of the type of research undertaken in the context of the Carnegie Tech program appeared as early as 1955, when Modigliani and Sauerlender (1955) presented a paper at the NBER conference on short-term economic forecasting entitled "Economic expectations and plans of firms in relation to short-term forecasting" based upon research conducted at Illinois. Modigliani had by this time moved to Carnegie Tech. In their comment on the paper, Cooper and Simon (1955: 355–9) described the approach they were developing at Carnegie Tech "in connection with a project on intra-firm behavior" and showed how it *complemented* that of Modigliani and Sauerlender. According to them (1955: 355–6), Modigliani and Sauerlender introduced the informational aspect of "feed-forward (or predictive) control" into "the model of production and inventory behavior". As they put it "at the present time, t, an estimate is formed of how conditions will appear" a number of "units hence". They continued on to say "on the basis of this expectation, and by means of comparison with current outputs, corrective information is carried back to be translated into a change in production or input schedules". Cooper and Simon went on to diagrammatically illustrate (1955: 357) what they saw as the "servomechanical" analogy used by Modigliani and Sauerlender and also distinguished on this basis between "rational" and "adaptive" economic behavior.

According to Cooper and Simon (1955: 357–8) "human behavior probably exhibits elements of both the 'rational' and the 'adaptive'" and the approach they "suggested" was "a combination of 'adaptive' and 'rational' behavior", or as they put it, optimization via "maximization of discounted expected gain" combined with *continual* behavioral adjustment "to changes in external conditions rapidly enough and successfully enough to avoid trouble", that is a "minimax" adjustment "principle".

Another example of the Illinois–Carnegie Tech connection is the *Quarterly Journal of Economics* paper by Modigliani and Weingartner (1958) entitled "Forecasting uses of anticipatory data on investment and sales". In their view (23), this paper was "an outgrowth of the project 'Expectations and Economic Fluctuations' financed by a grant from the Merrill Foundation ... and carried out at the University of Illinois under the direction of the senior author [Modigliani]". The research reported was also "supported in part by a research grant from the Graduate School of Industrial Administration [GSIA]" and "the paper was completed at the Carnegie Institute of Technology in May, 1957".

But the *most important* example of the Illinois–Carnegie Tech connection is the now classic paper by Grunberg and Modigliani (1954) entitled "The predictability of social events". Both authors were then at Carnegie Tech, but in a footnote (1954: 465, n. 2) Modigliani wrote "my contribution to this paper is an outgrowth of the research on 'Expectations and Business Fluctuations' financed by a grant from the Merrill Foundation", that is that same grant that financed most of the Illinois expectations research program.

In their paper, Grunberg and Modigliani acknowledged that Simon's "contributions" were "too numerous to be listed" (1954: 465, n. 1). Almost three decades later, in his collected works, Simon (1982: vol. I, 405) noted that his *own* paper on the possibility of public prediction (1954) "was stimulated by conversations with them about their work". In their article, Grunberg and Modigliani (1954: 465–78) challenged the previously generally accepted view that a publicly made economic forecast could be proven wrong since economic agents would change their behavior as a result of the public forecast itself. They proposed instead that expectations could be self-validating. In their view (1954: 470)

> it is reasonable to anticipate that as consistently correct public predictions are made, "learning" occurs, so that the expectations function will, over time, undergo continuous, or more likely, discontinuous change until it takes the form [expected price = publicly predicted price]. Agents will then act upon warranted expectations and will no longer be (agreeably or disagreeably) disappointed.

In his collected works, Simon (1982: vol. II, 405) noted that "Muth, in his famous paper on rational expectations (1961), refers to the Grunberg–Modigliani article" and continued on to say that while their 1954 approach "falls far short of stating the full rational expectations thesis (it actually states an adaptive expectations hypothesis)", it still "shows that the problem to which that thesis is addressed was in the Pittsburgh [Carnegie Tech] air as early as 1954".

Almost a decade later, in his autobiography, Simon (1991a: 249–50) summarized the development of the Carnegie Tech expectations research project in concise and lucid terms. Simon counterpointed his own theory of *bounded rationality* – which he developed at Carnegie over the period 1952–60 – with the theory of *rational* expectations developed by Muth *over* the period 1958–61 *while also at Carnegie Tech*, which Muth, according to Simon "explicitly labeled" as "a reply to my doctrine of bounded rationality" (Simon 1991a: 271). Simon, for his part, had developed his approach within the framework of the behavioral theory of the firm and Organization theory that had evolved during the 1950s in the GSIA at Carnegie Tech (Simon 1991: 164–5, 249–51, 270–1). But, as Simon put it (1991a: 164) "By the early 1960s the Golden Age of Organization theory and the behavioral theory of the firm had ended at Carnegie Institute of Technology".

Over the period 1954–60, Simon was also involved in what he called (1958 [1955]: 52, n. 6) "a rather extensive program of research into the theory and practice of dynamic programming" along with Charles Holt (from Chicago), Franco Modigliani (from Illinois), and John Muth (then at Carnegie Tech). According to Simon (1991a: 167), the "main direct product" of "the dynamic programming project" was the book by the "HMMS research team" (1991a: 249–50) entitled *Planning Production, Inventories and Work Force* (Holt *et al.* 1960). But, in Simon's view (1991a: 167) "it also had an indirect product-rational expectations". As Simon recalled in his autobiography (1991a: 249–50), John Muth

> as a graduate student, had been a valuable member of the Holt–Modigliani–Muth–Simon ... team in the dynamic programming research ... In our project, he investigated techniques for predicting future sales and generally for dealing with uncertainty. Shortly, after completing his dissertation, which was related to the project, Jack [Muth] published in *Econometrica* in 1961 a novel suggestion for handling uncertainty in economics. He clearly deserves a Nobel for it, even though I do not think it describes the real world correctly. Sometimes an idea that is not literally correct can have great scientific importance.

Simon continued

> The theory of rational expectations offered a direct challenge to theories of bounded rationality, for it assumed a rationality in economic actors beyond any limits that had previously been considered even in neoclassical theory.

Simon went on to relate that Lucas and Sargent, both at the GSIA of Carnegie Tech in the early 1970s "brought the theory of rational expectations into national and international prominence". He then noted that

> It is not without irony that bounded rationality and rational expectations, two of the major proposals after Keynes for the revision of economic theory (game theory is a third) though entirely antithetical to each other, were engendered in and flourished in the same small business school at almost the same time.
>
> Not only did they flourish, but they were represented, along with Keynesian theory, in a four-man team that worked closely and amicably together for several years on a joint research project. . . .

which, as Simon put it "harbored simultaneously two Keynesians (Modigliani and Holt), the prophet of bounded rationality (Simon), and the inventor of rational expectations (Muth) – the previous orthodoxy, a heresy, and a new orthodoxy".

While Simon won the Nobel Prize in Economics, he was not a supporter of the mainstream neoclassical maximization theory regarding economic agents. Indeed, his theory of bounded rationality is in direct opposition to it, and Simon himself described (1991a: 270) his conflict with the mainstream in terms of "combat", "hostilities", and "war". As he recalled in his autobiography (1991a: 270–1).

> The first hostilities took the form of counterattacks from the opponents of bounded rationality: from Edward S. Mason (1952 [1951]) and Fritz Machlup (1946), the former claiming that my revisions of the theory of the firm were not very relevant to economic theory, the latter that people, whatever the appearances, really maximized. But the blame for the war is not easily assigned . . . Certainly my colleagues in economics at Carnegie soon knew of my skepticism. Franco Modigliani, while remaining a close friend during his Pittsburgh years and ever since, never mistook me for an ally in matters of economic theory. And Jack Muth, in his announcement of rational expectations in 1961, explicitly labeled his theory a reply to my doctrine of bounded rationality. Lunchtime debate with my colleagues . . . undoubtedly contributed to the gradual escalation of my conflict with the profession.

However, as will be seen below, "lunchtime debate" and discussion between others involved in the evolution of rational expectations actually stimulated its development and the debate over its analytical efficacy; and this *even before the publication of Muth's pathbreaking 1961 paper.*

Projects and personalities: from Birmingham to Carnegie Tech

The problem of expectations was at the forefront of economic inquiry not only in the US. Prior to the Second World War expectations had received treatment by members of the "Stockholm School", such as Myrdal, Lundberg, and Lindhal; by Dutch economists such as Tinbergen; by English economists, such as Pigou, Robertson, Hawtrey, Keynes, Harrod, Hicks, and Shackle; and also by economists of Austrian origin, such as Hayek and Morgenstern, among others. In terms of *including* expectations in models of economic behavior, that is *modeling* expectations and their formation – explicitly or implicitly – as early as 1952, Hahn and Gorman, while at Birmingham University in England (Hahn 1952: 806, n. 1) had developed a "general dynamic equilibrium model" based upon the introduction of a "'notional' system" constructed "on the assumption that all expectations are fulfilled" (Hahn 1952: 806). As Hahn remarked in a letter to one of the authors of this book some four decades later (Hahn 1991) "although Muth proposed an econometrician's rational expectations equilibrium, there were of course many predecessors with perfect foresight. Harrod was one. So was Pigou. So, for that matter, was I (*Economic Journal*, December 1952)".

It is important to recall here that at Birmingham, Hahn and Gorman had supervised the doctoral dissertation of Edwin Mills and thus also influenced his treatment of expectations, which turned out to be quite similar to that of Muth, as will be seen below. While not a formal research program per se, the approach developed by Hahn and Gorman while at Birmingham is *crucial* to the history of rational expectations (RE). This is best illustrated by the "'notional' system" of expectations that are "*consistent*" which they proposed (Hahn 1952: 807–8). Indeed, their approach not only foreshadowed that of Mills and Muth, but their notion of expectations that are "consistent" actually foreshadowed the RE terminology favored by Simon in his "Ely Lecture" to the American Economic Association some 25 years later (Simon 1978a: 2, 10). For example, Hahn (1952: 807) wrote that

> Decisions are taken by a multitude of individuals. The first requirement for the existence of expectation functions compatible with the notional system is that expectations should be consistent in the sense that there are conceivable actual events which would allow all expectations to be fulfilled simultaneously.

He then went on (1952: 807–10) to specify "a system of expectation equations" and the conditions for what he later called a "rational expectations equilibrium" accordingly (Hahn 1991).

During the 1950s and early 1960s two former students of Hicks at

Oxford University – Richardson at Oxford itself and Clower at Northwestern – also turned their attention to the problems of expectations, information, and knowledge. Hicks had greatly influenced Richardson, and as he said in the preface to the first edition of his book *Information and Investment* (1960), Hicks had "read the whole book in both its present and in an earlier form" and gave him "very valuable advice" regarding his work, besides helping and encouraging him from his "undergraduate days" at Oxford onwards. Richardson's stated object, as he put it in the preface to his book, was to attain a "satisfactory explanation of the attainment of equilibrium positions" in a market economy "grounded" on a "theory of the formation of entrepreneurial expectations". In order to do this, he linked expectations to information by stating the fact, as he saw it "that expectations are based on information, and that the availability to entrepreneurs of the required information is, in part, dependent upon the nature of the market structure or system of relationships within which they operate" (1960: preface); thereby extending themes he had developed as early as 1953 and 1956 and had extensively discussed in his somewhat overlooked June 1959 *Economic Journal* paper entitled "Equilibrium, expectations and information". Richardson's 1960 book on the subject has received increasing attention (Loasby 1986; Richardson 1990: 2nd edn), and will not be discussed in detail here. Suffice it to say, however, that his *ongoing work* (1953, 1956, 1959, 1964) has *not* received the attention it deserves (Young and Lee 1993).

A good example of this is his little known albeit quite important introductory textbook entitled *Economic Theory* (Richardson 1964) published in the Hutchinson series edited by Harrod. In this book, Richardson stressed (1964: 123, 136–42) that the lack of what he called the "informational requirement" needed "for efficient adjustment" in a market economy was a key element in the "unorthodox" critique of "the theory of perfect competition" which he called "logically unsound" (1964: preface, 7); referring the student back to his own 1960 book. However, both Richardson's books have been overlooked.

In an interview (Richardson 1993), Richardson recalled the origins of his 1960 book and Hicks' reaction to it. As he put it

> The central idea of *Information and Investment* was that businessmen need to have certain information to take investment decisions and that information is a function of the market structure assumed and the market structure affects the availability of information. That idea came to me while walking around St. John's College [Oxford] gardens. It didn't seem to have any other intellectual origin. Hicks didn't like the ideas of *Information and Investment* very much. He read it all. But he was pretty unsympathetic to it because he was rather committed to the perfect competition model, as he says explicitly in *Value and Capital*. So I can't find any sort of parentage. I suppose Hayek's ...

> famous article called "Economics and knowledge", which I think I read ... while I was writing the book had a great influence on my thinking ... Hicks was a very good tutor from this point of view, that he didn't tell you to read the latest articles. He told you to go back to the main writers on the subject. He got me to read Walras. And it is clear that Walras, and of course Edgeworth too, knew that they hadn't proved how there exists in the *real* world a *tendency* to equilibrium, hence these curious devices – *tatonnement*, *prix de crie*, *recontracting* and so on ... And the more I thought about it, is that if you stick with the perfect competition model, you just *cannot* attain equilibrium [his emphasis].

Clower, as a graduate student, was supervised by Hicks while at Oxford in the early 1950s, and was greatly influenced by him. Later on, between 1957 and 1959, Clower put together a number of works that dealt in part with problems involving expectations formation. For example, in his 1957 book with Bushaw entitled *Introduction to Mathematical Economics*, Clower dealt with price expectations in the framework of a "generalized theory of price determination" (Bushaw and Clower 1957: 176–85) and "parametric" pricing (1957: 184) that is, where *sale* price is *identical* to the *estimated* price (1957: 180–1, 184). Clower was also involved in a research project at Northwestern University sponsored by the US Navy's "Office of Naval Research" (ONR) entitled "Temporal Planning and Management Decisions under Risk and Uncertainty". In fact, "the research underlying" his paper entitled "Some theory of an ignorant monopolist" published in the December 1959 issue of *Economic Journal* "was undertaken for the project" (Clower 1959a: 705, n. 1). In addition, the paper he presented at the 24th Annual Conference of the Western Economic Association in 1959 "Oligopoly Theory: a dynamical approach" (Clower 1959b) and that at the December 1959 Washington meeting of the Econometric Society entitled "Inductive Inference and Business Behavior" – of which more will be said below – were also, it would seem, outcomes of this project.

The object of his 1959 *EJ* paper was, according to Clower (1959a: 705) "to encourage study of learning processes and delayed responses *within the framework of traditional economic theory*" [Clower's emphasis]. In this regard he developed the concept of "conjectural" functions for demand, supply, price, profit, marginal revenue, and even "market clearance" (1959a: 708–10). According to him, the system he proposed "clearly tends towards the 'true' equilibrium point ... where the conjectured position of the price function is consistent with realized results" (1959a: 711). Clower went on to draw parallels between his proposed approach and "cobweb" models (1959a: 711–12) and maintained that his approach was superior. As he put it (1959a: 714–15) "models which yield abrupt changes in the values of theoretical variables are hard to reconcile with known sets of economic data; hence it is desirable to avoid building models in which 'cobweb' phenomena are, so to speak, part of the basic structure".

The paper Clower presented to the December 1959 Washington, DC meeting of the Econometric Society (1959c [1960])was a *generalization* of the approaches he proposed in his *EJ* paper (1959a) which dealt with "learning processes" and monopoly theory and in his Western Economic Association Conference paper (1959b), which dealt with "learning processes" and oligopoly theory respectively. In this paper (1959c [1960]: 685–6), Clower argued that instead of simply dynamizing "traditional price theory" on the one hand, or instituting "a revolution in the foundations of the theory rather than a further evolution of its superstructure" on the other, what was needed, in order to overcome "the shortcomings of traditional theory", as he put it, was "an approach which lies somewhere between the two extremes".

Clower continued (1959c [1960]: 686)

> Perhaps the most promising possibility in this regard is to introduce into various traditional theories explicit assumptions about the way in which market participants learn from experience. This leads to logically precise "learning" models of output and price formation which are strictly traditional in flavor but whose empirical implications are not so clearly contradicted by causal empirical observation.

He went on to "specify rules of inductive inference to be followed by market participants under conditions of limited information" accordingly. Interestingly enough, Clower noted (1959a: 716) that most of the models he had outlined in his *EJ* paper "have the econometrically convenient properties of linearity and identifiability". However, it was the models that Muth and Mills presented *at the very same* 1959 Washington, DC conference of the Econometric Society, and *not those of Clower*, that reached the stage of *econometric testing*, as will be seen below.

Working independently, in 1952 while at Johns Hopkins University, Fritz Machlup published a textbook directed mainly at intermediate and advanced students (1952: v) which he called *The Economics of Sellers Competition* and which was subtitled "Model analysis of seller's conduct". Some three decades later, in a little known article that appeared posthumously, Machlup asserted (1983: 172–3) that the approach to expectations he took in his 1952 book foreshadowed rational expectations. In the preface to his 1952 book (vi–vii), Machlup mentioned that "some sections of the present book have been published elsewhere", including "most of Chapters 7 and 8 as an article under the title 'Competition, pliopoly and profit' in *Economica* (n.s.) vol. IX (1942), 1–23 [February] and 153–75 [May]".

Interestingly enough, the seeds of Machlup's 1952 approach to expectations as seen in his 1942 two part paper *do* have much in common with the themes underlying rational expectations. For example, in his 1952 book, Machlup stressed the "induced revision of subjective expectations" via "the inevitable learning experience of the market participants" (Machlup 1983: 173). In this context, Machlup distinguished between what he called "objective" and "subjective" as regards "changes and ... expectations" (1952: 206–7, 280; 1983: 173). This distinction was based upon that which he made in his earlier paper (1942: 2, n. 1) where he said

> A sensible distinction between "subjective" and "objective" ... can be made by distinguishing between the status of the persons making a judgment. The judgment of the seller or any other acting person ["economic agent"] who is the subject of the economist's observation is always "subjective" whereas the judgment of the observing economist may be called "objective" – as long as he is a disinterested ("scientific") observer only.

Machlup then went on (1942: 2–3) to also distinguish between the "expectations of the observed sellers" and the "expectation of the observing economist" and talked about "a probability concept, which is in the first place in the mind of the outside observer [the economist] although it may also become an expectation of the sellers themselves".

In his 1983 paper entitled "The rationality of 'Rational Expectations'", Machlup was *quite critical* of what he called "the 'strong form'" or "strong hypothesis" of rational expectations (RE), calling it "inconceivable" and "ill-conceived", "fantastic", "self-contradictory", and a "logical impossibility" (1983: 176, 180–1). We will not go into his critique here, but suffice it to say that it deserves *careful consideration by all economists*. What we consider as *crucial* in Machlup's almost completely overlooked 1983 paper are two fundamental points. First, as he noted (1983: 179) "the theory of RE was first used in an explanation of *microeconomic* adjustment" [our emphasis] and second that "the 'weak' assumption of the formation of 'rational' expectations is *quite reasonable*" (1983: 180) [our emphasis]. What must be stressed here is that in *both* his 1942 papers and 1952 book Machlup was "groping" – to borrow a phrase from Jaffe – toward the "'*weak*' assumption" of the *formation* of "RE", in which, as he put it (1983: 180)

> a rational decision-maker will consider all information that he can get without undue cost provided that he believes it, or believes that many others (say competitors in selling or buying) believe it, and provided further that, according to his lights, he regards it as relevant. "His lights" may, of course, change, over time, as he learns from experience, his own and other persons.

Now, much has been written about how the RE approach was applied at the *macroeconomic* level and the debate between its protagonists and critics is well documented in both the economic and "history of thought" cum "methodology" literature. What has *not* been dealt with up to now, however, is the "ancient history" – as Marc Nerlove put it – or as Michael Lovell called it, the "genesis" of the *microeconomic and microeconometric* oriented Muth–Mills approach to rational *and* implicit expectations and its aftermath in terms of the *events and interactions between the personalities involved.* And, as will be seen, the story is essentially one of *independent and parallel development* albeit with elements of contact between those involved with the work of *both* Muth and Mills over the 1950s and early 1960s. A number of key personalities can be mentioned at the outset, who influenced – via direct or indirect contact – *and in turn were influenced by the approach of Muth and Mills.* These include Laidler, Meiselman, Holmes, Bailey, Nerlove, Lovell, Simon, Cyert, Griliches, Modigliani, and Bronfenbrenner, among others, or as we prefer to put it, the "Chicago–Hopkins–Cowles–Carnegie axis".

The public finance and money workshops at Chicago

According to David Laidler's recollections (Laidler 1995), the Public Finance workshop at Chicago "was run by Harberger and Martin Bailey". Laidler recalled that "I was Bob Lucas's exact contemporary at Chicago, and we wrote our theses in the same (Public Finance) workshop". Laidler also recalled that Bailey's "macro textbook of that vintage [*National Income and the Price Level* 1962, 1971] has a chapter on expectations and adjustment, and, as I recall, hints that error learning might be consistent with maximizing behavior ... also relevant to Chicago macroeconomics time series applications of expectations would be David Meiselman's thesis on the term structure, finished in around 1961". In his own recollection of the period, David Meiselman wrote (Meiselman 1995) "some of my own work in the area was included in my dissertation, *The Term Structure of Interest Rates*, which was published by Prentice-Hall in 1962. Not long after that I published another paper where I revived the Fisher thesis about the relationship between inflation expectations and interest rates ('Bond yields and the price level: the Gibson Paradox Regained', *Monetary Essays in Commemoration of the Centennial of the National Banking System*, 1963)".

Laidler continued on to say (Laidler 1995)

> My thesis was on housing, so the rest of the committee consisted of Margaret Reid and Richard Muth – John's brother. They made sure that I knew more than I ever wanted to know about the regression fallacy and its relationship to the errors in the variables model in terms of which Friedman had motivated the permanent income hypothesis. I suspect Friedman also covered some of this in his price theory course, which everyone took. With benefit of hindsight, of

course, in that application permanent income is a rational expectation of current income, and the mix of economic and econometric theory is as seamless as in any later work. No one understood that at the time, I think. The practical implication I took away from all this was to be very careful about how I selected my data in order, as far as possible, to eliminate transitory elements from my income measures; and when in doubt to run the regression both ways.

I also recalled Jim Holmes (who was, I seem to recall, a drinking buddy of Bob Lucas's before the latter's marriage), getting very worried because the errors created by applying error learning to time series data on income did not generate the randomness that was supposed to be the very essence of transitory shocks . . . Finally this was a period of "operation twist" on the term structure, and the Kennedy Administration's tax-cut proposals. We all knew very well that what would happen here would impact upon the way in which the policies affected expectations, and that in turn would depend, among other things, upon how long they were expected to last. Here a very informal version of what we now call the Lucas critique was pretty close to the surface.

All in all, then, I think that the informal discussion of expectations at Chicago in the early 1960's was a bit closer to RE than Bob Lucas recalls, although obviously, if it had been close enough, we'd all have seen its macro applications a decade earlier!

Jim Holmes also added another element to the expectations story when he recalled (Holmes 1995)

David Laidler's recollection is correct, I was very concerned with the residuals from the permanent income series satisfying Friedman's hypothesis when permanent income was estimated by an adaptive expectations scheme. In fact, I developed this into a paper "A condition for independence of permanent and transitory components of a series" [*JASA* 66: 13–15].

Bob Lucas and I were drinking buddies in graduate school and often discussed theoretical problems in economics. In addition to the one mentioned by Professor Laidler I recall developing and discussing a multiple island paradigm with distinct production and trading decisions associated with each island – which may have been developed by Bob into his famous piece on price misconceptions.

Finally, Martin Bailey also provided his detailed recollections of the public finance and money workshops at Chicago and his own contributions (Bailey 1995). As he wrote

the main stimulus to my interest in error learning, and that of others, came first from Phillip Cagan's doctoral research in the Money

Workshop on the topic of hyperinflation, which he was wrapping up while I was a post-doc there in 1955. I picked up on Cagan's (and Friedman's) analysis of inflation to develop my April 1956 article "The Welfare Cost of Inflationary Finance" in *JPE.* In the next year or so Marc Nerlove also got interested in the subject of "Koyck lags," including distributed-lag expectations, and published some work using it. In that period John Muth came to Chicago for a spell, writing first his 1960 article on error learning (Optimal Properties of Exponentially Weighted Forecasts) in *JASA*, and then two papers on rational expectations. His *JASA* paper further stimulated my interest, leading to my "Prediction of an Autoregressive Variable" published in *JASA* in 1965 after a long editorial process. I did more than "hint" at the idea in my macro book – I went over the top. Look at pages 227–267 in the first edition or pages 205–246 in the second edition of *National Income and the Price Level*, to see what I mean. In the pages just prior to those I also talked about adjustment delays, and their similarity to error learning. As I recall, Nerlove did a better job than I did of sorting out the differences.

At the same time, I knew of Muth's work on rational expectations, and taught something similar in my macro course. The main place that I had something along that line was my treatment of government deficits, where I presented the "Ricardian Equivalence" hypothesis (see the second edition of *National Income and the Price Level* at pages 156–158). I thought that the notion that people foresaw the future more or less accurately was much more sensible than treating them as creatures of mindless habit, but cannot claim to have elaborated the idea in any creative way.

In all this, one must not overlook Milton Friedman's contributions. First, he had to some extent anticipated rational expectations in his theory of permanent income and consumption, and specifically used an error learning model. Second, there is his Nobel lecture on the Phillips curve, where he said that you can't fool all of the people all of the time.

Thus, I think Friedman, Cagan, Nerlove, and Muth the main contributors to the developments . . . centering around the Money Workshop more than the Public Finance Workshop.

The Hopkins–Cowles–Carnegie connection

Marc Nerlove became "familiar with Mills' work" as early as 1958 when, as he recalled in a letter to one of the authors (19 November 1991a)

> I taught part time at [Johns] Hopkins Fall Semester 1958–59, and had lunch with Mills nearly every week. I recall objecting to Mills' idea [implicit expectations] because realized future prices could only

> measure expectations with an error which would, at best, lead to estimates of their effects in behavioral relations biased toward zero. But Muth's idea corrected that problem by substituting conditional expected values (expectation in the statistical sense).

When asked about his time as a graduate student at Johns Hopkins in the early 1950s, the influence of Machlup, and whether he thought Machlup had developed an "early" version of the RE approach in his 1952 book, as mentioned earlier, Nerlove replied in a further letter (5 January 1992)

> I was a graduate student at Hopkins 1952–54 and took all my economic theory from Fritz Machlup. We graduate students were enlisted to proofread the *Economics of Seller's Competition*, but I don't recall anything like rational expectations. I no longer have my copy of the book so I can't check and have never seen Fritz's *Kredit und Kapital* paper . . . My guess however, is that Fritz may have had something like *perfect foresight* [Nerlove's emphasis] which is close to Mills' implicit price expectations, but not at all the same thing as rational expectations.

Nerlove continued on to say

> From my standpoint, the key thing about rational expectations was its connection to the *stochastic* specification [Nerlove's emphasis]. This is why a conditional expectation, based on information up to the time the action is taken, is an improvement over implicit expectations. *Perfect foresight is a concept applicable only in the context of deterministic models* [our emphasis]. Fritz was not very "stochastically" oriented, so I'm not sure he would have appreciated the distinction.

Edwin Mills, for his part, recalled in a letter to one of the authors (27 November 1991c) that

> I read the *Economics of Seller's Competition*, but I cannot tell you when. Probably when I was teaching industrial organization at [Johns] Hopkins in the late 1950s. I have no recollection of anything in it that approximates the rational expectations hypothesis, but I have not read it in several decades. It certainly did not directly affect my work, but most important ideas in economics float around the literature for some time before they are defined precisely and incorporated in formal models. Machlup's book may fit in that category. I know that I never thought that I was influenced by the book in my thinking on the subject, and I am sure I never discussed the issues with Machlup. I knew him well; he was very kind to me as a junior faculty member. I also knew him when we were both at Princeton.

Michael Lovell also became involved with the work of both Mills and Muth quite early in his own career. With regard to Mills's early work, Lovell recalled in a letter to one of the authors (18 September 1991a) that

> My interest in the topic of expectations stemmed from my research into the contributions that fluctuations in inventories make to economic fluctuations and by the desire to test empirically the Lundberg–Metzler mode of the inventory cycle; I wrote a term paper on this topic jointly with Richard Day (now at USC) in the spring of 1956 at Harvard when we were both taking a statistics course offered by Guy Orcutt. Day and I were much interested in the paper by Modigliani and Sauerlender [1955] ... Two years later, while I was working on my dissertation, Franco [Modigliani] visited Harvard for a year; while I did not take Franco's course, I talked to him on a couple of occasions about my research and participated in a seminar on inventories which he attended along with Raiffa and Schlaifer, Albert Ando and John Meier that was held most Saturday mornings at the Harvard Business School.

Lovell continued

> I became acquainted with Ed Mills's articles on inventories in connection with my own thesis research [Mills 1954–55]. Later I got to know him quite well when he visited at the Cowles Foundation [Yale] for a semester. I thought that my assumption that the forecast error might be proportional to the observed change, which I attributed to Keynes, seemed to work better than his "implicit expectations". Ed finished his book while at Cowles, and *I thought then and think now that his contribution has been underappreciated, particularly by those who do not follow Muth in restricting "rational expectations" to the case in which the forecast error is distributed independently of the prediction* [our emphasis].

And, as Lovell recalled in a subsequent letter (10 December 1991b): "I cited Mills 1954/55 paper in my thesis and his 1957 *Econometrica* article in my July '61 *Econometrica* article".

As for his contact with Muth, Lovell recalled in his letter of 18 September 1991 that

> I met Jack Muth when he visited Yale for the 1961–62 academic year [Lovell was a staff member at the Cowles Foundation and on the faculty at Yale at the time] – he helped me on a sticky point in a paper I was writing about seasonal adjustment; we talked some about inventories, the Carnegie Tech quadratic modeling of production scheduling and inventory behavior, and rational expectations; I had my

> doubts about rational expectations because the evidence that I had seen up to then was that forecasters did not obtain as much precision as they could have obtained with readily available information. I was asked to referee [review] Ed Mills's book [Mills 1962] for *Econometrica*, but because of time pressures passed it along to Jack; Jack intended to run the inventory regressions in the reverse direction from Mills, which was the implication of rational as opposed to implicit expectations ... he punched the data on IBM cards but before testing his own approach he ran Mills's model. Jack found he could not replicate the results that Ed had reported in his book.

When asked about this in correspondence with one of the authors, Mills replied (6 November 1991b)

> I do not remember if Jack Muth reviewed my 1962 book. I do remember that he contacted me saying he could not reproduce some of the regressions in my book. I redid the regressions and found that the published estimates were indeed in error. My recollection attributes the errors to a very crude piece of computing machinery ... I still have the reestimated equations. They would have not made me write anything very different in the book.

In correspondence with one of the authors on this and other issues, John Muth wrote (14 March 1992b)

> You asked whether I ever did get to review Mills' 1962 book. While I visited the Cowles Foundation at Yale, I started to review it, but in the process of moving back to Carnegie-Mellon [Carnegie Tech] in Pittsburgh, the review fell through the cracks. So, although I did a lot of preliminary work on the review of it, the review was never completed. When I found that I could not replicate his results I did contact him and he replied to me.

Muth went on to say

> Mills' expectations model did not really sink into my consciousness until I read his book [Mills 1962] and Mike Lovell published his book on sales anticipations and inventories [Hirsch and Lovell 1969]. *I now believe that Mills' work has been very much underrated in the literature and that a combination of implicit and rational expectations, sometimes called noisy rational expectations is in better agreement with the facts than either model alone* [our emphasis].

The Chicago–Carnegie connection

With regard to the Chicago-Carnegie Tech axis and his own experience with Muth, Simon, Cyert, March, Lucas, Rapping, and Sargent there, Lovell – who was an Associate (1963–66) and Full Professor (1966–69) at the GSIA – recalled in his letter to one of the authors (18 September 1991a) that

> I went to Carnegie-Mellon in 1963 rather than stay at Yale for a while longer in part because I was impressed by Jack Muth, Herb Simon, by Dean Richard Cyert and by Jim March – this was long after Franco [Modigliani] had departed to Northwestern (which turned out to be only a one year stepping stone) and MIT. Lucas, Kamien, and Lave all arrived directly from earning their PhDs that same year; Rapping had been there for a semester or so. This was my first real contact with members of what people at Harvard and Chicago had called the "Chicago School" and their first contact with a "Keynesian" – indeed I was rather lonely as a minority house Keynesian at Carnegie-Mellon, particularly given my feeling that Keynes had been dead for some time. I urged Dick Cyert, a wonderfully understanding Dean, to get someone without a Chicago orientation, and he recruited Tom Sargent from Harvard – Bob Lucas and I, who talked together with Tom when he visited us for an interview, were equally enthusiastic about having Tom on board. Sargent left after a year to go into the Air Force under the terms of an ROTC commitment.

Lovell continued

> Jack Muth patiently reviewed with me the appropriate tests that Al Hirsch and I should run of rational expectations on our Commerce Data [Hirsch and Lovell 1969] – but while everyone knew all about Jack's skiing trips, he did not talk about his current research; the senior faculty decided not to give him tenure, but then promoted Lovell the next year, which strikes me as an excellent counter example to the RE hypothesis. At GSIA I worked on my inventory project pretty much alone, talking about it primarily with my co-author Al Hirsch ... I talked to my colleagues a lot at GSIA, including Simon and Lucas, *but I was not able to interest them in the topic of expectations* [our emphasis]. The book with Al Hirsch [1969] was reviewed favorably in *JEL* [Journal of Economic Literature], *but didn't attract much attention, perhaps because at the time there seemed to be little interest in inventories, business cycles or expectations* – and partly because there was little going on, I moved to other topics [our emphasis].

Interestingly enough, it was Mills who reviewed the Hirsch and Lovell volume in *JEL* [Mills 1971]. In his review, Mills wrote that their work was "certainly the most important empirical study of expectations in many years". Mills also said that in the Hirsch and Lovell study the question was posed "whether Ferber's law of expectations formation provides a better explanation of the ... data than does Nerlove's adaptive expectations hypothesis" (Mills 1971: 108). Mills then said (108) that he was "surprised that both hypotheses seemed to fit the data quite well". He went on to say (108) that in the Hirsch–Lovell volume

> Further analysis tests the structural hypothesis of Ferber and Nerlove against Muth's rational expectations hypothesis, Mills' implicit expectations hypothesis, and Lovell's weighted average of static and perfect forecasts. The Muth and Mills hypotheses perform better than the Ferber and Nerlove hypotheses at the industry level, but not as well at the firm level. But Lovell's hypothesis seems to outperform both sets of alternative hypotheses.

The crucial thing to recall here is that the OBE Commerce Department data used in the Hirsch and Lovell study *was microeconomically based.* That is, as Mills wrote (107) it was based on "quarterly data on sales and inventories from a sample of ... manufacturing firms" and "in addition to actual sales and inventories", the firms reported "anticipated sales and inventories one and two quarters in advance"; while at the industry level, the data was "aggregated into seven durable and seven non-durable industries" respectively. Indeed, *the Hirsch–Lovell study was one of the most important microeconometric tests of the Muth–Mills approach to expectations up to that point, as noted by Mills himself in his* JEL *review of it.*

In a letter to one of the authors (4 December 1991), Zvi Griliches also recalled additional aspects of the Chicago–Carnegie connection regarding the Muth–Mills approach to expectations. As he put it

> In 1957 and 1958, I think, I shared an office with Jack Muth at the University of Chicago. I was finishing my dissertation while he was a postdoc (with a still unfinished dissertation) from Carnegie Mellon. *We talked a lot about his work. I thought it very good but not revolutionary. But then one rarely does, when one is standing too close to it* [our emphasis]. I was vaguely familiar with Mills' work.

Griliches continued on to say

> I think that Muth's work should be seen against the background of two related strands of work; Modigliani on expectations first at Illinois (overlapping with Brady and Reid) and Eisner (the Hopkins connection for Mills), and then at Carnegie, where the Holt–Simon–

> Modigliani–Muth volume on inventory control preceded Muth's specific contribution, and the permanent vs. transitory income stream starting from Friedman's contribution to the Kuznets and Friedman volume, the work by Dorothy Brady and Margaret Reid on income and consumption surveys, Cagan's adaptive inflationary expectations model (under Friedman's supervision), Nerlove's extension of it to agricultural price expectations (a PhD thesis at Hopkins and another connection to Mills), Theil's bringing Koyck's model to Chicago, and my own subsequent work on distributed lags.

Griliches continued

> Against that background, the first Muth paper [1960] was memorable by showing when adaptive expectations were reasonable. What started out as a reasonable approximation was given a rigorous theoretical backing, a desirable property for the empirical part of the Chicago School aspiring also to live by Cowles Commission goals. The second famous paper [1961] was interpreted more as a demonstration that if you don't assume that people are fools and/or can be fooled all the time, you don't get stupid results (such as repeated cycles). *But that was already the Friedman–Cagan–Nerlove message, and hence the paper itself did not feel revolutionary to us. Nobody at that time took seriously the interpretation that economic actors use the econometrician's models to form their forecasts. That was either a debating point or a technical move to insure the intellectual consistency of the argument. The general Chicago opinion about the quality and relevance of the existing macro models was rather low at that time (and later on) and did not really see its way towards using this idea constructively. It was left to Lucas (and Rapping) to rediscover the traces of these ideas, both at Carnegie and Chicago, and push them to their logical conclusion* [our emphasis].

One additional recollection deserves to be related at this point regarding the *microeconomic origins of the rational expectations approach*. In a letter to one of the authors (19 August 1992) Martin Bronfenbrenner recalled that

> I was a visiting Professor at Carnegie [Tech] in 1955 (substituting for Franco Modigliani) while Jack [Muth] was working on his "rational expectations" dissertation. We talked on several occasions, and I can tell you why I, at least, underestimated the significance of what Jack was doing. The reason was that Jack's oral explanation to me – I was not on his thesis committee – *was exclusively in connection with microeconomic problems* [our emphasis], and I was not smart enough to see the possible macroeconomic applications of his work, as Bob Lucas would do some years later, also at Carnegie.

Finally, with regard to the influence of Simon and Modigliani on the development of Muth's ideas, there is a problem in establishing "direct" as against "indirect" influence. In a letter to one of the authors (2 December 1991) Simon wrote that John Muth

> undoubtedly *felt* [Simon's emphasis] challenged by my views on bounded rationality (and says so in his REH *Econometrica* paper) . . .
>
> Muth, Modigliani, Holt and I were jointly engaged in a study of production smoothing that eventuated in our book on the subject. Muth, then a graduate student, was assigned the task of looking at the problems of prediction of future sales that were involved in the projects, and in the course of this work made his start toward the findings reported in his *JASA* paper [1960].
>
> Jack, along with the economic faculty, were very well aware of my bounded rationality views and my skepticism about neoclassical theory, but that had nothing to do with this particular project, which proceeded with the neoclassical paradigm . . . a little earlier, Modigliani, together with Emil Grunberg wrote their paper on the possibility of economic predictions (would they be falsified by reactions if they were published?), and I was closely involved in that project, providing (as indicated in a footnote) a proof of their central theorem using Brouwer's fixed-point theorem. I did not co-author that paper, however, but published a parallel one on election predictions, based on the same theorem. The fixed-point here is very closely related to the rational expectations equilibrium, and some (e.g. Chipman) have thought that in these papers Grunberg, Modigliani, and I laid the groundwork for REH. I will let history judge that, but if true, it is ironic. In any event, those two papers may have had some influence on Jack's thinking about forecasting.
>
> What clearly did have influence on his thinking was, without any challenge, his disagreement with bounded rationality, and his belief that "people are more rational than Simon thinks they are".

Richard Cyert, who was Dean of the GSIA at Carnegie Tech at the time also replied in a letter to one of the authors (9 December 1991) that

> Jack Muth was on the faculty at Carnegie Tech where I was also a faculty member, so I know a great deal about the paper . . . *I don't think any of us thought Jack's paper was revolutionary at the time it was published. It was viewed as an answer to discussions and arguments that we had on the faculty, stimulated by Herbert Simon's attack on the concept of rationality in economics. Jack wrote the paper in a spirit of rebellion, Jack always being a rebel. He wanted to show that Herb was not only wrong, but that economists should emphasize rationality even more* [our emphasis]. I don't think that he himself saw the

> potential of using the concept in dynamic economics as though it had more validity than other ad hoc assumptions.

But let us leave the last word regarding these points to John Muth himself. In a letter to one of the authors (14 March 1992b), Muth replied to an assertion made in a letter from Marc Nerlove (19 December 1991b) in which Nerlove said "the story I recall is that the REH originated at Carnegie in the late 1950s in the form of a dare: Herbert Simon challenged Muth to come up with a theory of information use as 'rational' as the theory economists used to explain the allocation of other resources". In his letter to one of the authors dated 14 March 1992, Muth maintained that Nerlove's assertion

> that Herbert Simon challenged me to come up with a theory of information as rational as the theory economists use to explain the allocation of other resources is definitely not true. There never was any such challenge. The only thing even remotely resembling that is when Franco Modigliani assigned a problem in class to explain executive salaries. Herb Simon presented a model to explain that phenomenon. As a member of Modigliani's class, I tried to develop one too, but it wasn't very good.

The historiography of the Muth–Mills approach to expectations, then, is replete with many strands regarding its origins and development, as has been shown. Perhaps one of the most problematic is the issue of "precursors" – and especially one interpretation of an early article by Tinbergen (1932) as a precursor to Muth (Keuzenkamp 1991). Moreover, the *evolution* of the approaches of *both* Mills and Muth during the 1950s deserves extensive consideration here, and it is to these and related issues that we now turn our attention.

4 Muth, Mills, and Tinbergen

Muth's classic 1961 *Econometrica* paper has been cited many times since the so-called "RE revolution in macroeconomics". A number of economists even view it as representing the explicit re-introduction of expectations into macroeconomics after its having been put to "one-side" in the short-run neo-Keynesian analysis as represented by the IS-LM approach. But much more is involved in the story surrounding the origins and development of Muth's 1961 paper than has appeared in either the economics or the history of economics literature. When Muth *first* presented and circulated the *original* version of his paper (Muth 1959a, 1959b) reaction to his approach was somewhat "quiet". While a number of "rising stars" of economics and econometrics who have since come to prominence, and even some who were already established figures in the profession actually attended the session at the December 1959 Washington meeting of the Econometric Society, where Muth gave the *original* version of his 1961 paper, it still made no *immediate* impact on economics or economists, as will be seen in Chapter 5. In the decade following the *original* 1959 presentations by Muth and Mills, however, what could be considered to be a "quiet revolution" in *microeconomics* occurred, albeit *this* has been overlooked by most economists.

For example, the papers presented by Muth and Mills in 1959 generated discussion and debate in one of the foremost economic journals, the *Quarterly Journal of Economics* in May 1961, and this even *before* Muth's article appeared in *Econometrica* in July 1961. In addition, Negishi's 1964 note in *Econometrica* may be seen as a *crucial* "missing link" in the transition from the Walrasian microeconomic to the Walrasian General Equilibrium macroeconomic application of the RE approach. Moreover, Negishi's 1965 book *Kakaku to Haibun no Riron* (Theory of Price and Allocation) and an important article by Radner (1967) in French shows the extent to which the micro-based RE approach of Muth and Mills influenced microeconomics and microeconomists. Finally, Hirsch and Lovell (1969) illustrates the extent of *microeconometric testing* of the approaches of both Muth and Mills; and this even *before* the so-called "RE revolution in Macroeconomics" began.

In this chapter, we attempt to unravel some of the strands in the RE story relating to the origins and development of Muth's 1961 paper and to outline the evolution of Mills's approach to expectations over the 1950s and early 1960s. We then go on to deal with the ostensible "relationship" between the work of Muth and Mills on expectations and Tinbergen's earlier 1932 paper postulated by Keuzenkamp (1991).

Muth and Mills 1954–62

As noted above, John Muth presented the *original* version of his 1961 paper at the December 1959 Washington meeting of the Econometric Society (1959a). Moreover, Muth's 1959 paper was also circulated as a Carnegie Tech/ONR research memo (1959b) and the original unpublished paper was cited by, among others, Mills (1961) and Nerlove (1961b) in their debate in the *Quarterly Journal of Economics* over the efficacy of adaptive as against implicit expectations. But were there other influences upon Muth besides his teachers and colleagues at Carnegie Tech? Some indication as to the development of his ideas may be seen in his lectures at the University of Chicago in the Spring of 1957, on "Special Topics in Mathematical Economics (Dynamics and Uncertainty)" [in Friedman Papers]. In dealing with the issue of "moving equilibrium", for example, Muth referred the student to the works of Hicks, Modigliani and Brumberg, and Marschak, among others. In his lectures on "models of adaptive behavior", dealing with dynamics and the stability of equilibrium, he referred his students to the works of Samuleson and Metzler, among others. When dealing with "stochastic equilibrium (statics)" he directed the students to the works of Arrow, Friedman and Savage, Markowitz, and Hart, among others. For his next topic, "stochastic disequilibrium (dynamics, uncertainty)", Muth told his students to read Hart, among others. The final subject Muth dealt with was what he called "purposive behavior with ignorance", which he divided into three sub-topics: "searching", "learning", and "gaming", and advised his students to read von Neuman and Morgenstern and Simon, among other references.

From 1954 onwards, Edwin Mills had been working on his own *implicit* expectations approach which made the same link, in an even more *general* way than Muth, specifying it in *explicitly* mathematical terms so as to operationalize and test it (Mills 1954–55, 1957a, 1957b, 1959a, 1959b, 1961, 1962). And, at the same 1959 Washington meeting of the Econometric Society and on the very same day, 30 December, that Muth presented the original version of his 1961 paper at an afternoon session called "New approaches to old problems" chaired by Edwin Kuh, Mills also presented a paper outlining his implicit expectations approach at a morning session chaired by Robert Clower (Mills 1959b). Moreover, Mills's implicit expectations is not only more general than Muth's RE approach, but Muth himself, among others – such as Lovell and Nerlove – have come to see implicit expectations as a very good alternative to the RE approach to model expectations formation at the *micro*-level. (Muth 1985; Lovell 1986; Nerlove 1991a, 1991b). How then, did Mills's work on expectations evolve?

Mills's *earliest* expectations paper was based upon his doctoral dissertation "the theory of inventory decisions" submitted in 1955 at Birmingham and supervised by Hahn and Gorman. In fact, Hahn suggested that Mills work on this topic. Indeed, as Mills recalled, when Hahn had told him to "study inventories", Mills focused upon their micro aspects. It was only after Mills had finished his dissertation that Hahn told him "I meant macro" (Mills 1995).

In this paper, which was entitled "Expectations, uncertainty and inventory fluctuations" published in the *RES* (1954–55), Mills first outlined a "total supply" equation and then went on to develop a notion of "optimal inventory" in which an RE *equilibrium was implicit.*

The "total supply" equation specified by Mills in this paper was of the form:

$$y_t = u_t + I_{t-1} \qquad \text{(1954–55: 18, "equation 2")}$$

where u_t is production or output, y_t is "total supply" and I_{t-1} is inventory at the end of period t of the firm. In order to ensure consistency of notation with his later published work on this topic (Mills 1957a, 1962) which will be discussed below, this equation can also be expressed as:

$$y_t = z_t + I_{t-1} \qquad \text{(1957a: notation)}$$

where z_t is production, and, in terms of Mills's 1962 notation

$$x_t^S = z_t + I_{t-1}$$

where x_t^S is "total supply". Mills then went on to define what he called "optimum inventory" as "the difference between optimum supply, y^*, and the mathematical expectation of demand" (1954–55: 19), and specified an "optimal inventory equation" of the form

$$I^* = y^* - x_{t-1} \qquad \text{(1954–55: 19, "equation 7")}$$

"where", as he put it "x_{t-1}" is the actual demand of the previous period, which was assumed to be the mathematical expectation of demand in the current period" (18), that is to say, x_t. He then substituted "equation 2" into "equation 7" and obtained

$$u_t = x_{t-1} + (I^* - I_{t-1}) \qquad \text{(1954–55: 19)}$$

or, in terms of the notation of his later paper (1957a)

$$z_t = x_{t-1} + (I^* - I_{t-1})$$

Now, Mills obtained this result by *assuming* $y^* = y$, so that *given*

$$y_t = u_t + I_{t-1}$$

$$I^* = y^* - x_{t-1}$$

$$I^* + x_{t-1} = y^*$$

if $y^* = y$, that is if *optimum supply equals actual supply*, then

$$I^* + x_{t-1} = y = u_t + I_{t-1}$$
$$\text{and } u_t = x_{t-1} + (I^* - I_{t-1})$$

Indeed, in this paper he noted (1954–55: 16) that "equilibrium occurs ... when $x_t = x_{t-1}$ ...". It should also be noted that if $I^* = I_t$, that is if *optimal inventory is equal to actual inventory*, then

$$u_t = x_{t-1} + I_t - I_{t-1}$$

where u_t is z_t, in the notation of his later paper (1957a). And, if $x_{t-1} = x_t$, where $x_{t-1} = E(x_t)$, as defined by Mills (1954–55: 18), then

$$z_t = x_t + I_t - I_{t-1}$$

again, in the notation of his later paper (1957a: 223, "equation 3.2"), or in the notation of his 1962 book, if $x_t^S = x_t$, that is *supply equals demand*, then

$$x_t^S = z_t + I_{t-1} - I_t \qquad \text{(1962: 71, "equation 19d")}$$

In terms of the "RE equilibrium" *implicit* in his 1954–55 paper, *given demand as a function of price*, that is to say $x = f(p)$, if $x_t^e = x_{t-1}$, and if $E(p_t) = p_{t-1} = p_t$, that is $p^e = p_{t-1} = p_t$, then $E(x_t) = x_{t-1}$, that is $x_t^e = x_{t-1}$, and if $x_t = f(p_t)$ and $x_{t-1} = g(p_{t-1})$, then $p_t^e = \lambda p_{t-1}$, where $\lambda = 1$ indicates *constant price, which is the result of rational expectations under inventory speculation as manifest in "equation 4.1" of Muth* (1961: 323).

In his 1957 *Econometrica* paper entitled "The theory of inventory decisions" (Mills 1957a), Mills specified a "demand" equation of the form

$$x_t = E_t + u_t \qquad \text{(1957a: 223, "equation 2.1")}$$

where E_t is the "known" component of demand and u_t is the "uncertainty component" (1957a: 223). He also specified a relationship of the form

$$E_t = a - bp_t \qquad \text{(1957a: 223)}$$

where p_t is price. This being so, then by substitution we can readily see that

$$x_t = a - bp_t + u_t$$

which, in the "updated notation" proposed, for example, by Keuzenkamp (1991), could also take the form of

$$C_t = a - bp_t + u_t$$

where C_t is demand. We will return to the importance of this *derived* demand relationship below.

In this paper, Mills then went on to specify a "supply" equation of the form

$$y_t = z_t + I_{t-1} \qquad \text{(1957a: 223, "equation 3.1")}$$

where y_t is "total supply", z_t is production in t, x_t is demand in t, and I_t is inventory at the end of period t; or in the notation of his 1962 book

$$x_t^S = z_t + I_{t-1}$$

where x_t^S is "total supply" or production. Mills then specified a "sales" equation as

$$z_t - x_t = \Delta I_t \qquad \text{(223: "equation 3.2")}$$

Now, in this paper, price was "held constant" (1957a: 223), while Mills said that he intended to deal with variable price "in a later paper" (1957a: 224).

In a hitherto overlooked paper published in the October 1957 issue of *Management Science* entitled "Expectations and Undesired Inventory" (Mills 1957b), Mills presented a more sophisticated version of his approach, which included what he called a "micro-model" of a firm's output based on a "forecast" or "best guess" of "demand for its product" during a period (1957b: 105). Mills specified the output or "total supply" equation as

$$z_n = \beta_1 E_n + \beta_2 z_{n-1} + \beta_2 I_{n-1} + \beta_0 \qquad \text{(1957b: 105, "equation 1")}$$

where z_n is the "amount produced (production) in the nth period"; I_n is "inventory *remaining at the end of the* nth *period*"; and E_n is the *forecast* of demand (1957b: 105). Expressed in another way (1957b: 105, n. 1)

$$z_n = E_n + a(k + bE_n - I_{n-1})$$

that is, "the firm produces an amount equal to its best guess of demand [E_n] plus a fraction, a, of the difference between 'equilibrium' inventory ($k + bE_n$) and *actual inventory*, I_{n-1}" (1957b: 105, n. 1) [our emphasis].

Mills went on to say that "demand in period n, x_n, will in general be forecast somewhat inaccurately" (1957b: 106). In this context, he asserted that

$$\varepsilon_n = E_n - x_n \qquad \text{(1957b: 106, "equation 2")}$$

where ε_n is "the error of the forecast" (1957b: 106). Mills continued on to say that it was reasonable to "further suppose ... that there is no bias toward over or under prediction" and therefore "ε_n can be interpreted as a random variable with zero mean" (1957b: 106). He then eliminated E_n from "equation 1" by recourse to "equation 2" and obtained

$$z_n = \beta_1 + \beta_2 z_{n-1} + \beta_3 I_{n-1} + \beta_0 + \beta_1 \varepsilon_n \qquad \text{(106, "equation 3")}$$

Mills then went on to express this in terms of I_n by applying the "identity"

$$I_n = I_{n-1} + z_n - x_n \qquad \text{(106, "equation 4").}$$

Following from this, we can obtain

$$z_n = I_n - I_{n-1} + x_n$$

and thus

$$x_n = z_n + I_{n-1} - I_n$$

Now, *if* $x_n = E_n$, that is, if there is *no forecast error*, $\varepsilon_n = 0$; then $x_n = x_n^S$, that is, demand is equal to "total supply", or in the notation of his 1962 book

$$x_n^S = z_n + I_{n-1} - I_n \qquad \text{(Mills 1962: 71, "equation 19d")}$$

The object of *this* paper, according to Mills (1957b: 105) was actually to present a "model ... with the aid of which an estimate, however crude, of the amount of undesired inventory in the economy is made from market data". In his paper, Mills first presented "the Micro-Model" (1957b: 105ff) and then, in the section he called "the Macro-Model" (1957b: 107ff) went on to obtain an estimate of economy-wide undesired inventory. This he did as follows. In his words (1957b: 106): "Eliminating z_n from equation (3) by equation (4) we get

$$I_n = -(1-\beta_1)x_n + \beta_2 z_{n-1} + (1+\beta_2)I_{n-1} + \beta_0 + \beta_1\varepsilon_n \quad \text{(106, "equation 5")}$$

He went on to say (1957b: 107) that "estimates of the amount of undesired inventory in the economy are obtained by fitting equation (5) to the postwar national income statistics of aggregate production, sales and inventories". Mills used "the quarterly seasonally adjusted components of Gross National Product at annual rates" (1957b: 107) for this purpose and went on to even further improve his estimating procedure by "using not equation (5) but rather period to period changes", that is first difference form, so as to get around the problem of autocorrelation of the residuals. As he put it (1957b: 107) "better estimates of the coefficients are likely to be obtained if the residuals are randomly distributed through time". Mills reported (1957b: 107) that the actual first difference form of the equation he estimated by "traditional least squares" showed "no autocorrelation". By combining his supply-demand and inventory analysis with an analysis of the error structure involved in forecasting demand and its implications for inventory adjustment, Mills had actually outlined, for the first time, his "implicit expectations" approach in this almost totally overlooked, albeit crucial paper and actually applied it to the macro-economy. Perhaps if more attention had been given to Mills's ongoing work over the period 1954/55–1957/59, the so-called "RE Revolution in Macroeconomics" would have taken place over a decade earlier than it actually did!

In the February 1959 issue of *Quarterly Journal of Economics*, Mills published a paper entitled "Uncertainty and price theory", the contents of which he discussed with Solow, Kuh, Machlup, Domar, and Lerner respectively (1959a: 116). In this paper, he said that the firm "is unable to predict x [demand] in advance because it does not know which of its possible values u [the random term] will take" (1959a: 117).

It should also be noted here that Mills's model in his paper "Expectations and Undesired Inventory" has a random error term for the forecasts (1957b: 106). His *QJE* paper "Uncertainty and price theory" (1959a) also has a random term, u. In addition, in this paper Mills also makes the apparently self-conscious obliteration of Knight's distinction between risk and uncertainty when he writes (1959a: 117, n. 1) "In the following sections the terms 'risk' and 'uncertainty' are used interchangeably". Mills also presents a random variable u_t is his paper "The theory of inventory decisions" (1957a). The important thing to remember here is that these papers are *synchronous* to Muth's work and thus suggests *multiple discovery*.

By 1959, then, Mills had fully developed the "implicit expectations" model he presented at the December 1959 Econometric Society meeting in a paper entitled "Expectations, inventories and the stability of competitive markets" (Mills 1959b), which forms the *core – according to Mills himself* – of his 1962 book *Price, Output and Inventory Policy* (Mills 1962).

Interestingly enough, *as early as 1960* Muth cited Mills's 1959 Econometric Society paper in his own *unpublished* paper entitled "Estimation of economic relationships containing latent expectations variables" that only appeared in the 1981 Lucas and Sargent volume *Rational Expectations and Econometric Practice* (Muth 1960 [1981]: 325). As Muth put it in this paper (1960 [1981]: 322) "I have suggested elsewhere (Muth 1959a, 1959b) some reasons to believe that expectations are just as rational as other aspects of individual behavior". He went on to show given that "expectations are not much different from the prediction of the model itself, as rationality would imply" how "the parameters [can] be estimated from observable data" (1960 [1981]: 322–7). In the second section of this paper entitled "Estimation under more general conditions", Muth discussed the applicability of his proposed "rational model" in the case "if expectations for a longer horizon than one period are relevant".

Now, Muth's *unpublished* 1960 paper can be considered as a *crucial* "missing link" between the *microeconomic* basis and emphasis of his 1959 (and thus his 1961) paper and the *later macroapplications* of his "rational model"(1960 [1981]: 324). For example, in his 1960 *unpublished* paper, Muth mentions Cagan's work on macroeconomic expectations in the context of hyperinflation, and also that of Friedman, along with that of Modigliani and Brumberg, on the role of expectations in the consumption function. This indeed *confirms* the observations of *both* Griliches and Modigliani regarding the influence of these works on the development of Muth's approach, as mentioned in Chapter 3 above. However, in his 1959, that is, in his "1961" paper, Muth *did not* mention the possible applicability of his "rational model" to "long expectation spans" at the macroeconomic level.

Muth, Mills, and Tinbergen, 1932–62

In an article in the *Economic Journal* (Keuzenkamp 1991), an early paper by Tinbergen (1932) – originally published in German – was cited as a "precursor" to the rational expectations (RE) approach presented by Muth (1961). In his article, the author – who ostensibly studied "the early history of expectations analysis" (1991: 1245) – made a number of statements which highlight the problems surrounding the history of "expectational economics", as Hart called it, and especially of rational expectations. As in the cases of IS-LM and growth theory (Young 1987, 1989), the case of the RE approach presented in Muth's 1961 paper has been shown to be one of *sequential multiple discovery* and the very process of its discovery and diffusion as multifaceted and complex. Moreover, the number and identity of possible "precursors" to the RE approach which was *originally presented by Muth himself in 1959* (Muth 1959a, 1959b) – and the immediate and ostensibly "belated" reaction of economists to it – is surprising indeed, as will be seen in Chapter 5.

In this section, we attempt to deal with the relationship between Muth's 1961 paper and Tinbergen's earlier 1932 paper on the one hand, and relate both to Mills's approach as manifest in his ongoing work between 1954–55 and 1962, as outlined in the previous section. We will also briefly deal with Tinbergen's *own* early approach to expectations (Tinbergen 1934), and then go on to deal with the *problematic* treatment of these issues by Keuzenkamp in his article. These are illustrative both of the difficulties that arise from focusing on *specific* published work *only* when dealing with the history of "concept formation" in economics and the economics profession's *lack of knowledge, interest, and understanding regarding the history of its own "core concepts"*. In fact, it will be shown that Tinbergen (1932) is actually a "precursor" of *Mills's ongoing work between 1954 and 1962 on "implicit" expectations, rather than of Muth's "rational" expectations approach.*

First of all, Keuzenkamp asserted that "many economists wonder why rational expectations did not show up in macroeconomics directly after John Muth's pathbreaking 1961 paper" and also that "in 1961 … Muth reinvented rational expectations" (1991: 1245–6). Second, Keuzenkamp maintained that "Tinbergen was the first and, for nearly thirty years the only one who made the link between dynamic economic theory, expectations and uncertainty, and probability theory" and that "the step from uncertainty about future variables to expectations and probability theory may seem natural. (It certainly is for the 'post-Muth generation'), but these steps were not yet made, and were not made again until 1961" (1246–7). Third, Keuzenkamp claimed "it seems that even Tinbergen himself forgot about his Rational Expectations model" (1991: 1252). Finally, and perhaps most strikingly, Keuzenkamp concluded that Tinbergen's 1932 model was a "precursor" to Muth's 1961 RE model, albeit recognizing that there is a "divergence between the articles … as Muth concentrates on autocorrelated processes whilst Tinbergen only discusses the … case with serially independent disturbances", and that "the difference between Tinbergen and Muth is that Muth proceeds with serially independent disturbances throughout" (1248, 1250).

Now, the first and second statements made by Keuzenkamp have already been shown to be in error, as manifest in the ongoing work of *both* Muth and Mills, in the former case, starting in 1959, in the latter case, from 1954–55 onwards. As for his third statement, in this context, while Keuzenkamp mentions Tinbergen's 1933 *Econometrica* paper in which "the model of 1932 is very briefly repeated", he goes on to say that "In his later work in building dynamic macroeconomic models Tinbergen never referred to his theory of rational expectations", citing Tinbergen (1937) as an example of this (1991: 1252). However, Keuzenkamp has simply *overlooked* Tinbergen's 1934 *Econometrica* paper entitled "Annual survey of significant developments in general economic theory". In his survey, Tinbergen *not only verbally restated his 1932 approach, but explicitly referred the reader to his 1932 paper.* Moreover, in this survey, Tinbergen even proposed what could be called an "expectations research project", albeit with a *microeconomic* focus (1934: 28–9). Tinbergen concluded by saying that "a *wide field seems open, also, in slightly different directions, for successful investigations as to a more systematic knowledge of the fundamentals for expectances*" [our emphasis].

As for the last of Keuzenkamp's problematic statements regarding Muth and Tinbergen, while his "central message" is that Tinbergen's 1932 model is a "precursor" to Muth's 1961 RE model, Keuzenkamp has *simply not realized the fundamental difference between them as manifest in the nature and characteristics of the "error" term of the respective models, and thus has not recognized the close similarity between Tinbergen's 1932 approach and Mills's "implicit" expectations model.* In order to compare Mills's approach to that of Tinbergen on the one hand, and that of Muth on the other, in Table 1 below we have replicated Keuzenkamp's "Table 1" (1991: 1251) in the first two columns of our table, which reproduces the equation systems of Muth (1961) and Tinbergen (1932), and also added a *third* column, which contains corresponding equations posited by Mills in his 1962 book (see 71–2) which are based on the paper he presented on the morning of the same day Muth presented the original version of his own RE paper at the December 1959 Washington Meeting of the Econometric Society. For ease in comparison and comprehension, Mills's notation *has been converted to that used in Keuzenkamp's "Table 1".* Now, following from the RE equilibrium assumptions he made in his 1954–55 paper, Mills's "equation 21" in Table 1 below is readily derived. And, as has been shown above, Mills *initially* specified the *demand equation* given as "equation 20" in Table 1 below in his 1957 *Econometrica* paper (Mills 1957a).

As can be seen in Table 1, Tinbergen and Mills consider serially uncorrelated disturbances (given (v)). Muth, however, specifies disturbances which are serially correlated with the past history of *u* (see (i)). In light of the *dis*-similarity, then, in the treatment of the error term between Tinbergen and Muth, and the *similarity* between Tinbergen and Mills, it could be said that Mills either re-discovered or re-invented Tinbergen's 1932 approach, or rather that he *independently* discovered a very similar *micro-based* approach and that Tinbergen is, therefore a "precursor" of Mills and *not* of Muth.

The *crucial* significance of Mills's pathbreaking work on implicit expectations, however, lies not only in its "rediscovery" of Tinbergen's 1932 approach – and this in light of the fact that in an interview, Mills said he had indeed read Tinbergen' s 1932 paper "in German" (Mills 1995) – but in its relationship to Muth's own work on RE, since not only were *both* "spinoffs" of formal and informal expectations research projects at

Table 1 Comparison of Muth, Tinbergen, and Mills models

Muth		*Tinbergen*		*Mills*	
$C_t = -\beta p_t$	(30a)	$C_t = f(p_t) f' < 0$		$C_t = a - bp_t + u_t$	(20)
$P_t = \gamma p_t^e + u_t$	(30b)	$P_t = \bar{P} + u_t$		$P_t = p_t^e / c$	(19a)
$I_t = \alpha(p_{t+1}^e - p_t)$	(30c)	$I_t = g(p_{t+1}^e, p_t)$		$I_t = \max\{(p_{t+1}^e - p_t) / r, 0\}$	(19b)
$C_t + I_t = P_t + I_t$	(31)	$C_t + I_t = P_t + I_{t-1}$		$C_t + I_t = P_t + I_{t-1}$	(22)
$u_t = \sum_{i=1}^{\infty} w_i \mu_{t-1}$	(i)	$P_{t+1}^e = E(P_{t+1}) = \bar{P}$ (the mean)		$x_t^S = P_t + I_{t-1} - I_t$	(21)
$E(\mu_j) = 0$	(ii)	$u_t = \mu_t$	(v)	$u_t = \mu_t$	(v)
$E(\mu_i \mu_j) = \sigma^2$ if $i = j$	(iii)				
$= 0$ if $i \neq j$	(iv)				

Note

Where: C refers to demand, p to prices, P to production, p^e to expected prices, I to inventories, $\bar{P}$ to the mathematical expectation of next year's production, c to marginal production cost, r to inventory cost, x^s to total supply, and t to the time period, β, γ, α, g, a, b are constants, u is disturbance terms, w_i are weights and μ_t are serially uncorrelated random variables with zero mean, constant variance σ^2 (as stated in (ii) to (iv)).

Carnegie Tech and Johns Hopkins respectively, as has been shown above, but Muth himself and others have come to adopt Mills's approach as a *better* way of modeling expectations at the *micro*-level due to measurement and measurement error problems relating to Muth's 1959/61 approach (Muth 1985; Lovell 1986).

In light of the above, it is indeed surprising that a very recent paper on Muth's contributions did not mention those of Mills, except for a passing reference to his "discussion on how to model expectations with Nerlove", despite the timely admonition of the author that "historians of economics cannot wash their hands of contemporary developments in economics and let economists write their own histories" (Sent 2002: 304, 315). Perhaps "historians of economics" should listen more carefully to economists and their "histories", especially when "multiple discovery" and what we have called above "independent parallel development" are involved.

5 December 1959 and its aftermath

The fact that *both* Muth and Mills presented the *original versions* of their respective approaches to expectations at the December 1959 Washington, DC meeting of the Econometric Society has been overlooked by "historians" of economic thought in general, and even by ostensibly "comprehensive observers of the history of rational expectations" itself. Indeed, the aspect of "multiple discovery" involved in the development of the rational and implicit expectations approach goes beyond the issue of "precursors", since many observers have simply *overlooked* Mills's work. One example of this has already been seen in the case of Keuzenkamp's *Economic Journal* article (1991), as shown above. Another can be seen in Niehans's book *A History of Economic Theory* (1990), where he explicitly states that as regards rational expectations "no multiple discovery has yet come to light" (1990: 509).

In a compilation entitled *A Reader's Guide to Rational Expectations* subtitled, "A survey and comprehensive annotated bibliography", Redman did notice the aspect of "multiple discovery" as regards RE, stating for example that "John Muth first introduced the concept of rational expectations to economists in his article ... published in *Econometrica* in 1961. At approximately the same time Edwin S. Mills (1957a, 1957b, 1962) introduced the very similar concept of implicit expectations" (1992: 5); and also stating that "implicit expectations are so closely related to rational expectations that Mills deserves to be credited with developing the concept" (1992: 140). But what Redman *omits* in this "comprehensive" work, or rather what has been simply overlooked – besides the fact that the approaches *are formally distinct in the mathematical sense*, albeit similar in their underlying assumptions – are the following points, which are crucial to an understanding of the evolution of the Muth–Mills approach to expectations:

1 the paper given by Mills at the Econometric Society meeting in Washington, DC at the session called "Economic Theory III" on "Wednesday morning, December 30" 1959, with "Robert W. Clower, Northwestern University, Chairman", at which "papers were discussed

by Gerard Debreu, Yale University and Mitchell Harwitz, Northwestern University" (Report 1960: 698–9) *comprises the core of his 1962 book, according to Mills himself* (Mills 1991a).

2 there was an important exchange between Mills and Nerlove, who attended both the session at which Mills presented his paper, and that at which Muth presented the *original version* of his now famous paper, on the relative efficacy of the use of implicit and rational expectations as against adaptive expectations *in microeconomics* in the May 1961 issue of *Quarterly Journal of Economics*, and this, *before Muth's paper was even published* (Mills 1961; Nerlove 1961b).

3 Mills started to work on his own approach to expectations *before* 1957, as shown above (Mills 1954–55).

4 Negishi published an important albeit overlooked paper linking rational expectations and general equilibrium theory in 1964 (Negishi 1964). Moreover, his 1965 book *Theory of Price and Allocation* (in Japanese) and an important article by Radner (1967) in French shows the extent to which the *microeconomically-based* RE approach of Muth and the implicit expectations approach of Mills had influenced "fertile minds" in the field of microeconomics.

5 that there were indeed a number of "precursors" to Muth and Mills, such as Tinbergen (1932) and Machlup (1952), whose work has been discussed above, and also Lindhal (1939, 1957), who influenced Hart's work.

Now, the role of "Conferences" and "Meetings" in the dissemination of new knowledge and approaches in economics and new methods of economic analysis is indeed problematic. On the one hand, new ideas are *sometimes introduced* on such occasions, with papers usually circulated prior to, at, or even after their presentation. On the other hand, as Robert Solow put it in a letter to one of the authors (2 December 1991) regarding the issue: "I think that the Econometric Society meeting is the wrong place to look. Nobody ever learns or understands new ideas at those meetings. In fact the sessions are very sparsely attended, except for the occasional blockbuster. The most anyone ever learns is that there is a paper that he or she might like to read. Nothing is absorbed. The presentations are too short; and as soon as one is over it is followed by another". Or, as Robert Clower also asserted in a letter (19 December 1991): "Let me assure you, that nothing revolutionary ever appeared in a paper given at the Econometric Society. Revolutions are not in the papers. They come about because someone, or a group of people, later on find something exciting and form a school around it".

Clower is indeed correct in his assertion. But, the important thing to stress is the *impression that new ideas make on fertile minds* at conferences and meetings. Thus, while most economists who attended the Muth and Mills sessions *did not* take up the rational and implicit expectations approach, or as will be seen, were not too impressed by them even *after* they were published, Lovell, Nerlove, Negishi, and Radner, besides Mills and Muth, still used it to model expectations formation or as a benchmark for comparison of the relative efficacy of alternate approaches to expectations *at the microeconomic level.*

In the first section of this chapter we focus on the sessions at the December 1959 meeting of the Econometric Society where, on the same day, 30 December, Mills gave his implicit expectations paper entitled "Expectations, inventories, and the stability of competitive markets" at a morning session, while Muth gave his now famous paper "Rational expectations and the theory of price movements" at an afternoon session called "New Approaches to Old Problems", chaired by Edwin Kuh. The recollections of Muth and Mills regarding the sessions at which they gave their respective papers, along with those of discussants and participants in the sessions, will be presented. We then go on to present the *retrospective* impressions and assessments of a number of prominent *mainstream* economists of the Muth–Mills approach, that is rational and implicit expectations. In the second section of the chapter, we discuss the outcome of December 1959 and the linkage between microfoundations and macroapplications of the Muth–Mills approach.

The Econometric Society meeting, December 1959

The "Report of the Washington meeting December 28–30 1959" of the Econometric Society was published in the July 1960 issue of *Econometrica*, where an abstract of Muth's now famous paper appeared (Report 1960: 704). In this abstract, Muth wrote

> In order to arrive at a fairly simple explanation of the way expectations are formed, we advance the hypothesis that they are essentially the same as the predictions of the relevant economic theory. In particular, the hypothesis asserts two things: (1) information is scarce, and the economic system generally does not waste it, and (2) the way expectations are formed depends specifically on the structure of the entire system. Methods of analysis, which are appropriate under special conditions, are described in the context of an isolated market with a fixed production lag. The interpretive value of the hypothesis is illustrated by the introduction of commodity speculation. Finally, it is shown that the rational expectations hypothesis is in good agreement with the facts, at least if one views the empirical results generously.

An abstract of Mills's paper, on the other hand, did *not* appear (Report 1960: 699). Albert Hart was the discussant for Muth's paper, while Gerard Debreu was the discussant for Mills's paper (Report 1960: 698, 704).

As Muth recalled in a letter regarding his 1959 paper and other aspects of his RE approach (2 August 1991a)

> My recollection is that the presentation was the early part of the 1961 paper: the basic model involving an isolated market. Albert Hart was the discussant at the 1959 meeting, and he gave me a page of his typewritten comments ... My recollection is that Hart emphasized only that the variables used in the paper are deviations from equilibrium values, not absolute quantities.

In the *published* version of the paper (Muth 1961), Muth had mentioned that Modigliani had commented on his 1959 paper. In this regard, Muth recalled

> The comments of Modigliani were mostly the sort that you get when you circulate the paper among respected colleagues. My recollection is that he did not have any substantial criticism or suggestions, only some of a stylistic and minor nature. He had no problem with the basic concept of the paper, because the model itself is extremely simple, not involving great technical intricacy. (The implications of the theory on monetary theory had, of course, not yet been drawn by Lucas, Sargent and Wallace, and others).

As regards the influence of Grunberg and Modigliani's paper (1954) and that of Simon (1954) on his own 1959 paper – taking into account that the former *was* cited by Muth in the published version of his 1959 paper (Muth 1961) – Muth replied

> Concerning the Grunberg and Modigliani 1954 *Journal of Political Economy* paper (see also Herbert A. Simon's *Public Opinion Quarterly* paper), certainly I was aware of the problem and their results. One must draw a distinction, however, between their concerns and those of the rational expectations model. Their primary interest was the question, is it necessarily true that "in reacting to the published prediction of a future event, individuals influence the course of events and therefore falsify the prediction"? The forecast is treated as an exogenous variable in a static, deterministic world. According to the rational expectations hypothesis, expectations are determined by the structure of the system. The forecasts are endogenous. In addition, the model assumes a system which is dynamic and stochastic.

Muth continued

> Some authors have referred to rational expectations as self-fulfilling expectations. Self-fulfilling expectations are expectations in which

> "confident error generates its own spurious confirmation" (Robert K. Merton: *Social Theory and Social Structure*, Free Press, 1957, 128). The important word is "spurious". The expectation is an exogenous variable in this model, as well, and thus differs from the rational expectations model.

In a subsequent letter (5 September 1991b) Muth dealt with the influence of Herbert Simon on his work and his 1959 paper. He wrote

> I was a student of Herbert Simon while in the graduate program at Carnegie Tech in 1952–1956. I took a management course from him in 1953, based largely on his book on public administration; also, a course on mathematical social science in 1955, which involved a number of readings such as his articles in economics, including part of a book by Andronov and Chaikin on the theory of oscillations. I also participated as a graduate student in a project sponsored by the Office of Naval Research on aggregate scheduling. The faculty members involved in that were Charles Holt, Franco Modigliani, Herbert Simon, and initially Robert Schlaifer.
>
> At this time Simon's work was mostly in organizational theory and economics. It was before he got involved in the simulation of cognitive processes, which started around 1956 or 1957. Needless to say, with all this exposure he has had a very important general influence on me.
>
> However, there is very little direct influence on my work in expectations. Indeed, the rational expectations model runs counter to his main beliefs about appropriate types of economic models and his own modeling technique in two ways. (1) Rational expectations involves notions of equilibrium, while he favors a process, or algorithmic, model of steps taken by decision makers. (2) Rational expectations obviously involves rational choice in its purest form, while he advocates approaches based upon aspiration level models of search.
>
> A major project I have been working on recently is much closer to the process and search approach in modeling economic activity, although it does not use the aspiration level model.

Finally, with regard to Mills's 1957 paper on implicit expectations and his view of Mills's approach and its relation to his own work, Muth wrote (2 August 1991a)

> Implicit expectations were introduced by Edwin Mills in his 1957 *Econometrica* paper. I was familiar with the paper but had not studied it carefully enough to notice his expectations model. Several years ago, Michael Lovell [Hirsch and Lovell 1969] pointed out the distinction between rational and implicit expectations. In rational expectations the error is uncorrelated with the forecast, while in implicit

> expectations the error is uncorrelated with the realization. I now feel that a combination of the two is a closer approximation to reality (see my 1985 *Eastern Economic Journal* paper).

Mills, for his part, also recalled, in a series of letters, some aspects of the session at which he presented his own paper in 1959. As he said (26 September 1991a)

> Until the Econometric Society meeting at which, by coincidence and at separate sessions, he and I presented our papers, I did not know John Muth.

He continued

> I do not have a copy of my paper, but the substance appears in my book *Price, Output and Inventory Policy* (NY: Wiley, 1962) Ch. 3 et seq ... I do recall that Marc Nerlove directed me to Muth's paper and pointed out the similarity of approaches.

In a further letter (6 November 1991b), Mills added

> I do not remember if I attended Muth's Econometric Society Session, or if he attended my session. I certainly read a draft of his paper not long afterward ... Gerard Debreu discussed my paper. I recall a comment "I believe that if Mills' result is correct, it is true under much more general conditions than he analyzes". This could be a figment of my memory, but it is certainly a nice Debreu-like comment.

Debreu, for his part, in a letter (22 November 1991) wrote that

> I have no reason to doubt the *Econometrica* report on the session I attended. I do not have, however, a copy of Edwin Mills' paper or of the comments I might have made after his presentation. The sentence that Edwin Mills quotes in his letter of November 6, 1991 to you sounds plausible, but I cannot remember uttering it.

Debreu continued

> Again it seems likely, given the program of the meeting, that I attended the afternoon session at which John Muth spoke. I am certain that I listened at least once to his presentation of his paper at about that time, and I distinctly recall finding its main ideas quite stimulating. I do not believe, however, that I perceived them or Mills' ideas as "revolutionary," nor do I remember noticing the "similarity" between the two papers.

Marc Nerlove, who as Mills recalled "directed" him "to Muth's paper", in a letter (19 November 1991a) also recalled some aspects of the sessions at which Muth and Mills gave their respective papers. As he wrote

> I do recall the Washington meetings, but I was familiar with Mills' work before then ... I did go to both presentations, made a lot of comments from the floor (I was pretty brash) and even introduced the two (I also knew Muth slightly through his brother Richard F.). Later I refereed both Muth's *JASA* and *Econometrica* papers for their respective journals.

Nerlove continued

> Muth's idea was terribly appealing, at least to me ... One reason the idea probably didn't take off until much later is that it was almost impossible to implement empirically. This is later corrected by the modification called "quasi-rational expectations" discussed in my 1979 book [Nerlove *et al.* 1979].

Now, while Edwin Mills did not remember attending John Muth's session, it would seem that Muth, for his part, *did* attend that of Mills. For, as Muth wrote in a letter to one of the authors (14 March 1992b)

> I don't really recall very much in detail about Mills' session at the December 1959 meeting of the Econometric Society. After all, it was over thirty years ago. Also, I don't recall seeing a copy of his paper entitled "Expectations, Inventories and the Stability of Competitive Markets", which eventually became chapter 3 of his 1962 book. I think my brother, Richard F. Muth, did review one of his articles for publication somewhere. Mills' expectations model did not really sink into my consciousness until I read his book and Mike Lovell published his book on sales anticipations and inventories.

William Cooper also attended the Muth session, and while in a letter said that his memory was "at best hazy" (5 December 1991), also went on to say that

> My main memory is that Albert Hart (who I knew both at Chicago and Columbia) served as the discussant of Jack's paper and really only talked around it. It may be that Hart was influenced by his collaboration with J.R. Hicks on a text which dealt with a national income approach to economics – a very good text which I used in the course I taught at Chicago. You may recall that the topic of expectations is discussed at length in Hicks' *Value and Capital* and it also formed a central theme in Hart's doctoral dissertation ... This was probably the

> reason he was selected as a discussant but, nevertheless, he didn't seem to understand (or at least he didn't direct himself) to what Muth was saying on *rational* expectations – probably because neither he nor Hicks had considered the topic from that standpoint.

Richard Eckaus, who also attended the Muth session, wrote (2 December 1991) that "Hart rather offhandedly dismissed" Muth's paper and that he recalled "thinking that there was more to it than Hart acknowledged". Irma Adelman attended both the sessions of Muth and Mills (letter of 14 January 1992) and wrote

> I remember attending the presentation of both the Muth paper and the Mills paper. But my feeling at the time was merely that it offered an interesting variant on adaptive expectations. The revolutionary aspect of rational expectations comes in only when the impact of government policy is included in the rational expectation formation of all institutional actors in the economy, not just inventories. As I remember, these tie-ins were not made in the Mills and Muth papers.

Now, when viewed *in the perspective* of the so-called "RE Revolution in Macroeconomics", the "revolutionary aspect of rational expectations" *when it first appeared was indeed overlooked by many prominent observers.* Alternatively, *it was not deemed as being revolutionary, then or now.* For example, in a letter (2 December 1991) Solow wrote

> I am also pretty sure that I read Muth's paper when it came out. And I must have known what Ed Mills was up to because we were friends and colleagues. I did not then think of the concept of rational expectations as revolutionary. To tell you the truth, I would not describe it that way now. My guess is that it picks up some extra aura from being associated with the reversion to complete and perfect market-clearing in macroeconomics, although the two ideas are conceptually entirely distinct.

Other prominent economists also recalled their initial reaction to Muth's RE approach. Phillip Cagan, for his part, while not having attended the Muth session at the 1959 meeting still wrote in a letter (28 November 1991)

> I certainly did not attend Muth's paper. However, I was a visiting professor at Carnegie Mellon in the early 1960s where Muth was teaching, and I became aware of his paper. I was especially interested because it extended the concept of expectations that I had introduced in a study of hyperinflations. At that time Muth's contribution was not of course referred to as a revolutionary new concept of "rational expectations".

> It was interesting but did not seem particularly important. It became important, as I see it, when more and more of the literature was taken over by the modelers of theoretical constructs who needed some way to handle expectations. Someone noticed that expectations could be modeled by assuming that agents expected what the model predicted. Eureka! The theoretical modelers were off and running – ever since.
>
> Some of us have doubts about the usefulness for empirical work of rational expectations (see my article in the December 91 issue of *Journal of International Macroeconomics*), though this in no way takes away from Muth's insightful contribution. Nevertheless, it has obviously been a boon for the theoreticians.

While he also did not attend the session at which Muth presented his paper, in a letter (26 November 1991) M.L. Burstein wrote

> I do recall that Jack [Muth] worked on his dissertation [at the University of Chicago] in the same room I – and other members of the Harberger Public Finance Workshop worked (Zvi Griliches, Yehuda Grunfeld, Bill Niskanen, Marc Nerlove, Lester Telser, *et al.*) . . . I can report this:
>
> i I had no idea that Jack Muth's work was monumentally important – and it is such.
> ii I clearly recall the cobweb theory orientation of his study – and picked up the flaw in cobweb theory (very important then in what passed for advanced economics) that was thus revealed. But the larger issues, the amplitude of his discovery, completely passed me by. I did get the hang around 1974. Thus I doubt if my 1968 book was significantly influenced by this result.
> iii That said I and others wrote about the ineffectiveness of tax-policy and refunding operations in the early 1960s. See my 1963 book – but I don't think I had Jack's framework in mind.
>
> On net, I am not proud of my record of reception of RE – not until 1974 when I became solidly enmeshed.

Harold Watts, who was Assistant Director of the Cowles Foundation at Yale (1958–61) and stayed on at Cowles until 1963 – spanning the time during which both Muth and Mills were there respectively – also wrote in a letter (10 December 1991)

> While I do not have any recollections about the ES sessions in December 1959, I was acquainted with both Jack Muth and Ed Mills shortly after that time . . . I was familiar with much of the expectational literature, having discussed a paper by Marc Nerlove that involved both

> stock adjustments and adaptive expectations. I also worked informally with Bob Eisner when he visited at Cowles and was working on plans and expectations in connection with investment forecasting.
>
> My general recollection is that rational expectations were met with relatively little interest because there seemed to be many more interesting and relevant things to do at the time. It even seems to me that the originators concurred in that assessment. The basic ideas were interesting and original, but did not seem to be revolutionary (and still don't in my estimation).

On the other hand, G. Edward Schuh, in a letter (3 December 1991) actually "broadened" the "puzzle" of the *initial acceptance* of the RE and implicit expectations approach when he wrote

> You are correct that I did participate in the 1959 meetings of the Econometric Society ... In fact, I gave a paper at that meeting – the first professional paper of my career! However, I did not participate ... in either of the sessions to which you refer.
>
> I have some thoughts for you, however, for whatever they might be worth. Part of these is directed to broadening the puzzle. *To be specific, the work of Koyck and Nerlove with distributed lag models should have set the stage for more ready acceptance of the rational expectations model. In the case of both authors, they emphasized that these models could be interpreted either as a means to use past information from the economy to make predictions about the expectations for the future, or as a means of measuring the lag in response to information generated in the current period* [our emphasis].

Schuh continued

> From my own perspective, I was using these new distributed lag models in my dissertation research at the University of Chicago. My dissertation was completed on the job at Purdue University, so it took me a couple of years to completion. I remember reading Muth's article and trying to draw on it in the context of the models I was using. In fact, I may well have made reference to it in both my thesis and the journal articles that came out of it. As a young professional, however, I must confess to not appreciating the significance of what he did, although later in my career I repeatedly reminded students that the root of the rational expectations approach went back to Muth's article.
>
> Why did people like me not recognize the significance of this early work? I think in part it was because we didn't find using an expectations model in principle all that significant. After all, most of us were forced to read Keynes, even at the University of Chicago(!) [Schuh's

> emphasis], and he talked a lot about expectations. In effect, so what was new other than a means of taking them into account in empirical research by means of the distributed lag models. *One of the puzzles to me is that a professional as bright as Nerlove seemed so close to stumbling onto the rational expectations approach and did not seem to grasp it – in retrospect* [our emphasis – but see below]. He did, however, realize the horrendous identification problem involved in using the Koyck model.
>
> I also think it was in part a consequence of the failure to recognize the full implications of the rational expectations perspective for policy *and for econometric estimation* [our emphasis – but also see below].
>
> For what it is worth, the professors at the University of Chicago *who reviewed my thesis, and they included Friedman and Griliches, did not seem to recognize the significance of the Muth article – or of the work of Nerlove and Koyck which pointed in that direction* [our emphasis].

In his letter of 5 December 1991 cited above, William Cooper made the following salient points regarding the *initial* reception of Muth's RE approach. As he put it

> You may want to take note of the rule that Jacob Marschak once told me about: it takes 20 years, on average, for a new idea to become adopted in economics. This may also be true in other sciences and may have something to do with generation gaps, generation turnovers and like phenomena. In addition you can add that Jack was young and relatively unknown at the time and it was not even clear that he was an economist, as the term was used in those days, and in fact he subsequently turned more towards management science and operations research.

Moreover, in a letter (2 December 1991) Stanley Lebergott actually broadened the question regarding the initial reaction to and early adoption of RE when he wrote

> You ask why "rational expectations ... (was) not immediately adopted by the economics profession" in 1959?
>
> Aside from any other reasons it appeared in the midst of many other signals, most of which were also plausible and were more in line with prior expectations.
>
> I do not remember the original 1959 presentation but you could also ask: why was it not adopted even a decade later? I was a member of an FRB Consultants Committee, and we sponsored the Econometrics of Price Determination Conference, October 31, 1970 (Published June 1972 by the FRB).
>
> Lucas presented a paper on the Natural Rate hypothesis, adopting Muth. You can read (p. 113) Frank Fisher's dismissal: "Lucas appears

to believe that the notion that one cannot fool all the people all the time implies one cannot fool all the people even some of the time ... when policies change average expectations will (not necessarily) be right in the short run".

Time dating is obviously not trivial. And where you predict what the outcome will be, between the short run and the limit, depends on your prior perspective. In this instance it also was confounded with

a Those of us involved in say the SSRC–Brookings model were still trying to work out the awful empirical fitting. Persistently going back to every first principle was not the up front task when the sub-optimizing was so onerous. Do note (in the FRB volume) the extended paper by Nerlove had to face the rational expectations critique, and really did not. Shirley Almon's article also appeared in *Econometrica* in 1965 – well after Muth – and did not. (Both were included, even handedly, in Zellner's *Readings in Economic Statistics and Econometrics* (1968).) Surely that forcibly suggests adaptive applications [expectations] was alive and well at Harvard and Chicago. (And Nerlove was at Yale somewhere in this period.)
b Theil's insights still prevailed. Adopting a new paradigm, in sum, was mixed up with the war between Keynesians and monetarists. But Frank Fisher's point about dating expectations was not trivial, may even still be with us.

Franklin Fisher, for his part, wrote (5 December 1991)

> So far as I can remember I did not attend either of the sessions at the 1959 meetings in which you are interested.
>
> For what it is worth, I did read Muth's paper when it was published. My view of why it had so little impact is (although I have not reread it) that it is quite obscurely written. It does not convey the sense of something truly important.

And, as for how he saw the "empirical validity" of the RE approach when it first appeared, Wassily Leontief wrote (2 December 1991): "Let me admit that I must have been, at that time, skeptical of the empirical validity of the theory of rational expectations as I am now".

In contrast to all this, Arnold Zellner, while not being able to recall having attended either of the sessions "at which Muth and Mills presented their papers" still wrote (30 December 1991)

> However in 1961, I read the Muth paper in *Econometrica* and was quite impressed by it since it put forward a novel and attractive approach. I included the paper in my advanced graduate course in

> econometrics, Dept. of Economics, U. of Wisconsin at Madison and then in a 1968 book, *Readings in Economic Statistics and Econometrics*, Little, Brown and Co., Boston that I edited.
>
> *I was just as surprised as you are that Muth's ideas did not have an instantaneous impact. Perhaps his paper was somewhat difficult to read or many were taken up with adaptive expectations. In any event, the profession was slow to recognize Muth's contribution* [our emphasis].

But let us leave the last word on this issue to Muth himself, who in a letter (28 February 1992) give us his views regarding the initial acceptance of RE:

> I would like to react to a statement made by Mike Lovell that rational expectations finally took hold after lying dormant for a decade. A similar view was expressed by Robert Lucas and Thomas Sargent in the introduction to their readings book, *Rational Expectations and Econometric Practice* (University of Minnesota Press, 1980). The editors' introduction opens with the statement: "After a remarkably quiet first decade John Muth's idea of 'rational expectations' has taken hold, or taken off, in an equally remarkable way".
>
> The *Social Science Citation Index* lists 17 references to my paper for the years 1966–70, their first years of publication. The paper was referred to, but not used, by Kenneth Arrow in his "The Economic Implications of Learning by Doing" (*Review of Economic Studies 29* [1962], pp. 155–173). It was also reprinted in 1968 by Arnold Zellner (*Readings in Economic Statistics and Econometrics*, Little, Brown). This attention is not much compared with that of later years, but it does not really qualify as neglect.
>
> Having said that, there is indeed a time lag in adopting new concepts and ideas in economics. Maybe something weird was happening during the decade of the 1960's. Perhaps new ideas take hold only as the older generation is gradually replaced by the new. Most of my former teachers at Carnegie-Mellon have only very limited enthusiasm for the rational expectations hypothesis, even though it is now commonplace in financial and macroeconomics.

Based upon the material presented above and that to be discussed below, we would agree with Muth that after their *initial* presentation (1957–59) and publication (1961–62), the reaction to his RE and Mills's implicit expectations approaches *cannot* be characterized, in his words "as neglect". What was *actually* overlooked were their *macroeconomic* implications. For, over the period 1959–69, *both* the RE and implicit expectations approaches *did* affect microeconomic and microeconometric analysis, as will now be shown.

Utilization 1959–69

In an article "Rational expectations in microeconomic models: an overview" (Jordan and Radner 1982) published over two decades *after* Muth and Mills presented their original papers on RE and implicit expectations, economists were reminded by Jordan and Radner (1982: 203) that Radner, for his part, had introduced the notion of an RE *Equilibrium* in his seminal paper *in French* (Radner 1967; also see Radner 1968). Despite this, Radner's 1967 paper was *not mentioned* in Pesaran's important book *The Limits to Rational Expectations* (1987), nor in Hamouda and Rowley's work *Expectations, Equilibrium and Dynamics* (1988).

But this is not all, for there is also no mention in Pesaran's book of Mills *at all*, nor of the Mills–Nerlove *QJE* debate in 1961. Moreover, Negishi's important 1964 paper linking RE and General Equilibrium (GE) is not mentioned by Pesaran, nor is Radner (1968), Hirsch and Lovell (1969), or even Muth (1985). In Hamouda and Rowley (1988), for their part, there is *also no mention* of Negishi (1964) or Hirsch and Lovell (1969). And, for that matter, *neither* Muth (1985) nor Lovell (1986) are mentioned by them, although other *much less important* articles *do* receive attention. Indeed, it is as if the literature on RE and on its microeconometric testing over the period 1959–69 and even later has been simply *overlooked*, even by those whose object it was to ostensibly provide a comprehensive survey of the development of expectational economics in general and of the RE concept in particular.

In this section, we focus, therefore, on what we consider to be the *seminal* works on RE and implicit expectations on the microeconomic and microeconometric levels over the period 1959–69 which comprise what we call "the Missing Decade". In this context, we will also consider the three "missing links" between the micro- and macroapplications of the notion of RE, Negishi (1964, 1965) and Radner (1967, 1968) which linked RE to GE theory, and that of Phelps (1966), which linked "endogenous expectation formation" to macroanalysis of inflation and unemployment processes, thus providing them with appropriate microfoundations.

Now, the *original* version of Muth's 1961 paper, was actually circulated as "Carnegie Institute of Technology ONR Research Memo No. 65" (Muth 1959b) and Nerlove, for one, cited it *at length* in his 1960 Conference paper "Time-series analysis of the supply of agricultural products" (Nerlove 1961a) published in the conference proceedings edited by Heady entitled *Agricultural Supply Functions* (1961). *Indeed, it would seem that it was this "Research Memo" that was submitted to* Econometrica *for publication by Muth, being the written and expanded version of the paper he had presented at the December 1959 Econometric Society meeting; this, in light of the fact that Muth could not find a copy of his original conference paper and also was not sure if a written version existed* (letter of Muth to authors, 2 August 1991a). For, as Nerlove recalled as cited above, he refereed

Muth's paper for *Econometrica.* And the fact of the matter is that in his 1960 Conference paper, Nerlove wrote (1961a: 47–8)

> From the standpoint of economic theory, the rational expectations hypothesis is the most attractive hypothesis concerning the formation of expectations which has been formulated to date and which is sufficiently simple to be used in connection with time-series analysis.

He went on to list three reasons why the REH appeared to him to be "far more reasonable than it first sounds". As Nerlove wrote (1961a: 48–9)

> the rational expectations hypothesis does not require that every farmer or businessman formulate a correct and relevant economic model. Economists cannot even do that! What it does require is that the representative firm behave *as if* it had made predictions on the basis of the same economic model used by the economist to analyze industry behavior. It implies expectations which are constructs of the same nature as "certainty equivalents", "adaptive expectations", and "supply functions" – indeed almost any other economic concept. Furthermore, the expectations thus generated will be entirely consistent with the economic model used and will have the additional advantage of not assuming less rationality in the formation of expectations than in other forms of economic behavior. If one is prepared, for the purposes of a predictive model, to assume that on average producers maximize profits, it does not make sense to assume that they err greatly in making forecasts on the average, or at least err *more* than the model used to predict their behavior. The rational expectations hypothesis [is] an attractive one from the aesthetic standpoint and because of its consistency both with general economic theory and the particular economic model underlying the statistical analysis undertaken [Nerlove's emphasis] ... it is possible to introduce elements of irrationality into the picture. Such deviations from rationality are, of course, unimportant when they are unsystematic. This is what we mean when we speak of rational expectations "on the average". But if the deviations are systematic, biased expectations may result. Muth [here Nerlove is referring to Muth's *Research Memo*] gives an example of how such biases may be introduced.

Interestingly enough, in his "debate" with Mills on the efficacy of adaptive versus rational and implicit expectations Nerlove wrote (1961b: 336, n. 2) that in his treatment of Muth's model "the discussion here follows the somewhat simple derivation of the appropriate rational expectations given in my paper [Nerlove 1961a]" as it appeared in the conference volume mentioned above. In fact, as early as in his 1961 "debate" with Mills, Nerlove had made a number of *crucial points* regarding the Muth–Mills approach to expectations. Nerlove concluded (1961b: 338)

> it may be said that Mills has left an important element out of his analysis, namely the stochastic. When this element is introduced, it is possible to exhibit circumstances under which adaptive expectations are "always wrong whenever the market is out of equilibrium", but they are *not* [Nerlove's emphasis] "wrong in a very simple and systematic way" . . . It follows that Mills is quite right concerning the unsatisfactory nature of adaptive expectations in general. *It remains to be seen, however, how successful we will be in introducing the general principles stressed by Mills and Muth into econometric practice and the analysis of stability problems* [our emphasis].

Mills, for his part, in his 1961 paper "The use of adaptive expectations in stability analysis: comment" asserted (1961: 330)

> An important problem in economics, which has received little systematic study, is to decide how much information decision makers should be assumed to possess in making price, output, purchase and other decisions. At the extreme, some writers argue that it is best to assume that decision makers are always right in the sense that they know the true probability distribution of the variable they are trying to predict.

Mills added in a footnote (330, n. 1)

> This position has been taken independently by John Muth in an unpublished paper . . . [referring to Muth's *Research Memo*, it would seem] and by the author in a forthcoming book [referring to Mills 1962].

Mills went on also to take issue with Nerlove's *earlier QJE* paper on "Adaptive expectations and cobweb phenomena" (Nerlove 1958) and said (Mills 1961: 333–4) "it is not plausible to assume that a decision-maker, who is otherwise assumed to behave rationally, continues to form expectations in a way which is continuously contradicted by experience in a mechanical and easily perceived fashion". In response to this, Nerlove mathematically showed (Nerlove 1961b: 338) "that under certain circumstances adaptive expectations are not subject to the objection which Mills raises". He did this by comparing the stability conditions in the Muth–Mills approach and the concomitant expectations generated with, as he put it "the stability conditions given in my earlier paper [Nerlove 1958]". He concluded (1961b: 338) that "it is easy to see that instability is impossible *when the adaptive expectations are rational*" [our emphasis].

Indeed, in this exchange with Mills, Nerlove (1961b) *actually repeated arguments he made in his 1960 conference paper mentioned above* (Nerlove 1961a: 53) in which he mathematically generated adaptive expectations which "are also *rational* ones" [Nerlove's emphasis], and said that "the estimation techniques proposed for models based on adaptive expectations are inappropriate in the case of rational expectations, *despite the fact that rational expectations turn out to be of the adaptive form*" [Nerlove's emphasis]. Nerlove concluded (1961a: 53)

> it may be said that rational expectations are difficult to find even for very simple economic models. This does not mean, however, that they are not worth finding. They have the property of being entirely consistent with the economic model into which they are introduced. The little qualitative evidence developed supports the rational expectations hypothesis. There is clearly a need for more evidence of a quantitative character.

It should also be noted that besides those interested in its microeconomic and microeconometric *applications*, Muth's RE article (1961) also generated other reaction in *Econometrica*, that is a somewhat overlooked – albeit important paper by Bossons and Modigliani (1966) entitled "Statistical vs. structural explanations of understatement and regressivity in 'rational' expectations". Now, while dealt with in Hamouda and Rowley (1988: 59, 93–4), neither the *problem* of "regressivity" nor the article by Bossons and Modigliani (1966) are even mentioned by Pesaran (1987) in his book, which ostensibly dealt with "the limits to RE". This omission would not be "that significant", if not for the fact that, as Muth himself recalled in a letter (14 October 1991c)

> The article by Bossons and Modigliani pointed out that I had misinterpreted the regressivity phenomenon and identified it improperly with the regression effect (underextrapolation in their terminology). Bossons was primarily responsible for the article. We had discussed it while it was still in draft form. He got me cold.

Perhaps the most significant microeconometric testing of RE and implicit expectations over the period 1959–69 was that undertaken by Hirsch and Lovell (1969), at least according to Mills – who reviewed their volume for *JEL* (Mills 1971: 107), as noted above – and to Muth himself. Indeed, as Muth indicated in correspondence with one of the authors, the Hirsch and Lovell volume did influence him, although he was not at Carnegie Tech when it was written, and did not participate in the reviewing process of the manuscript, as others – later to be very actively involved in the so-called "RE Revolution in Macroeconomics" – were. For, in his letter of 14 October 1991 cited above, Muth also wrote that

> By the time the Hirsch and Lovell book was being written, I had already moved to Michigan State from Carnegie Tech, and so was not as conveniently available for review of the manuscript even if Lovell had wanted me to do it. At that time both Sargent and Prescott were at Carnegie Tech. I later read the book and enjoyed it.

In a subsequent letter (14 March 1992b), as we have noted above Muth added that "Mills' expectations model did not really sink into my consciousness until I read his book [Mills 1962] and Mike Lovell published his book on sales anticipations and inventories [Hirsch and Lovell 1969]".

It is indeed interesting that Muth mentioned the fact that both Edward Prescott and Thomas Sargent were at Carnegie Tech at the time Lovell was writing his book with Hirsch, for both Prescott and Sargent actually read and made "constructive comments on preliminary drafts of the manuscript" (Hirsch and Lovell 1969: preface, vi). In fact, when queried as to the nature of his "constructive comments" on the manuscript of the Hirsch and Lovell volume, and his view of RE and the results they published – *which did not support either Muth's RE or Mills's implicit expectations approaches* (Hirsch and Lovell 1969: 169–81), Prescott replied, in a letter to one of the authors of this book (30 September 1991)

> I do not remember exactly the nature of my discussions with Mike Lovell concerning rational expectations. I believe that we discussed the meaning of the question "What is your expectation of . . ." My position is that this is an ambiguous question and that we as economists should not treat answers to this question as measurements of anything.

Prescott went on to say

> In taking this position, I was influenced by what I learned in a statistical decision theory course that Morris H. DeGroot taught on the question of eliciting priors. For this question to have meaning, the loss function of the respondent must be known. Another problem is that what people say they would do in a given situation is often not what they actually do in that situation. I adopted the Lucas position that rational expectations, or for that matter maximizing behavior, is not something that can be tested. A model with rational expectations properties can be tested, but not rational expectations itself.

Prescott concluded

> Muth displayed genius in proposing the rational expectations requirement for economic models.

In fact, here Prescott was repeating his argument that the REH cannot be directly tested empirically. For, as he said almost fifteen years before (Prescott 1977: 30)

> Like utility, expectations are not observed, and surveys cannot be used to test the rational expectations hypothesis. One can only test if some theory, whether it incorporates rational expectations or, for that matter, irrational expectations, is or is not consistent with observations.

For his part, Sargent in a note to one of the authors of his book wrote, in answer to the same questions put to Prescott (17 September 1991)

> I can't remember my reactions to Lovell's findings in detail. Lovell was the person who first taught me about rational expectations. I have thought for a long time that the line of work he started is a good one, and that it deserves attention. Dave Ruble at the Minneapolis Fed has done some very interesting and good stuff along these lines recently. The measurement problems and measurement error problems are continuing to receive attention.

In our view, the approach of and results reported by Hirsch and Lovell in 1969 regarding both RE and implicit expectations deserves detailed consideration here, for their study represents the culmination of a period over which those at the *forefront* of the "RE Revolution in Microeconomics" (Nerlove, Negishi, Radner) and in Macroeconomics (Lucas, Sargent, Prescott) *familiarized* themselves with the Muth–Mills approach. Indeed, as Robert Lucas wrote in a letter to one of the authors (30 August 1991)

> I got the idea of rational expectations from John Muth, who was a colleague of mine at Carnegie Tech in the mid 1960s. The first use I made of this construct was in a 1966 working paper entitled "Optimal Investment with Rational Expectations" which was published as chapter 5 of a book Thomas Sargent and I edited *Rational Expectations and Econometric Practice*. Edward Prescott and I used rational expectations in our 1971 *Econometrica* paper, "Investment Under Uncertainty".

Lucas continued

> I know nothing of the history of this idea before Muth's work. I had been influenced by work at Chicago on expectations by Phillip Cagan, Marc Nerlove, and Milton Friedman, but none of them was very close to rational expectations. According to Muth, Edwin Mills ... was

closer, but he didn't have it either. I was not aware of Hart's work, or (except through Muth) of Modigliani's.

Lucas concluded

> I must say, I continue to be amazed at the originality of Muth's formulation. I just do not know of any predecessors that were at all close. I have no idea how he came up with it.

Hirsch and Lovell opened their discussion of what they termed "'rational' or 'implicit' expectations" by saying that (1969: 169)

> in contrast to the behavioral models of Ferber and Nerlove, the rational expectations hypothesis advance by Muth [1961] is a *normative* [our emphasis] proposition rather than a theory of how expectations are actually formed. Muth reserved the term "rational" for expectations possessing certain desirable attributes.

They went on to say (1969: 170)

> Is it reasonable to expect that respondents will report anticipations that are rational in the sense in which Muth defines the term? A brief review of three types of forecasts [considered in section 4.2.2 (of their book)] will remind us that this is an empirical question that cannot be resolved solely on the basis of theoretical consideration.

Hirsch and Lovell continued

> We shall first consider the empirical question of whether observed anticipations satisfy certain restrictions that Muth imposed in formulating his concept of rational expectations then [in section 5.4.2 (of their book)] we shall examine empirical evidence concerning Mills' [1957a, 1962] conjecture that the actual realization can be fruitfully employed as an implicit proxy for *ex ante* variables in econometric applications whenever anticipations are not directly observable.

In their test of Muth's RE approach as applied to Office of Business Economics microeconomic data (recall the discussion of Mills's review of their book cited above), Hirsch and Lovell concluded (1969: 175–7)

> In summary, it appears that firms do not rationally employ the information provided by past sales experience in preparing either their short or their long sales forecasts ... Unless the decision maker has a long history of experience with the nature of the forecasts that are being provided to him, he is unable to achieve the degree of

> forecasting precision suggested by Muth's definition of rational expectations.

Now, when dealing with "actual realizations as a proxy for anticipations", i.e. implicit expectations, Hirsch and Lovell wrote that in a *generalized* RE equation (1969: 169, "equation 4.1") where P = the forecast, A = the actual realization, and where "the discrepancy between the forecast P and the actual realization, A *should* be a random variable with zero expected value" and that "the forecast error *should* be uncorrelated with P [their emphasis]" (1969: 169) suggested (1969: 177)

> that actual realizations may be employed as a proxy for anticipations in econometric work when observations on expected sales are not available. This is the "implicit expectations" approach utilized by Edwin Mills [1957a, 1962] in his pathbreaking investigations of the production decision.

In a note to their statement (1969: 177 n. 32), Hirsch and Lovell said that

> Mills' concept of "implicit expectations" involves an alternative specification from Muth's of the stochastic properties of the disturbance [of equation 4.1 as given above], for Mills requires that ε be distributed independently of A rather than P. If the forecast is derived from a survey of the firm's customers the disturbance will have the desired property; "implicit" as opposed to "rational" expectations will be obtained.

Hirsch and Lovell went on to say (1969: 177) "the fruitfulness of the 'implicit' expectations concept depends, in part, upon how precise firms are at predicting sales volume" and found (1969: 185) that "the use of the actual realization as an implicit proxy fails only at the individual firm level" and also that "Lovell's [1961] slightly more complicated proxy procedure for approximating anticipated sales" worked better than that of Mills at the *aggregate* level (1969: 185–92).

With regard to *his own 1961 paper* entitled "Manufacturer's inventories, sales expectations and the acceleration principle" *which was also originally given at the December 1959 Washington DC meeting of the Econometric Society and was also published in the same issue of* Econometrica [July 1961] *as Muth's paper*, Lovell recalled in a letter (10 December 1991b) the comments of the discussant, John Meyer, and also those of Arthur Okun regarding it. As he wrote

> I checked my back files and found a letter from John Meyer responding to a query from me to elaborate on the comments he made on my

> inventory paper at the Washington meetings – his question had to do with the accuracy of the commerce data on inventories rather than about expectations. I also found a comment by Art Okun, a colleague at Cowles, suggesting that I should allow for the possibility that production levels might be revised during the three month observation period, which enters into the interpretation of the expectations coefficient in my model.

Lovell also said that he was indeed familiar with Mills's work, having cited Mills [1957a] in his own *Econometrica* paper (Lovell 1961). In this letter, Lovell went on to say

> I looked in the latest *Social Science Citation Index* and observed that Muth's paper on "Properties of some Short-Run Business Forecasts", *Eastern Economic Journal* July–September 1985, is not being cited. This is a revised version of the paper that he presented at a session I organized of the Eastern Economic Association ... I think this is unfortunate, because Jack made some important modifications of his original theory.

Lovell is indeed correct in focusing upon Muth's 1985 *EEJ* paper, since Muth also referred to its importance in the *ongoing development of his own approach to expectations*, as he wrote in his letters cited above. For example, in his letter dated 2 August 1991, Muth referred to his 1985 paper when he said that "I now feel that a combination of the two [rational and implicit expectations] is a closer approximation to reality". In his subsequent letter, dated 14 October 1991, Muth expanded on this when he wrote

> I have myself done a little bit of empirical work and the results were not entirely favorable to the rational expectations hypothesis. This article appeared in the *Eastern Economic Journal* ... I wrote Lovell about my results and he invited me to present them at the 1985 Eastern Economic Association in Pittsburgh and also in the AEA meeting in NY the following winter.

Now, this is not the place for a comprehensive discussion of Muth's 1985 paper, which is, as Lovell wrote (10 December 1991b), a paper that unfortunately "is not being cited". Suffice it to say, however, that we would agree with both Lovell and Muth as to its importance, since as Lovell noted in his own *American Economic Review* paper "Tests of the rational expectations hypothesis" (Lovell 1986: 117) "Muth was led by the negative empirical evidence to substantially modify his *original* model of rational expectations" [our emphasis].

Negishi, for his part, did not attend the sessions of Muth and Mills at the 1959 Washington meeting of the Econometric Society, but as he recalled in a letter (9 December 1991)

> I recognized, however, the significance of their contributions soon after they were published, at least in my own way of interpretations. I published a small note "Stability and Rationality of Extrapolative Expectations" in *Econometrica* (1964) in which I referred to Muth's 1961 *Econometrica* paper. Also, in the Chapter on Rational Expectations of my 1965 book *Kakaku to Haibun no Riron (Theory of Price and Allocation)* I referred to Mills' 1962 book as well as Muth's 1961 paper.

In fact, Negishi's 1964 "small note" *is quite significant*, for in it he used Muth's approach to "give some rational basis to extrapolative expectations" (Negishi 1964: 649). In other words, Negishi proposed RE as the basis for the *endogenous* expectational assumption underlying "the dynamic stability of multiple markets" in the system *originally* proposed by Arrow and Debreu (1954) as manifest in Enthoven and Arrow (1956). In fact, Negishi *actually extended* Muth's approach in this regard. As he put it (Negishi 1964: 649)

> The rational expectation hypothesis advanced by Muth ... is that expectations are essentially the same as the predictions of the relevant economic theory; that the economy generally does not waste information; and that expectations depend specifically on the structure of the entire system. However, since there is cost of information and computation, expectations may also be called rational when they are formed as the prediction based on a simplified and approximated version of the economic theory, using only limited amounts of information on a part of the system. Extrapolative expectations will be derived below as the prediction of the equilibrium by the use of estimated excess demand functions, and it will be shown that the coefficients of expectations thus derived are such that the system of multiple markets is stable when gross substitutability and tatonnement are assumed.

By making RE the *expectational* basis of the Arrow–Debreu general equilibrium (GE) model, Negishi provided *fertile ground* for Radner to *further develop* the Arrow–Debreu approach. For, as Radner wrote in a letter to one of the authors (5 February 1992)

> My own interest in the subject arose from my attempt to extend the Arrow–Debreu model to the case of incomplete markets. The first results of this attempt were published in 1967 [Radner 1967] ... This paper dealt simultaneously with two aspects of "rational expectations": consistency in the expectations of future prices, and making

inferences about other agents' information from equilibrium prices. I like to think it had little impact because it was published in French!

In fact, Radner expanded on this the next year *in English* in his seminal paper in *Econometrica* entitled "Competitive equilibrium under uncertainty" (Radner 1968). This paper, as Radner later noted (Radner 1991: 452, n. 11–12) "explored the consequences and problems of extending the AD [Arrow–Debreu] model to the case in which different agents have different information" and in it he "argued that heterogeneity of information among agents would lead to incomplete markets, and hence to a sequence of markets".

Finally, as regards *the extension of the application of endogenous expectation formation, we turn to Phelps (1966) as the "missing link" between micro and macro analysis of inflation and unemployment.* For, in this highly significant Cowles Discussion Paper, Phelps *initiated the process of establishing "dynamic" microfoundations* for the macroeconomic analysis of inflation and unemployment (1966: 2, 59) *by providing an endogenous expectational basis for public prediction of policy making by economic agents* (1966: 63). As Phelps recalled in a letter to one of the authors (7 October 1991)

> I conceived of the expectations-augmented Phillips curve in 1965, possibly in the spring, and waited to get to work on it until my work on growth theory was finished and my sabbatical leave began (January 1, 1966). I worked singlehandedly on it in Room Q at LSE from mid-January until May. After a long refereeing process, this work appeared as Discussion Paper 214 in the Cowles Foundation Series, August 25, 1966. This became the *Economica* paper (1967).

Phelps went on to say

> But I had not come up with a real model, or even a concrete image, of how expectations drive price setting and wage setting. In the summer, at Sidgwick Avenue in Cambridge, I struggled with the problem of how to model wage-setting in a way giving a central role to expectations. At first I focused on *price* expectations as a factor – but always these formulations failed to satisfy me. Finally, in Philadelphia, probably in October, I realized that the firm's wages will be conditioned by its expectations of other firm's wages – in view of its concern about its competitiveness in the labor market, hence its quit rate, etc. This led to the at places clumsy model of the wage-wage spiral and the equilibrium unemployment rate, which was first a Discussion paper at Penn ... published as a supplement to the July–August 1968 *JPE*.

Phelps went on to describe those who influenced him as follows

> Influences? Fellner on expectations – but he didn't have the *spatial* dimension, *across* firms. I had to dream that up myself. Much later, Alchian's paper suggested that this spatial aspect was in Keynes' *General Theory*. But I had not understood that! And Keynes' model was quite different.

To this he added

> I had not read Hart, nor the Modigliani–Grunberg piece. I may have seen the Richardson piece, but I don't remember. Simon? No influence. Through Fellner I acquired an appreciation for Lindahl and for Hayek, so through Fellner I became a vessel ready to carry the continental emphasis on expectations to the "econometric" terrain of wage and price dynamics. Of course, the econometric modeling by Cagan, Nerlove, and Mills must have given me *some* [Phelps' emphasis] support in embarking on an expectational approach. But those papers, while containing a x^e somewhere, did not point to the conception of the informational imperfection of the labor market that I was finally drawn to.

Phelps concluded

> Because Friedman's model was easier, it got more attention than mine – but it was *not* a model of *unemployment* [Phelps' emphasis], and it was of modest empirical appeal. I felt that the Lucas–Rapping model suffered the same limitations, and it contained a theoretical flaw (see my May 1969 AEA *Papers and Proceedings* piece). For those who continued to want to use a market-clearing approach I suggested the *islands parable* in that 1969 essay.

Now, as noted above, Modigliani was the discussant of the Hart paper. Between 1949–52 he had been (geographically) a "Chicago" economist attached to both the Cowles Commission and the University of Illinois, and was associated with research project at both Illinois and Carnegie. Modigliani (1995: 150) described the "exciting atmosphere" at Carnegie, with Herbert Simon being the "key figure" and "genius". Muth (1961) is regarded as having "formalized" the 1954 essay by Grunberg and Modigliani (Begg 1982: 26). Eleven years after Hart's paper, on 30 December 1959, Muth (1961) presented his famous paper on "Rational expectations and the theory of price movements". Muth (1961: 315, n. 1, 316) acknowledged comments from both Modigliani and Hart, and the third assertion of his hypothesis stated that "a 'public prediction' in the sense of Grunberg and Modigliani (1954) will have no substantial effect on the economic system (unless it is based on inside information)". Modigliani (1995: 150) regarded Muth as one of his "great students". Muth's (1961: 316, 318) hypothesis was based on the view that "dynamic economic models do not assume enough rationality". This was "exactly the opposite point of view" to that held by Simon (1959). Muth's rationality implied that "if the prediction of the theory were substantially better than the expectations of the firms, then there would be opportunities for the "insider 'to profit from the knowledge'". This profit opportunity would not exist when "the aggregate expectation of the firms is the same as the prediction of the theory". At that point, economists (the "insiders") have no further potential "arbitrage" possibilities.

Samuelson was the chairperson of the December 1948 Hart–Marschak session. On 28 December 1959, two days before Muth delivered his paper, Samuelson and Solow (1960: 186–7, 192–3) delivered their paper formalizing "the Fundamental Phillips Schedule". Using "Rees's data" they plotted observations and a "roughly estimated" Phillips curve. Their paper came with a "caution. All of our discussion has been phrased in short-run terms . . . what we do in a policy way during the next few years might cause [the curve] to shift in a definite way". Specifically, picking a low inflation point on the Phillips curve might "so act upon wage and other expectations as to shift the curve downwards in the longer run". Thus, they clearly identified the importance of the "invariance" critique. In "Rational expectations and the Theory of Economic Policy", Sargent and Wallace (1976: 172, 174) outlined their version of the "invariance" critique (expressed a more formal econometric language) using Samuelson's advocacy of "look at everything" policy discretion as a whipping post. Sargent and Wallace explained that it was common to find reduced form equations which contained parameters "that depend partly on the way unobservable expectations of the public are correlated with the other variables on the right hand side of the equation, which in turn depends on the public's perception of how policy makers are behaving. If the public's perceptions are accurate, then the way in which its expectations are formed change whenever policy changes, which will lead to changes in the parameters . . . of the reduced form equation. It is consequently improper to manipulate that reduced form as if its parameters were invariant with respect to changes in [the parameters]". As for Lucas, his proposed aggregate supply function explains the business cycle through expectational errors, which cause deviations. In contrast, Hart (1948: 180) sought to "correct the widespread tendency towards treating 'Psychological' factors in fluctuations solely in terms of 'errors' – a bias which wastes the Keynesian and Swedish insights about the role of self-filling expectations patterns in giving an upswing or a downswing momentum" Muth (1961: 315) was self-consciously in the Hartian tradition: The second sentence of his paper referred to "the 'ex ante' analysis of the Stockholm School" as a "highly suggestive approach short-run problem". In his famous critique of econometric policy evaluation, Lucas attributed an early version to Marschak. Marschak was present when Hart outlined his research agenda, which could well have led to the Lucas Critique. And it was Muth's rational expectations that provided the necessary link.

In summary, following in the footsteps of the Hart Research Agenda, over the decade 1959–69, a growing number of economists became aware of RE (especially those who were later at the forefront of the "RE Revolution in Macroeconomics"), albeit it was first applied at the microeconomic and first tested at the microeconometric level only. Over the period 1964–67, the link between RE and GE was made by Negishi and Radner. During the mid-1960s, Sargent had been taught RE by Lovell on his own account, and both Sargent and Prescott had commented on the manuscript of the Hirsch and Lovell volume (1969) – in which RE and implicit expectations were empirically tested at the microeconometric level. As early as 1966, Lucas had applied RE to model expectations formation regarding investment at the macroeconomic level, according to Lucas himself. Finally, between 1966 and 1969, Phelps extended the endogenous approach to expectations to deal with problems of analyzing inflation and unemployment. Thus, by the early 1970s the outcome of the extensive microeconomic and microeconometric utilization of RE and implicit expectations that had occurred over the 1960s was its extension beyond the microeconomic sphere of inquiry, bringing about the so-called "RE Revolution in Macroeconomics". In other words, there was a continuity in the process of diffusion and dissemination of RE and implicit expectations, rather than a discontinuity between their early microeconomic history and their eventual utilization in macroeconomics.

6 Patinkin, expectations, and Chicago

Money, Interest and Prices [*MIP*] is unambiguously one of the most important economics treatises of the twentieth century. It is clearly in the tradition of Hicks's *Value and Capital* and Keynes's *General Theory*, both of which Patinkin tried to extend in the various editions of *MIP* (1965: xxiv–xxv). Moreover, according to Patinkin, *MIP* is based upon the ideas first presented in his 1947 Chicago doctoral dissertation and "further developed in a series of articles published in various journals and anthologies through the years 1948 to 1954" (1965: xvii). In order to understand Patinkin's treatment of expectations in the various editions of *MIP*, therefore, reference must be made to the influences upon his ideas regarding them, and his papers over the period 1948–54, in which he utilized them.

In this chapter, we present and analyze Patinkin's ongoing treatment of expectations, from his early papers (1948–54) through the three editions of *MIP* (1956, 1965, and the abridged 2nd edition, 1989), and also place Patinkin's approach in the perspective of the variant approaches to expectations of his teachers and colleagues at Chicago. The issues we will deal with, therefore, include: the relationship between Patinkin's treatment of expectations and those of his teachers and colleagues, such as Frank Knight, Albert Hart, George Stigler, and Oskar Lange; how Patinkin's approach to expectations developed from 1948 onwards; and the types of expectations he utilized in the "micro" and "macro" models in the various editions of *MIP*.

In the first section of the chapter, we will survey the approaches to expectations which may have affected Patinkin's own approach, that is, of his teachers and colleagues at Chicago, especially Knight, Hart, Stigler, and Lange. In this section, we also focus upon three of Patinkin's early papers which we think form the main basis for describing his pre-*MIP* treatment of expectations on the micro and macro levels. These are "Price flexibility and full employment" (1948 [1981]); "Involuntary unemployment and the Keynesian supply function" (1949) and "Keynesian economics and the quantity theory" (1954). In the second section of the chapter, a detailed comparison will be made between the first and second editions of *MIP* so as to assess the evolution of Patinkin's approach to expectations between them. And all this, in order to try to explain why, despite the existence of rational expectations and its applicability to the *MIP* framework – at least in the second edition – Patinkin himself preferred using adaptive expectations.

Knight, Hart, Stigler, Lange, and Patinkin on anticipations

The Chicago approach to expectations was eclectic, to say the least, and its variant strands affected Patinkin via the direct or indirect influences of Knight, Hart, Stigler, and, in our view, to the greatest extent by Lange. Lange, for his part, was influenced by the approaches of Hicks (1939a) on the one hand, and Samuelson (1941) on the other. But in his Cowles monograph and subsequent book *Price Flexibility and Employment* (1944a, 1945), and the mathematical appendix, which also appeared as a separate Cowles paper under the title *The Stability of Equilibrium* (1944b), Lange went beyond their contributions. Lange's treatment of expectations has been somewhat overlooked and we will outline it below. But before doing this, the approaches of Knight, Hart, and Stigler must first be dealt with.

In his retrospective pieces "Frank Knight as Teacher" (1973 [1981]) and "Reminiscences of Chicago, 1941–47" (1981) published in his *Essays on and in the Chicago Tradition* (1981), Patinkin described his memories of Knight as one of his mentors over the period while he was an undergraduate and graduate student at Chicago. According to Patinkin, Knight, as one of his "teachers of economic theory ... devoted much attention to probing ... into the meaning of the basic definitions and assumptions of the analysis" such as "perfect foresight", among other terms. Patinkin continued "Knight was basically not sympathetic to the new developments in economic theory (read: Keynes and Hicks) – and even, I would say, instinctively critical of them – Lange was an early convert as well as an efficient expositor and refiner" (1981: 25–6). Now, it should be remembered that his essay "Knight as a Teacher" was originally published in the *AER* in December 1973, and was written in Chicago in 1972 – just after the *JPE* symposium in which Patinkin assaulted Friedman's reminiscences of Chicago for the second time (Lucas first presented his "Econometric policy evaluation" paper in April 1973). In other words, Patinkin was getting very agitated about Chicago at that time (Leeson, 2003).

These are clearly understatements on Patinkin's part, as attested to by the fact that Knight went far beyond just "probing" the notion of "perfect foresight", or being simply "not sympathetic" and "instinctively critical" of Keynes and Hicks. With regard to the latter issue, Knight wrote in his American Economic Association Presidential Address (1951 [1963]: 252) "The latest 'new economics,' and in my opinion rather the worst for fallacious doctrine and pernicious consequences, is that launched by the late John Maynard (Lord) Keynes, who for a decade succeeded in carrying economic thinking well back to the dark age." A decade before, in his 1941 paper "The business cycle, interest and money", Knight had also virulently attacked Hicks's *Value and Capital* (1939a). Knight wrote (1941 [1963]: 222)

> In a discussion of the influence of speculation in the future value of money on the rate of interest on loans – under any possible conditions – the most essential fact is that there is no functional relation between the price level and any rate of interest. Consequently, no monetary change has any direct or permanent effect on the rate. On this point such writers as Keynes and Hicks fall into the simple methodological fallacy ... confusion of the power to "disturb" another value magnitude with a real functional connection of causality.

In a note to this, Knight added (1941 [1963]: 222, n. 18)

> Hicks's *Value and Capital* ... does not seem to give a quotable statement of a liquidity–preference–function theory of interest ... But present purposes do not call for an examination of the *manifold confusions of which unfortunately this book largely consists* [our emphasis].

With regard to the former issue – "perfect foresight" – which is more relevant for our purpose here, in his 1941 paper Knight wrote (1941 [1963]: 208) "We should always keep in mind in economic reasoning that perfect foresight is theoretically as well as practically impossible, unless all partners plan collusively in advance all details of their procedure and adhere to the agreed plan". Indeed, Knight even used the examples of agricultural markets and the "corn-hog cycle" to illustrate his viewpoint, albeit reaching a conclusion diametrically opposite to that of Muth two decades later (Muth 1961).

In his attempt to generalize and extend both Keynes (1936) and Hicks (1939a), therefore, Patinkin had, in effect, either to "free himself" – to paraphrase Keynes – from Knight's views on their respective works, or alternatively, to go beyond Keynes, that is, to become "more Keynesian than Keynes", as Patinkin himself put it (*MIP*, 2nd edn, 1965: 340). With regard to anticipations, however, Patinkin seems to have accepted Knight's rejection of "perfect foresight", as will be seen below.

Stigler versus Hart on anticipations, and Stigler on expectations, 1942 onwards

The final sentence of Albert Hart's (1936: 57) unpublished University of Chicago dissertation on "Anticipations, business planning and the cycle" reads: "where there is ground for evaluating the effect of proposed measures of policy upon anticipations (or where that effect may be presumed to be neutral for the question in hand) the tools of the economic theorist may prove very useful in judging the influence of such measures on the volume of employment and production".

As against this, Stigler, in his review of Hart's University of Chicago monograph, *Anticipations, Uncertainty and Dynamic Planning* (Hart 1940b) in the June 1941 issue of the *American Economic Review*, was skeptical about making much progress with respect to the theory of expectations: "the promised land to some economists and a mirage to others. The reviewer must admit that he leans towards the latter view: much of the literature on expectations consists of obvious and uninformative generalizations of static analysis". With respect to "the revision of anticipations ... progress depends much more on the accumulation of data (of a type almost impossible to collect!) than on an increase in the versatility of our technical apparatus" (Stigler 1941: 358–9).

While others were foreshadowing Rational Expectations, Stigler in his book *The Theory of Competitive Price* (1942: 95–7) was not. As he wrote (1942: 95–7) "All rational men base their anticipations of the future on their experience in the past; there is no other basis for prophecy ... There are also certain general grounds for questioning the importance of anticipations of price changes". It should be recalled here that Stigler's 1942 volume, *The Theory of Competitive Price*, formed the basis for the four editions of his book, *The Theory of Price*, which appeared in 1946, 1952, 1966, and 1987 respectively (Leeson 2000d). Interestingly enough, despite the position he took in 1942 regarding the efficacy of modeling price expectations, by the third edition of this book, published in 1966, Stigler came to utilize the *adaptive expectations* approach to analyze price expectations (1966: 29, n. 11). However, nowhere in this edition is there mention of "perfect foresight" or Muth, and this despite the fact that Muth's approach, and that of Mills (implicit expectations) had been utilized at the microeconomic level from 1958 onwards, as seen above.

Lange on expectations, 1944

In his 1944 Cowles monograph entitled *Price Flexibility and Employment*, Lange focused upon price expectations in a *general equilibrium* framework (1944a: 1). He started with *Hicksian* "static expectations", which he defined as the case where "entrepreneurs and consumers expect current prices to continue over that part of the future which is relevant to their decisions" (1944a: 1). He then formulated the notion of what he called "*effective* expected prices" [Lange's emphasis] (1944a: 31). The method by which he reached this notion was as follows. He first relaxed the assumption of certainty with regard to expected or future prices. He did this by asserting that "At best, the entrepreneur or consumer expects that a given future price can have a *set of possible values*" so that "his price expectations are subject to *uncertainty*" [Lange's emphasis] (1944a: 29). He then proceeded to define what he called "the most probable price" which exhibits a probability distribution over a *range* of values so that the definiteness of expectation of it would be inversely related to this range. In other words, "the range" could "be taken as a measure of the degree of uncertainty of the expectation" (1944a: 29).

Lange then defined what he called the "forward price". He said that it "represents the price a definite, certain expectation of which is regarded ... as equivalent to the most probable price actually expected with certainty" (1944a: 31), i.e. the most probable price actually expected with certainty. For expositional purposes, let us call this $E(p)$. Lange went on to define what he called the "effective expected price", as noted above. He defined these as "equivalent prices expected with certainty", i.e. "the most probable price minus the risk premium" (1944a: 31). Lange (1944a: 32) noted that Hicks, for his part, had called the risk premium "the uncertainty of expectation" (1939a: 126). Again, for expositional purposes, let us call this p_e. Interestingly enough, Lange then asserted that under one specific condition, "uncertain price expectations can be reduced to certain ones" (1944a: 31–2). This condition was *certainty of expectation*, that is to say, using the expositional notation above, if there is *certainty of expectation*, then there is also such a price so that $E(p) = p_e$. In other words, by extending Hicks's approach to expectations, Lange was groping toward an approach which could be considered a precursor to that of Muth. Hart had earlier objected to such an approach in his 1940 Chicago monograph (1940b: 55) when he asserted that it would *not* be "possible to find such a price as, if expected with certainty, would lead to the same actions of sellers and buyers as the actual expected price subject to uncertainty" (Lange 1944a: 32, n. 19). Lange replied to Hart's objection by actually proposing that it be empirically tested (1944a: 32, n. 19), foreshadowing the empirical testing of Muth's hypothesis on the *microeconometric* level some two decades later.

Now, the Mathematical Appendix to Lange's 1944 Cowles monograph also appeared in 1944 as *The Stability of Economic Equilibrium* in the Cowles Commission Papers "new series" (Lange 1944b). But the Appendix as published in Lange's monograph was actually only *part* of the larger Cowles paper. In fact, in the English version of his collected papers, a section from his 1944 *paper* which he called "*Forms of supply adjustment and economic equilibrium*" was published (Lange 1961 [1970]: 125–34). In this, Lange dealt with the relationship between price, supply adjustment, equilibrium, and price anticipations in the *general equilibrium* context by reference to the "cob-web theorem" and its limitations (1961 [1970]: 126).

The first point he made regarding price anticipations in the cob-web context was that "in order to be able to make any valid statement" regarding adjustment to equilibrium "additional information is required ... on the individual anticipations concerning the future price-level" (1961

[1970]: 127). He then went on to distinguish between supply adjustment to equilibrium in agricultural as against industrial production, which "follows an adjustment to equilibrium quite different from the case of the 'cob-web theorem'" (1961 [1970]: 127). In Lange's view, this is the ability of the major part of industrial production to undergo "a gradual or even continuous supply adjustment", in contrast to the case of agricultural production (1961 [1970]: 132–3).

As a result, in Lange's view, since "in the majority of production branches, the stability" of equilibrium "is guaranteed" by "gradual or continuous" adjustment in supply, "the anticipated future price-level by entrepreneurs" is not crucial. Rather, "it is quite sufficient that the entrepreneurs should adapt their production to the relative market price" (1961 [1970]: 133). Lange finally turned to deal with "the role of anticipation of the future price-level by entrepreneurs in the agricultural as against the industrial production sectors. In order to do this, he utilized "the Evans supply function", which specified that the quantity offered was a function not only of price but also of "the differential quotient of the price over time" (1961 [1970]: 134; Evans 1930: 36). Finally, Lange distinguished between the case of immediate, as against continuous or gradual supply adjustment in the context of price anticipations. According to him, it was the anticipation of future price that brought about *immediate* supply response to price change in the agricultural case, which exhibited inherent structural supply adjustment delays (relatively constant growing and production periods (1961 [1970]: 134).

To sum up, Patinkin was, by his own account, influenced by Lange as a teacher (1981: 8). However, he was also highly critical of Lange's 1944 Cowles monograph, both in his 1949 paper "Indeterminacy of absolute prices" (1949 [1981]: 140ff) and in *MIP* (1965: I.3, 625, n. 27). Thus, it is not surprising that Patinkin *did not* utilize Lange's 1944 approach to price expectations, for if he had, he might have utilized it in the first edition of *MIP*, and perhaps might have even mentioned Muth's approach in the second edition, rather than relying there solely on the adaptive expectations model, similar to Stigler (1966), but more about this below.

Patinkin on anticipations, equilibrium, and expectations, 1948–54

In order to understand the evolution of Patinkin's approach to anticipations, equilibrium, and expectations in the early papers that emanated from his thesis, we must recall the fundamental distinction between *exogenous* and *endogenous* expectations. In his 1948 *AER* paper, "Price flexibility and full employment", which he described as "an elaboration of the corresponding discussion in my thesis" (1981: 14, n. 19), Patinkin focused upon the importance of anticipations and expectations when he wrote (1948 [1951]: 273): "In dynamic analysis we must give full attention to the role played by price expectations and anticipations in general." But the expectations Patinkin was talking about were of the *exogenous* type. This is manifest in his references to anticipations that "progressively worsen" (1948 [1951]: 273) and to "adverse anticipations" (1948 [1951]: 278, 281). Moreover, as these were exogenously determined, Patinkin did not consider the issue of their *formation*. What he *was* concerned with was the nature of the link between "price flexibility", anticipations (expectations), "full employment", equilibrium and stability in a dynamic Keynesian system *as he interpreted it.*

The major points Patinkin made in this context were that the "real significance of the Keynesian contribution can be realized only within framework of *dynamic* economics ... the fundamental issue raised by Keynesian economics is the stability of the *dynamic system* ... what Keynesian economics claims is that the economic system may be in a position of underemployment *dis*equilibrium" (1948 [1951]: 279–80 [Patinkin's emphases]).

At this point we should recall the importance Patinkin placed on the issue of disequilibrium as against equilibrium in the "macro-system" he constructed from the "Walrasian general equilibrium system". As he wrote (1949 [1981]: 159–61)

> To start from fundamentals, it is clear that a complete explanation of the economic system can be presented only through a Walrasian general-equilibrium system ... it is immediately evident that the macro-system we have built up from our Walrasian system is one which can never be at equilibrium. For the income level Y_o, which equilibrates the demand side of the economy, leaves the supply side in disequilibrium. Conversely, the income level, which equilibrates the supply side, leaves the demand side in disequilibrium. There is no level of income which will simultaneously equilibrate both of these sets of forces in the economy. What is the economic interpretation of this inability to reach a consistent equilibrium position? ... it is argued that the inconsistency created by the explicit introduction of the aggregate supply function into Keynesian systems provides the key to the theory of involuntary unemployment implicit in Keynesian economics.

With regard to anticipations, price flexibility and the variants of the "Keynesian position", there were "three distinct theoretical formulations ... differing in varying degrees from the classical one" according to Patinkin (1948 [1951]: 281–2). In the static case, anticipations did "not matter", while in the dynamic case, anticipations "mattered", but their influence was related both to the speed of adjustment and the nature of equilibrium and its stability in the dynamic system. As he wrote (1948 [1951]: 281) "in a dynamic world of uncertainty and adverse expectations, even if we were to allow an infinite adjustment period, there is no certainty that full employment will be generated" and even if full employment were "eventually generated by a policy of price flexibility ... the length of time that might be necessary for the adjustment makes the policy impractical".

But even at this stage of his ongoing analysis, Patinkin still took expectations to be exogenous and not determined by the parameters of the economic system itself. It was only in the second edition of *MIP*, as will be seen below, that he changed his approach.

Now, it should be noted that in his 1948 *AER* paper, Patinkin had used the term "anticipations" rather than "expectations". In his 1949 *EJ* paper, "Involuntary unemployment and the Keynesian supply function", Patinkin referred to "dynamic expectation factors" (1949 [1981]: 174). More significantly, by his 1954 paper "Keynesian economics and the quantity theory", Patinkin used the term "destabilizing expectations" (1954: 136, 152); and this, prior to its appearance in *MIP* (e.g. 1965: 701).

What is puzzling, however, is that despite Patinkin's emphasis on general equilibrium, he did not develop his *own* approach to expectations in this framework. Moreover, Patinkin did not utilize Hahn's general equilibrium approach – as presented in his seminal 1952 *EJ* paper, "Expectations and equilibrium" – but more about this below.

Money, interest, prices, equilibrium, and expectations

A comparison of Patinkin's treatment of expectations in the first as against the second edition of *Money, Interest, and Prices* is quite revealing. But in order to understand what, in our view, occurred to change his approach, we must also consider the state of play regarding the treatment of expectations at the time Patinkin was putting together *MIP*. From the early 1950s onwards, expectations played a growing role in economic analysis, but *almost all* approaches up to 1956, the year of publication of the first edition of *MIP*, focused upon *exogenous* expectations formation. One very important, albeit somewhat overlooked contribution which focused upon *endogenous* expectations formation *in the general equilibrium context* was Hahn's 1952 *EJ* paper "Expectations and Equilibrium". Because of its relevance for our attempt to explain Patinkin's treatment of expectations, we will briefly present Hahn's main points here.

Hahn first made the linkage between expectations and equilibrium when he wrote (1952: 804) "The existence of equilibrium through time ... presupposes the existence of an expectation function of constant form". He went on to discuss "some of the conditions a general dynamic equilibrium model must fulfil". In order to accomplish this, he introduced a "'notional' system ... constructed on the assumption that all expectations are fulfilled" (806). He continued on to say "Decisions are taken by a multitude of individuals. The first requirement for the existence of expectations functions compatible with the notional system is that expectations should be *consistent* [our emphasis] in the sense that there are conceivable actual events which would allow all expectations to be fulfilled simultaneously" (807). And, in order to do this, he specified a "system of expectation equations", which he developed accordingly (807). Hahn then set out "a simple 'notional' model of the economy" in which "all expectations are continuously fulfilled" so that "actual and expected output, and demand and supply coincide" (810–11). He then considered the case where "individuals do not anticipate future events correctly" and the "sort of expectations function" this implied (811), and also dealt with the possibility of "multi-valued expectations" (818–19). With regard to the former case, Hahn asserted that expectations could indeed be "disappointed" during the "adjustment process" (815). He went on to say "This we have argued is inconsistent with a constant expectation ... function for any length of time. To prove ... that some permanent equilibrium will be established, we must show how and at what stage expectations change and become 'correct' " (815). As for the latter problem, he wrote (819)

> Our main pre-occupation in the analysis of equilibrium was to find a situation for which the behavioural equation could be regarded as remaining of constant form. We cannot observe expectation – only behaviour. Let us repeat what we mean by constant or routine behaviour. The latter is said to occur if the behaviour of the economic unit is the same whenever certain variables on which this behaviour is said to depend take on any same given values ... we have argued in this paper that the behaviour function will remain of constant form if, and only if (over a period of time), the routine behaviour it describes is successful ... It may, of course, be that even partial success will be sufficient to ensure the constancy of the behaviour function. Our main point here is that if the actual achievement differs (over time) from a successful achievement in a *systematic* way, then this constitutes new "experience" and attempts will be made to change behaviour [our emphasis].
>
> We can thus by-pass the problem of multi-valued expectations without invalidating our previous analysis.

Hahn's endogenizing of expectations is revealed in the final sentence of his paper, where he wrote "it is clearly essential to know something of the relationships between expectations and the routine adopted" (819). Now, in the first edition of *MIP*, Patinkin neither followed Hahn's lead regarding endogenizing expectations nor cited his paper. The reason for this becomes clear when we realize that Hahn's approach to expectations was based upon *general equilibrium*, while Patinkin's treatment of expectations in *MIP* follows from a *general disequilibrium* approach, which in his own view, was the "central message" of *MIP*. In other words, for Patinkin, since "dynamic expectations" were a *destabilizing* factor, the expectational *model* that he used to explain the *general disequilibrium* which he considered as *inherent* in the macroeconomy would have to bring about *disequilibrium*, and *not equilibrium*.

Now, in both the first and second editions of *MIP*, Patinkin delineated two sets of expectational types, "static" and "dynamic" expectations, and what he called "certain" and "destabilizing" expectations. According to Patinkin (1956: 87; 1965: 80) "An individual with 'static expectations' expects the prices and interest of future weeks to be the same as present ones; an individual with 'dynamic expectations' expects them to be different. These expectations can be held with or without certainty." However, between the two editions, there was a significant change in emphasis regarding the importance of expectations and their treatment, that is to say the *model of expectations formation* utilized by Patinkin. In both editions of *MIP*, Patinkin's concern with expectations emanated, at least in part, from their effect upon the theory of money, that is the demand for money and its role in the economy. As he wrote in the first edition (1956: 87)

> Since the following discussion is based on highly unrealistic assumptions, it is advisable to preface it with a statement of its intended context. This is actually a double one. At a lower level of significance we are concerned with a problem in pure logic: with showing that the argument of this book is internally consistent; with demonstrating that its assumption of a positive demand for money need not contradict its assumption of static, certain expectations – or even of perfect foresight – with respect to future prices, interest, and income; with proving, therefore, that the existence of dynamic or uncertain price and interest expectations is not a sine qua non of a theory of money.

In the second edition he wrote (1965: 80–1)

> Three further comments might be made, First, our concern ... is with the demand for money that would exist even if there were perfect certainty with respect to future prices and interest. Uncertainty does play a role in the analysis, but only uncertainty with respect to the timing of payments. Thus one by-product of the following argument is the demonstration that dynamic or uncertain price and/or interest expectations are not a sine qua non of a positive demand for money.

But, in the first edition, Patinkin deliberately neglected expectations in his approach to the demand for money (1956: 95). He further justified his argument when he wrote (1956: 180–1)

> Nevertheless, the assumption that the demand for money is motivated

> in part by dynamic expectations and interest and price uncertainty can invalidate these classical conclusions. This should certainly not surprise us. For in introducing these elements into the analysis we also introduce many additional "degrees of freedom." Hence, as long as these elements are not in some way tied down, we can – by endowing them with the appropriate properties – obtain any conclusion we might desire. Once the Pandora box of expectations and interest and price uncertainty is opened upon the world of economic analysis, anything can happen.

In the second edition of *MIP,* Patinkin changed his views and wrote (257–8)

> We might also note that the assumption that the demand for money is motivated in part by dynamic expectations can sometimes invalidate the classical invariance of interest even with respect to changes in the quantity of money. This should certainly not surprise us. For in introducing these elements into the analysis we also introduce many additional "degrees of freedom." Hence as long as these elements are in some way tied down, we can – by endowing them with the appropriate properties – obtain any conclusion we might desire. Only after we have specified the way in which individuals formulate their expectations can the analysis become determinate.

With regard to "destabilizing expectations", Patinkin dealt with these in the context of the negative real balance effect and rising prices, but he did not specify the expectations model which would stabilize the economic system (1956: 209). In the second edition, Patinkin again changed his views. While some of the text is virtually identical in the first edition and the second (1956: 209; 1965: 310), Patinkin went on to say, however, that (1965: 311)

> The plausibility of this argument is reinforced by the analysis ... which shows that the degree to which an individual wishes to anticipate future purchases of commodities is determined not by the mere expectation that prices will rise, but by the expected rate of increase of this rise. Thus if prices should rise at a constant rate, there will be no further increase in current demand as a result of inter-temporal substitution; at the same time this demand would be subjected to the ever-growing dampening pressure of a negative real-financial-asset effect. And in this way the stability of the system would be assured.

And, in a note to this, he wrote (1965: 311, n. 45) "The relevant macroeconomic system is described ... below. For simplicity, we have assumed here that the expected rate of increase equals the actual current rate. In the real world, however, the relationship is undoubtedly more complicated. See the next paragraph in the text."

At this point in the second edition of *MIP* (1965: 311) Patinkin introduced the *expectations model* he advocated, which he thought would ensure the *stability* of his *disequilibrium* macroeconomic system (1948 [1951]: 280–2; 1965: 337–8). As he put it (1965: 311)

> More generally, if we take account of the fact that expectations are not pulled out of the air, but are related to past price experience; and if we further assume that this relation expresses itself in the fact that the expected price is a weighted average of past ones (where the weights decline as one goes back in time) – then it can be shown that a system stable under static expectations will remain so even after these are replaced by dynamic ones.

In a note to this, he cited Arrow and Nerlove (1958) and Arrow and Hurwicz (1962) on "adaptive expectations".

Patinkin, disequilibrium macroeconomics, and rational expectations

In the introduction to the first and second editions of *MIP*, Patinkin noted two major themes. The first was the development of the real-balance effect and its integration into economic theory at the micro and macro level. The second was the development of "the monetary theory of an economy with involuntary unemployment", i.e. Keynesian unemployment, which he interpreted, as early as his 1948 paper "Price flexibility and full employment" (Patinkin 1948 [1951]), not via a situation of static equilibrium but rather by the notion of *dynamic disequilibrium* (1948 [1951]: 280). In the introduction to the *abridged* edition of the second edition (Patinkin 1989), Patinkin expressed his disappointment that what he "considered to be a major novelty and contribution" of *MIP* – that is to say "disequilibrium economics" – "found little echo in the literature of the years that followed" (Patinkin 1989: xvii).

In the introduction to the abridged second edition, Patinkin also dealt with the issue of adaptive as against rational expectations. He started by criticizing Keynes' *General Theory*, which although it attributed "great importance to expectations" did *not* "develop a formal theory of the way in which they are formed" (Patinkin 1989: xxxv). He went on to say that such an approach "*also characterized the first edition*" of *MIP*, and "*the second one as well*" (1989: xxxv) [our emphases]. He then proceeded to say that "the 'rational expectations revolution' . . . was primarily a result of the internal dynamics of our discipline itself, motivated at least in part by the failure of macroeconomic econometric models in the 1970s to predict correctly" (1989: xxxv). But, as has been shown above, the rational expectations model was applied at the microeconomic and microeconometric level from the late 1950s onwards, and thus the model should at least have been *mentioned* in the second edition of *MIP* (Patinkin 1965).

However, a *close* reading of the introduction to the abridged second edition (1989) reveals why Patinkin chose *not* to use the rational expectations model. Patinkin asserted (1989: xxxvi)

> I think that it is fair to say that there is today a consensus in the profession that the assumption of rational expectations has had a salutary effect in calling into question the mechanical application of adaptive expectations. At the same time, an essential implication of such expectations has frequently been retained by substituting lags attributed to long-term contracts for those that had been attributed to the lagged adjustment of expectations. To this I must add that there is a consensus that, on the basis of both theoretical and empirical considerations, rejects the original overenthusiastic and doctrinaire application of rational expectations that led to the related contentions of a vertical Phillips curve even in the short run and the absolute neutrality of anticipated monetary policy.

Patinkin then turned to what he saw as the key problem in the use of the rational expectations model. As he wrote (1989: xxxviii)

> Let me turn finally to the problematic aspects of the assumption of rational expectations, a subject that has been much discussed in the literature ... I would like to add to this discussion from a different perspective, one that I presumptuously feel should emerge from the collective introspection of our profession. For this purpose I start not with the technical definition of rational expectations but with the commonsense justification that has frequently been given for this assumption: namely, that individuals "take account of all the information available to them" and that they do not make "systematic errors".

He then cited two examples of the "systematic errors" made by economists. The first involved the real-balance effect. As he put it (1989: xxxviii) "for at least two decades distinguished economists at one and the same time recognized the existence of the real-balance effect and yet espoused a 'homogeneity postulate' and a related dichotomy that contradicted it. Surely that warrants the term 'systematic error'". The second related to the Phillips curve, which showed (1989: xxxviii)

> the inverse relationship between the rate of change of nominal wages and unemployment; and this is what most of us (myself included) were also teaching our students. And on what after all, was Friedman's criticism ... based, if not on one of the elementary principles that we had

> ourselves all learned as students from the indifference-curve analysis of the choice between leisure and consumption-commodities: that the individual's decision was based not on the nominal wage rate but on the real one; that, to use one of the basic concepts of this book (which I too subsequently ignored in my teaching of the Phillips curve), the individual was free of money illusion. Surely that is a failure to "take advantage of all available information"; surely that is the perpetration of "systematic error".

Patinkin then concluded (1989: xxxviii) "Why should we economists assume that *homines economici* behave so differently?" Now, whether Patinkin was correct in calling this "systematic error" rather than "cognitive dissonance" is a moot point, but this is not the place for such a discussion (see Young and Darity 2000). Moreover, it is important to recall at this point that Cagan (1956) and Nerlove (1958) were utilizing Phillips' adaptive expectations formula given to Friedman by Phillips in May 1952, at both the micro and macro levels, and this prior to Patinkin's use of it in the second edition of *MIP*, as will be seen in Chapter 7 below.

To sum up, then, Patinkin objected to utilizing rational expectations. He thought it unsuitable for the *disequilibrium* approach he was trying to develop and make the "*central message*" and *core* of macroeconomics, by aggregating up from a labor market in *disequilibrium* (Patinkin 1959: 586; 1965: 340–2; 1983). This was because the "adaptive expectations" approach enabled stability in the *disequilibrium* macroeconomic system he advocated, as it *enabled* systematic error on the microeconomic level. Rational expectations would cause such a system to be in equilibrium, for if in disequilibrium, it would return the system to a *rational expectations equilibrium*, as it would *not* enable systematic error on the microeconomic level (Jordan and Radner 1982).

7 Expectations and the monetarist counter-revolution

Milton Friedman succeeded in, and by, placing expectations at the center of macroeconomic analysis. His contribution was, in part, constructive (it created a pivotal position for expectations) and, in part, destructive (it undermined the previous Keynesian orthodoxy). That orthodoxy had made significant progress with respect to the analysis of expectations; but the monetarist counter-revolution succeeded in creating the impression that orthodoxy was fundamentally flawed – in large part because of the supposed neglect of expectations.

Prior to the natural-rate counter-revolution, Friedman had made two major contributions. His 1953 methodology of positive economics was both an attack on the analysis of assumptions (a hallmark of the monopolistic competition revolution and to a lesser extent Keynesian macroeconomics) and an agenda for scientific research. His 1957 theory of the consumption function was both an assault on Keynesian faith in counter-cyclical fiscal policy and a fruitful way of extracting information about the varying component of income flows (Friedman 1953, 1957). Likewise, the natural rate expectations augmented Phillips curve was both a contribution to the analysis of expectations and a counter-revolutionary assault on the Keynesian hegemony.

Friedman's methodology and theory of the consumption function rapidly became part of the fabric of modern economics. Friedman concluded, in his famous methodological essay, that "The weakest and least satisfactory part of current economic theory seems to me to be in the field of monetary dynamics, which is concerned with the process of adaptation of the economy as a whole to changes in conditions and so with short-period fluctuations in aggregate activity. In this field we do not even have a theory that can be appropriately called 'the' existing theory of monetary dynamics" (1953: 42, see also 1950: 467). Prior to the expectations augmented Phillips curve, Friedman's macroeconomics had *not* been widely accepted by economists. Indeed, from the publication of *Studies in the Quantity Theory of Money* (Friedman 1956) to his December 1967 American Economic Association (AEA) Presidential Address, Friedman's macroeconomics had been regarded as peripheral if not eccentric.

All this was to change with the expectations augmented Phillips curve. Friedman (1968a: 8) added "one wrinkle" to the Phillips curve in the same way as Irving Fisher added "only one wrinkle to Wicksell". In so doing, Friedman predicted that the Phillips curve trade-off between inflation and unemployment existed temporarily, but not permanently. Friedman asserted that "Phillips' analysis ... contains a basic defect – the failure to distinguish between *nominal* wages and *real* wages". In his Nobel Lecture, Friedman (1977: 217–19) asserted that "Phillips' analysis seems very persuasive and obvious. Yet it is utterly fallacious ... It is fallacious because no economic theorist has ever asserted that the demand and supply of labor are functions of the *nominal* wage rate. Every economic theorist from Adam Smith to the present would have told you that the vertical axis should refer not to the *nominal* wage rate but to the *real* wage rate ... His argument was a very simple analysis – I hesitate to say simple minded, but so it has proved – in terms of *static* supply and demand conditions" [emphases in text].

The stagflation of the late 1960s and 1970s was regarded as evidence of the superior predictive ability of the monetarist model. Stagflation discredited the Phillips curve and the Keynesian macroeconomists who were associated with it. As a consequence, macroeconomics came to be organized around the natural-rate expectations augmented Phillips curve, developed by Friedman and Edmund Phelps (1970). This model contributed to the process by which Keynesianism (and faith in government intervention) was replaced by monetarism (and faith in market outcomes).

Prominent Keynesians, Paul Samuelson and Robert Solow (1960), had used A.W.H. Phillips curve to derive an inflation-unemployment policy trade-off for the United States. In academic year 1964–65, Samuelson pondered before a blackboard, and dismissed as doubtful an early version of the natural rate model (Akerlof 1982: 337). James Tobin (1968: 53) argued that the coefficient on inflationary expectations was less than 1: the worst outcome was that when inflationary expectations caught up with actual experience, unemployment would rise to its natural level. Solow (1968: 3), Harry Johnson (1970: 110–12) and Albert Rees (1970: 237–8) all continued to express faith in a moderate inflation-unemployment trade-off. But shortly afterwards, Keynesian stalwarts such as Tobin (1972: 9) felt obliged to question the validity of the original Phillips curve which came to be described as "an empirical finding in search of a theory". Solow (1978: 205) concluded that in the 1960s and 1970s the profession experienced a "loss of virginity with respect to inflationary expectations".

Other anti-Keynesians benefited from this discomfiture, especially the New Classical macroeconomists who placed even stricter emphasis on the role of expectations. The Old Keynesian high inflation Phillips curve supposedly misled the Western world into the inflationary maelstrom of the 1970s (Lucas and Sargent 1978). The 1970s was the decade of "The Death of Keynesian Economics" – and the collapse of the Phillips curve trade-off, its failure to recognize the subtleties of both inflationary expectations and the Lucas Critique play a major role in this "death rattle" (Sargent 1996: 543). As Robert Lucas (1980: 18; 1981: 560; 1984: 56) put it: "one cannot find good, under-forty economists who identified themselves or their work as Keynesian ... I, along with many others, was in on the kill in an intellectual sense". According to Lucas, the quarry subjected to this "kill" was the proposition that "permanent inflation will ... induce a permanent economic high ... [the] shift of the 'trade-off' relationship to centre stage in policy discussions appears primarily due to Phillips (1958) and Samuelson and Solow (1960)"; "We got the high-inflation decade, and with it as clear-cut an experimental discrimination as macroeconomics is ever likely to see, and Friedman and Phelps were right. It really is as simple as that"; "They went way out on a limb in the late '60s, saying that high inflation wasn't going to give us anything by way of lower unemployment". Robert Solow (1978: 203) detected in Lucas and Thomas Sargent "a polemical vocabulary reminiscent of Spiro Agnew"; but the revolutionaries doubted that "softening our rhetoric will help matters" (Lucas and Sargent 1978: 82, 60).

Friedman's analysis of expectations has a history that predates his AEA address. Following an exchange with Solow at an April 1966 University of Chicago conference, Friedman (1966) outlined the natural rate model. A few months later, in his *Newsweek* column on 17 October 1966, Friedman made the "prediction ... *There will be an inflationary recession*". Years before, Friedman (1958: 252) outlined the proposition that as inflationary expectations adjust to rising prices, the short-run advantages of inflation disappear: "If the advantages are to be obtained, the rate of price rise will have to be accelerated and there is no stopping place short of runaway inflation." In 1960, he outlined the natural rate model in full to Richard Lipsey during a visit to the London School of Economics. Friedman (1962: 284) informed his students that "Considerations derived from price theory give no reason to expect any systematic long-term relation between the percentage of the labour force unemployed and the rate at which money wages rise."

There were several other precursors to this type of analysis. Ludwig von Mises (1974 [1958]: 154, 159) argued that "Inflation can cure unemployment only by curtailing the wage earner's *real* wages" [emphasis in text]; unemployment increased as inflationary expectations were revealed to be lower than actual inflation. An almost identical analysis of the way incorrect inflationary expectations can temporarily reduce unemployment can be found in the work of Hayek (1958, 1972 [1960]: 65–97) and Haberler (1958: 140). William Fellner (1959: 227, 235–6) and Raymond J. Saulnier (1963: 25–7), both policy-influential economists, also worked out versions of the natural rate expectations augmented Phillips curve at this time.

This chapter will focus on another prehistory of Friedman's analysis. The adaptive inflationary expectations formula used to undermine the original Phillips curve was provided to Friedman by Phillips. Expectations had played an important role in the Keynesian orthodoxy that Friedman was assaulting. This chapter will examine the role that expectations played in Phillips' macroeconomic model and the process by which Phillips' formula was used to effect the monetarist assault on that model and the analysis derived from it.

The natural rate expectations augmented Phillips curve model

The natural-rate model can be described using the $ diagram, with the upper half representing inflationary macroeconomic policy and the lower half representing disinflationary macroeconomic policy. Inflation is measured along the vertical axis and unemployment along the horizontal axis.

Friedman accepted that the pursuit of high levels of economic activity might temporarily push the economy toward point B. But he also predicted that the equilibrating forces of neoclassical microeconomics would ensure that B was not a position of low unemployment equilibrium, but rather a position of unsustainable *dis*equilibrium. Friedman argued that BAD was one of a family of short-run Phillips curves (along which inflationary expectations were constant). The economy was in disequilibrium at all points along BAD other than A (where inflationary expectations were equal to actual inflation). Using macroeconomic stimulation to reduce unemployment below the natural rate would generate expectational disequilibrium. As agents realized that actual inflation was greater than expected inflation they would alter their labor supply behavior and the economy would return to equilibrium at the natural rate. As inflationary expectations were corrected the short-run Phillips curve would shift upwards and the economy would trace out the points BC (stagflation).

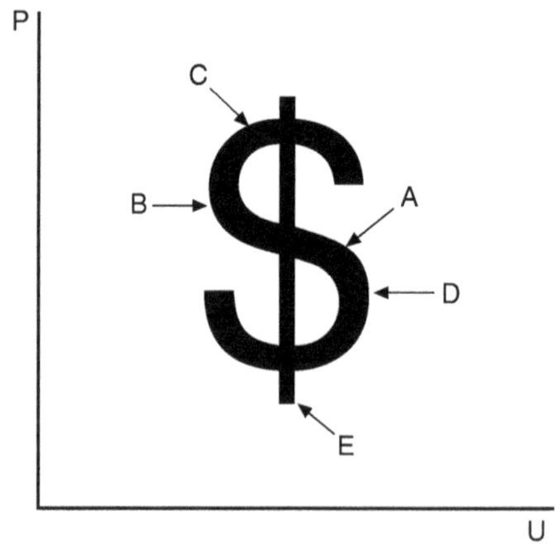

Figure 1 The expectations augmented Phillips curve model.

Unemployment, therefore, could not be permanently reduced through macroeconomic stimulation: the natural rate of unemployment (points E, A, or C) was the best that could be achieved in the long run. To reduce the natural rate required microeconomic reform, not macroeconomic stimulation.

In the $ model, measured unemployment (U) is no longer perceived as a macroeconomic target. Instead, by definition, it becomes identically equal to the natural rate of unemployment (U^N), plus or minus any "unnatural" component (U^{UN}). In the $ model, if policy makers pursue macroeconomic stimulation and measured unemployment is pushed below its natural rate, this "unnatural" deviation ($U^N - U$) is sustainable only so long as agents are deluded and there is a discrepancy between actual inflation (P) and expected inflation (P^e). Unemployment (U) would return to equilibrium (U^N) as soon as this delusion was overcome, and wage contracts ceased to be based on unrealistic calculations of future inflation. In equilibrium, $U = U^N$, and there is no "unnatural" component of unemployment ($U^{UN} = 0$).

Formally:

$$U = U^N + U^{UN}, \text{ and}$$
$$U^{UN} = f\,\theta\,[(P^e - P)]$$

Where θ = the speed of adjustment of incorrect inflationary expectations.

From the late 1960s, Friedman's theoretical gravitational forces became empirically observable. Western economies began to shift from B to C: inflation and unemployment increased simultaneously. Since predictive success was the judge and jury of Friedman's (1953) methodology of positive economics this gave his macroeconomic model a large degree of scientific respectability. As a consequence, monetarist economists recommended a disinflation strategy designed to push the economy out from A to D in the hope that the model was symmetric and that the equilibrating forces of dissipating expectational delusion would take the economy rapidly from D to E.

In both the US and the UK the journey from A to D was rapid. In the US the journey from D to E was also quite rapid (beginning in late 1982). But since this experience was complicated by the simultaneous macroeconomic stimulation caused by the large government deficits of the 1980s, it is difficult to infer that the US provided compelling evidence about the symmetry of the natural rate expectations augmented Phillips curve model. In the UK, point D was much further out than anticipated and the journey from D to E more prolonged than expected.

This prolonged recession could have predicted from the "expectations trap" that was present but unacknowledged in Friedman's model. Friedman (1976: 221–2; 1977: 454) expressed confidence in the Phillips curve as a short-run description of the macroeconomy during the previous century, where inflationary expectations had been constant, and equal to zero.

But in one crucial respect the diagram which Friedman presented (1976: 218, Fig. 12.3) bears little resemblance to Phillips' scatter diagram. Yet, it is Friedman's Phillips curve (not Phillips' or Lipsey's), which has dominated textbook representations of the short-run Phillips curve. If we compare the slope of Friedman's short-run Phillips curve to the right of the "natural" rate, with that of Phillips' and Lipsey's, Phillips curve becomes virtually a wage change floor at 5.5 percent unemployment. A 5 percent increase in unemployment, from 5.5 percent, to 10.5 percent, produces approximately a 0.5 percent reduction in the rate of change of money wage rates. Phillips (2000 [1958]: 254) also found that in the six years following the policy-induced recession associated with the return to the gold standard, unemployment rose from 12.5 percent in 1926, to 22.1 percent in 1932, but wage inflation fell by only 0.6 percent per annum. In Lipsey's post-1923 relationship, any increase in unemployment above approximately 4 percent produces no apparent reduction in the rate of increase in money wage rates; there is a wage change floor at +1 percent.

Since Friedman, like Phillips and Lipsey, did not see the translation from wages to prices as being troublesome, this implies that any policy-induced unemployment above 4 percent cannot reduce inflationary expectations, because these expectations are not being falsified. Friedman's diagram (1976: 226, Fig. 12.7) became the basis of the subsequently influential natural rate model. Yet the shape of the (short-run) Phillips curve at higher levels of unemployment has shifted from its original slope of nearly zero (in Phillips' and Lipsey's expositions) to a slope that is clearly negative. The mechanism by which policy-induced recessions can produce beneficial results is crucially dependent on this slope being negative. Yet the empirical curves to which Friedman added inflationary expectations – "only one wrinkle" (Friedman 1968a: 8) – contained evidence over a long period of data of an "expectations trap" which would thwart policy

The expectations trap does not render the natural rate model invalid in the inflationary zone (i.e. to the left in the "natural" rate). Also, if the Phillips curve has a non-zero slope in the disinflationary zone, then *some* divergence between actual and expected inflation may be deemed to exist; thus facilitating the process – at least at the level of textbook theory – by which the model may be said to plausibly represent the workings of an actual macroeconomy. The issue then reverts to a question of timing – how long would it take for inflationary expectations, and thereby measured inflation, and measured unemployment to fall?

Friedman (1968a: 11) calculated that full adjustment would take "a couple of decades". But there appears to be no ambiguity with respect to that portion of a Phillips curve that has a slope of zero. The existence of a wage change floor implies that no matter how high unemployment reaches, expected inflation (and therefore actual inflation and measured unemployment) cannot fall. Indeed, it is here – in the dis-inflationary region – that the very existence of expectations themselves undermines the validity of the "expectations augmented" natural rate model.

Partly as a consequence, economists have increasingly questioned the symmetry assertion that underpins the $ model as outlined above (the idea that disinflation is the mirror image of inflation). The "hysteresis" argument suggested that U^N might be gravitationally attracted to U rather than the other way round. The economy's stock of human and physical capital clearly deteriorates as factories close and unemployment increases (A to D). Since this capital stock presumably underpins the quantity of the natural rate of output it is possible that the natural rate (the vertical line CAE) shifts outwards toward D in addition to (or instead of) the actual rate of unemployment shifting inwards toward a fixed natural rate.

Phillips and expectations

In the late 1940s, Phillips (a sociology undergraduate) came to the attention of his economics teachers at the LSE by suggesting how a figure in Kenneth Boulding's (1948: 117, Fig. 9) *Economic Analysis* could be extended (Dorrance 2000; Barr 2000). The figure represented the process by which prices rise in response to excess demand, measured by the change in stocks in response to flow disequilibrium. Boulding's "liquid" model led to one of the first physical (and highly "liquid") macroeconomic models: the Phillips Machine (2000 [1950]: chapter 10).

Phillips' (2000 [1950]: 73, 76–7) first appearance in the literature involved a brief discussion of the destabilizing influence of expectations about prices: "This simple model could be further developed, in particular by making a distinction between working and liquid stocks, introducing lags into the production and consumption functions, and linking the demand curve for liquid stocks to the rate of change of price through a coefficient of expectations. Each of these developments would result in an oscillatory system. They will not be considered further here." The "simple model" assumed that prices were constant, or that values were measured in "some kind of real units". Phillips demonstrated that it was possible to "introduce prices indirectly into the system", allowing real and nominal magnitudes to be considered (and graphed) separately.

Dennis Robertson "practically danced a jig" when he saw the Phillips Machine in operation. When the Chancellor of the Exchequer and the Governor of the Bank of England attended a dinner at LSE, they adjourned to the Machine room where the Chancellor was given control of the fiscal levers and the Governor control of the monetary ones (Dorrance 2000). Robertson (correspondence to Meade 27 August 1950) complained that the "treatment of prices [referring to Phillips (2000 [1954: 294]: 76–7)] is so brief that I should like to suspend judgement as to how far it saves the god from the reproach of being a bottom-of-the-slump god, with all goods in perfectly elastic supply. But it is clear, isn't it? That when this last condition is not fulfilled, i.e. in anything like 'normal' times, the multiplier formula needs altering (and at full employment, on certain assumptions, becomes explosive ... can the god look after this?)".

Phillips (19 September 1950) replied to Robertson: "I agree entirely with your criticism of the multiplier formula under conditions of full employment ... But the machine will deal with curves of any shape ... If the price rise is so great that confidence in the monetary system is lost altogether, savings will actually drop to zero ... If now income rises beyond the region of full employment, the slopes of the curves, and therefore of the multiplier change. When the stage is reached at which, for a given increase in income, investment increases more than savings, the process becomes 'explosive' ... Machines could be designed by a competent engineer (but not by me!) to deal with far more complex price effects than this, if economists could agree on what they wanted to happen." In the operational notes accompanying the machine, Phillips wrote that "With this number of relationships and assumptions concerning the effects of price changes there is not much chance of getting very precise numerical multiplier results on the machine. But since, under conditions of rising prices there is not much chance of getting them in reality either, this is not a very great disadvantage from the point of view of exposition either" (cited by Vines 2000: 62).

Phillips told his colleagues that the curve was an extension of the unfinished research agenda of the Machine (Yamey 2000). He (2000 [1954]: 187) criticized Michel Kalecki's *Theory of Economic Dynamics* (1954) for attaching "no causal significance ... to price movements". The opening sentence of the theoretical Phillips curve (2000 [1954]: 134) addressed Robertson's letter: the method of "comparative statics ... does not provide a very firm basis for policy recommendations [because] the time path of income, production and employment during the process of adjustment is not revealed. It is quite possible that certain types of policy may give rise to undesired fluctuations, or even cause a previously stable system to become unstable, although the final equilibrium position as shown by a static analysis appears to be quite satisfactory. Second, the effects of variations in prices and interest rates cannot be dealt with adequately with the simple multiplier models which usually form the basis of the analysis." Thus Phillips' academic career was, from the start, associated with the attempt to explain the instabilities and discontinuities associated with rising prices. As David Vines (2000) put it in his discussion of the "Phillips tradition", there is "more in the Machine ... than is allowed for in macroeconomic conventional wisdom".

Phillips enrolled for a PhD under James Meade. His LSE colleagues turned to him for assistance with the analysis of inflationary expectations. Henry Phelps Brown, for example, acknowledged a specific debt to Phillips for "the form of the argument" about inflationary expectations and profit expectations – the situation where "the price level itself is taking the initiative, and moving under the influence of a preponderant expectation about the likelihood and feasibility of rises and falls in product prices, which has itself been built up by such factors as changes in … 'the market environment' … [which impart] a gentle but continuing motion to the price level" (Phelps Brown and Weber 1953: 279).

In recognition for his contribution to macroeconomic analysis (including presumably the analysis of inflationary expectations), Friedman (1955, no specific date) wrote to offer Phillips a visiting position in Chicago: "I only know how stimulating I would myself find it to have you around for a year; and I venture to believe that the change in environment might be stimulating to you as well." Friedman hoped that Phillips would teach a course in economic fluctuations and added that the theoretical Phillips curve (2000 [1954]: chapter 16) was "a stimulating prologue. The difficulty is that it could be a prologue to a number of different lines of work and I am led to wonder which of these you are in the process of pursuing. This is highly relevant from the point of view of its possible relation to various research undertakings in process here". Phillips (1955) declined on the grounds that he hoped to get "a small group together under Professor Kendall, to review the problems involved in obtaining better empirical knowledge of behaviour responses". It was Kendall who edited the volume in which Phillips first outlined his econometric policy evaluation critique.

Friedman tried to recruit Phillips again in 1960. Phillips (25 January 1961) declined: "The reason is that the theoretical work I have been doing over the last three or four years on dynamic processes and statistical estimation is still progressing and absorbing most of my energy and I have been forced to realise that I cannot do this intensive theoretical work alongside anything substantial in the way of empirical research. It will probably take another three or four years to push the theoretical work as far as I am capable of doing and I hope then to use it to get to grips with real problems in the way you are doing. I should like to do the two types of work together but physical and mental limitations prevent it, so I had better clear up what I can in the one field before having a try at the other." Phillips described Chicago as a "notable … centre of empirical research in economics", which Friedman (14 February 1961) appeared to take exception to: "Heaven preserve us if Chicago should not offer as hospitable an environment for theoretical as to empirical research, and conversely."

One of the reasons that Friedman was keen to recruit Phillips was that Friedman had just launched his Workshop in Money and Banking (1953), and Phillips had just solved a problem for Friedman concerning the analysis of inflationary expectations. At least one economist (pivotal to the second generation Chicago School) had previously despaired of the theory of expectations. In a review of Albert Hart's *Anticipations, Uncertainty and Dynamic Planning*, George Stigler (1941: 358–9) referred to expectations as "the promised land to some economists and a mirage to others.

The reviewer must admit that he leans towards the latter view: much of the literature on expectations consists of obvious and uninformative generalizations of static analysis". With respect to "the revision of anticipations ... progress depends much more on the accumulation of data (of a type almost impossible to collect!) than on an increase in the versatility of our technical apparatus". Friedman (1953 [1946]: 277–300) attacked Oskar Lange on similar grounds: "An example of a classification that has no direct empirical counterpart is Lange's classification of monetary changes ... An explicit monetary policy aimed at achieving a neutral (or positive or negative) monetary effect would be exceedingly complicated, would involve action especially adapted to the particular disequilibrium to be corrected, and would involve knowledge about price expectations, that even in principle, let alone in practice, would be utterly unattainable."

Robbins invited Friedman to deliver two lectures at the LSE on the first and sixth of May 1952 assuring him that "I think you find that there are so many people here who have questions to put to you that if you are willing to sit about and talk you'll never find any difficulty in filling the rest of your days" (4 March 1952). Friedman (correspondence to one of the authors 25 August 1993) had questions to ask as well, raising with Phillips the question of "how to approximate expectations about future inflation". Phillips then wrote down the adaptive inflationary expectations equation, which would later transform macroeconomics. At the time, economists were in no doubt about Phillips' implicit assumption about inflation: "*Implicitly* [emphasis added], Phillips wrote his article for a world in which everyone anticipated that nominal prices would be stable" (Friedman 1968a: 8). Friedman (correspondence to one of the authors 25 August 1993) explained that "the 'implicitly' is really needed ... Phillips himself understood that his analysis depended on a particular state of expectations about inflation ... Phillips' (2000 [1954]: chapter 16) *Economic Journal* article made a very real impression on me. However, his discussion of inflationary expectations in that article is very succinct."

In 1952 Friedman returned to Chicago where he provided Phillip Cagan with the adaptive inflationary expectations formula. Cagan (1956), Mark Nerlove (1958: 231), Arrow and Nerlove (1958: 299) used this formula to transform economic analysis. This formula is generally known as the Friedman-Phelps formula; but Cagan (2000) calls it "Phillips' Adaptive Expectations Formula". It was this formula which Friedman (1956: 19–20) predicted would transform whole sections of economics: Cagan's "device for estimating expected rates of change of prices from actual rates of change, which works so well for his data, can be carried over to other variables as well and is likely to be important in fields other than money. I have already used it to estimate 'expected income' as a determinant of consumption (Friedman 1957) and Gary Becker has experimented with using this 'expected income' series in a demand function for money."

In his PhD and a subsequent essay in the *Economic Journal*, Phillips

(2000 [1954]) stated that flexible prices are integral-type forces and he demonstrated the alarming consequences of integral-type policies generating a "dynamically unstable [system] ... In such a case the oscillations would increase in amplitude until limited by non-linearities in the system and would then persist within those limits so long as the policy was continued ... There may, however, be a tendency for monetary authorities, when attempting to correct an 'error' in production, continuously to strengthen their correcting action the longer the error persists, in which case they would be applying an integral correction policy ... It will be seen that even with a low value of the integral correction factor, cyclical fluctuations of considerable magnitude are caused by this type of policy, and also that the approach to the desired value of production is very slow. Moreover, any attempt to speed up the process by adopting a stronger policy is likely to do more harm than good by increasing the violence of the cyclical fluctuations."

The final and most crucial sub-sections of Phillips' stabilization model (2000 [1954]: 153–7) were "Inherent Regulations of the System" and "Stabilisation of the System" which began with: "Some examples will be given below to illustrate the stability of this system under different conditions of price flexibility *and with different expectations concerning future price changes* [emphasis added]." The theoretical Phillips curve was then tested against a variety of scenarios: inflationary expectations being a crucial factor in determining whether the system has satisfactory outcomes or not: "Demand is also likely to be influenced by the rate at which prices are changing, or have been changing in the recent past, as distinct from the amount by which they have changed, this influence on demand being greater, the greater the rate of change of prices ... The direction of this change in demand will depend on expectations about future price changes. If changing prices induce expectations of further changes in the same direction, as will probably be the case after fairly rapid and prolonged movements, demand will change in the same direction as the changing prices ... there will be a positive feed-back tending to intensify the error, the response of demand to changing prices thus acting as a perverse or destabilizing mechanism of the proportional type."

Even if Phillips saw inflationary expectations as destabilizing aggregate demand alone, this by itself would destroy the possibility of a stable trade-off because the expectation of further inflation "tend[s] to introduce fluctuations": "The strength of the integral regulating mechanisms increases with the increasing degree of price flexibility, while the total strength of the proportional regulating mechanisms decreases as demand responds perversely to the more rapid rate of change of prices, and both these effects tend to introduce fluctuations when price flexibility is increased beyond a certain point. When price expectations operate in this way, therefore, the system ... becomes unstable" (2000 [1954]: 155).

Phillips' pathbreaking contributions caught his contemporaries unaware: he pre-empted at least one research project. Charles Holt together with Franco Modigliani, John Muth, and Herbert Simon were working along similar lines to Phillips (Holt *et al.* 1960). When Merton Miller left the LSE and joined the Carnegie Institute of Technology, he prompted Holt to contact Phillips. Holt (2000) subsequently spent eighteen months working with Phillips at the LSE. The visit had been prompted by some correspondence: "Many useful techniques have been developed in Electrical Engineering and the field of Automatic Control which could profitably be translated into the field of Economics. Since prior to coming into Economics my background was in the fore mentioned fields, I was interested in doing this job. However, in many instances you have anticipated me and thus saved me the trouble" (Holt to Phillips, 6 July 1956).

Phillips (15 October 1956) replied to Holt: "Your work on the control of inventories and production by individual firms and the relation between these decisions and aggregate economic relationships seems to me of major importance. I have very much neglected these matters so far in my own work and concentrated on the sort of problem that would face a central bank or other regulating authority in attempting to control the aggregates in a system. I think this is justified in the early stages of an investigation and we are, I feel sure, only at the beginning of systematic research work in this field, but it will certainly be necessary to develop the analysis of the relation between micro- and macro-economic relationships." Phillips did not go on to provide these microeconomic foundations, but the Phelps (1970) volume was a continuation – not a critique – of Phillips' research agenda.

In the early 1960s, Phillips spent six months at the University of Wisconsin with Holt. Phillips' (2000 [1962]: 218) policy proposal was to locate the economy in the low or zero "compromise" zone, while "trying to shift the relation" inwards through labor market reform. Holt went on to examine *A Manpower Solution* to *The Inflation–Unemployment Dilemma* (Holt *et al.* 1971) – again, a continuation of Phillips' research agenda.

Thereafter he worked "on the central theoretical problems" of the Ford Foundation funded "Project on Dynamic Process Analysis" (May 1956–April 1963). The objective was to specify and estimate models for the control of economic systems. In this period, he presented some empirical illustrations of his stabilization proposals, while continuing to pursue the matter theoretically. The theoretical Phillips curve was published in June 1954; in the three years to June 1957, Phillips became familiar with the Nyquist stability criterion and experimented with electronic simulations of stabilization proposals using equipment at the National Physical Laboratory (NPL) and Short Brothers and Harland Ltd. From about 1952, Phillips interacted with Richard Tizard at the NPL; and, in 1956, Tizard resigned as Head of the NPL Control Mechanisms and Electronics Division to take up a two-year Fellowship at the London School of Economics to work full-time with Phillips (Swade 2000). These collaborations led

Phillips (2000 [1957]: 169) to conclude that "the problem of stabilisation is more complex than appeared to be the case". An empirical agenda was needed: "improved methods should be developed for estimating quantitatively the magnitudes and time-forms of economic relationships in order that the range of permissible hypotheses may be restricted more closely than is at present possible". It seems likely that around June 1957, he began to work on the first empirical Phillips curve (2000 [1958]: chapter 25).

Having pioneered the destabilizing effects of inflationary expectations, Phillips provided very little discussion of this topic in his 1958 empirical curve. His second explanatory variable (the rate of change of unemployment) in Phillips' (2000 [1958]: 243) model influenced wage changes through the expectation that the business cycle will continue moving upwards (or downwards). Lipsey (1960: 20) labeled this "an expectation effect ... the reaction of *expectations* [emphasis in text], and hence of competitive bidding, to changes in *u*". But there is no systematic analysis of inflationary expectations. It is possible that Phillips instructed Friedman, Phelps Brown, and others how to model adaptive inflationary expectations in their empirical work, but decided to ignore it in his own. An alternative explanation is that Phillips was primarily interested in the low inflation "compromise" zone where inflationary expectations are not a dominating force.

There is a distinct continuity between the 1954 theoretical Phillips curve, the 1958, 1959, and 1962 empirical Phillips curves and his growth model. In a "Simple Model of Employment, Money and Prices in a Growing Economy", Phillips (2000 [1961]: 201–2) described his inflation equation as being "in accordance with an obvious extension of the classical quantity theory of money, applied to the growth equilibrium path of a steadily expanding economy". His steady state rate of interest, r_s ("the real rate of interest in Fisher's sense, i.e., as the money rate of interest minus the expected rate of change of the price level") was also "independent of the absolute quantity of money, again in accordance with classical theory". His interest rate function was "only suitable for a limited range of variation of *YP/M*". With exchange rate fixity the domestic money supply (and hence the inflation rate) become endogenously determined; the trade-off operates only within a narrow low inflation band.

This was exactly how Phillips (2000 [1961]: 201) described the limits of his model: he was only "interested" in ranges of values in which actual output (Y) fluctuates around capacity output (Y_n) by a maximum of 5 percent: "In order to reduce the model with money, interest and prices to linear differential equations in x [$= Y/Y_n$], y_n and p it is necessary to express log Y ... in terms of log Y_n and x. For this purpose we shall use the approximation

$$\begin{aligned}\log Y &\cong \log Y_n + (Y - Y_n)/Y_n \\ &= \log Y_n + x - 1\end{aligned}$$

The approximation is very good over the range of values of $(Y - Y_n)/Y_n$, say from −0.05 to 0.05, *in which we are interested* [emphasis added]." Since Phillips (2000 [1961]: 196) stated that these output fluctuations were "five times as large as the corresponding fluctuations in the proportion of the labour force employed", this clearly indicates that Phillips limited his analysis to outcomes in the compromise zone of plus or minus one percentage point deviations of unemployment from normal capacity output. Phillips was re-stating the conclusion of his empirical work; normal capacity output (and approximately zero inflation) was consistent with an unemployment rate "a little under 2½ per cent" (2000 [1958]: 259).

Although Phillips drew an average curve representing the trajectory of the British economy as it swung from bust to boom and back again, at no stage did he suggest that *high* inflation would reduce unemployment for anything other than a temporary period. Yet Phillips' historical investigations had produced an average curve that encompassed 32 percent wage inflation and 22 percent unemployment (2000 [1958]: 253, Fig. 25.9). Wage inflation in excess of 27 percent occurred in 1918 and this observation falls on Phillips curve. But Phillips' empirical analysis also reveals that 1918 was followed by two decades of extraordinarily high unemployment – hardly an augury of a stable high inflation trade-off. Phillips did not state or imply that any point on his average curve could be targeted for stabilization purposes.

But underpinning the original Phillips curve was the argument that "One of the important policy problems of our time is that of maintaining a high level of economic activity and employment *while avoiding a continual rise in prices* [emphasis added]." Phillips explained that there was "fairly general agreement" that the prevailing rate of 3.7 percent inflation was "undesirable. It has undoubtedly been a major cause of the general weakness of the balance of payments and the foreign reserves, and if continued it would almost certainly make the present rate of exchange untenable." His objective was, if possible, "to prevent continually rising prices of consumer goods while maintaining high levels of economic activity ... the problem therefore reduces to whether it is possible to prevent the price of labour services, that is average money earnings per man-hour, from rising at more than about 2 per cent per year ... one of the main purposes of this analysis is to consider what levels of demand for labour the monetary and fiscal authorities should seek to maintain in their attempt to reconcile the two main policy objectives of high levels of activity and stable prices. I would question whether it is really in the interests of workers that the average level of hourly earnings should increase more rapidly than the average rate of productivity, say about 2 per cent per year" (2000 [1959]: 261, 269–80, [1962]: 208, [1961]: 201, [1962]: 218, [1958]: 259).

Like Phillips, Friedman (1968a: 9–11) described the initial expansionary effects of a reduction in unemployment. But when inflation became high enough to influence expectational behavior, Friedman later argued that expansion "describes only the initial effects". Modern macroeconomics has several explanations for the existence of a temporary trade-off (involving monetary misperceptions and intertemporal substitution). Friedman's version of the Phillips–Friedman–Phelps Critique suggested a temporary trade-off between unanticipated inflation and unemployment lasting "two to five years", taking "a couple of decades" to return to the natural rate of unemployment. Friedman's mechanism involved real wage resistance in response to the initial "simultaneous fall *ex post* in real wages to employers and rise *ex ante* in real wages to employees". Thus real wage resistance plays an equilibrating role in Friedman's version.

Unlike Friedman, Phillips was highly skeptical about equilibrating forces. In a Robbins seminar paper on "Stability of 'self-correcting' systems" (21 May 1957) Phillips examined a system in which the rate of change of prices was proportional to excess demand. Phillips concluded that "If the 'equilibrating forces' are too strong they will make the system unstable ... The argument extends without difficulty to any system, in which there are 'equilibrating' or 'self-correcting' forces operating through time lags".

Phillips' version of the Phillips–Friedman–Phelps Critique was a far more potent constraint on policy makers than Friedman's version: inflation had far more serious consequences for Phillips than for Friedman. For Friedman, the (purely internal) imbalance corrected itself through utility maximizing labor supply adjustments, as inflation ceased to be incorrectly anticipated. Only a temporary boom would result, and would soon be eroded by real wage resistance. But in Phillips' model, external imbalance (driven by only minor inflation differentials) could be addressed by exchange rate adjustment, leaving the internal imbalance in need of still greater attention. In addition, the role Friedman allocated to inflationary expectation was benign, whereas the role allocated to inflationary expectations by Phillips (2000 [1954]) was far more destabilizing, denying the possibility of a stable target in the presence of such expectations.

Not only was there "fairly general agreement" (Phillips 2000 [1962]: 207–8) that non-trivial (3.7 percent) inflation was intolerable; but the assumption of low (but unspecified) and stable inflation rates was commonly invoked by model builders in the pre-stagflation era. For example, the Lucas and Rapping (1969: 748) model of "Real Wages, Employment and Inflation" was assumed to hold "only under reasonably stable rates of price increase. To define what is meant by reasonable stability, and to discover how expectations are revised when such stability ceases to obtain, seems to us to be a crucial, unresolved problem." Friedman (1968a: 6, 1968b: 21) also stated that the "price expectation effect is slow to develop and also slow to disappear. Fisher estimated that it took several decades for a full adjustment and recent work is consistent with his estimate." Friedman presented evidence about the time it took for "price anticipations" to influence behavior that was "wholly consistent with Fisher's".

Phillips' opposition to inflation was axiomatic: an expression of one of the eternal truths that separate economists from monetary cranks. Nevertheless, he clearly stated the assumptions under which small amounts of inflation could be traded-off for small amounts of unemployment in the "compromise" zone. He did not suggest that a permanent trade-off existed outside the "compromise" zone.

In the 1950s Philips was aware of an explicit examination of the process by which inflationary expectations shifts a "Phillips curve". John Black (1959: 145, n. 1), the author of an article in *Economica* (of which Phillips was a co-editor) on "Inflation and long-run growth", thanked Phillips for "comments and suggestions". Black (1959: 147–50) apologized for being "unable to think of any other name" (other than aggregate supply curve) for his function relating the "behavior of prices over time which will result from any given level of employment". Black's "Phillips curve" was a rectangular hyperbola with full employment as one asymptote and a deflationary floor as the other. The location of Black's "Phillips curve" was dependent on three parameters: first, *A*, the size of the rectangle linking the curve to the asymptotes which was determined by (among other factors) the "strength or weakness of general fears of inflation"; second, *I*, an investment function; and third, *P*, "the price expectations function, which relates vertical shifts in the aggregate supply curve to the price changes experienced by price and wage setters in recent periods ... the position of the supply curve can be made to shift vertically in a way determined by the rate of change of the price level over some past period. This implies that as both buyers and sellers get attuned to regarding a given rate of increase of prices as normal, and come to expect it to continue, the whole supply curve shifts upwards ... The position of the aggregate supply schedule in any period, however, will itself reflect the effects of earlier price changes on price expectations ... the adverse effect on the level of output at any time via the upward shift in the schedule due to price increases in earlier periods". The possibilities for growth depended on the empirical size of the lags, including "the lags in the effects of current price changes on price expectations".

Phillips was also aware of Bent Hansen's *A Study in the Theory of Inflation* and recommended the text to Lipsey: "Bill first put me on to this source and I came to accept this view of the Phillips curve as being a Hansen-type reaction curve for the labour market" (correspondence from Lipsey to one of the authors 19 February 1993). Hansen (1951: 249, 139) offered the "explicit inclusion of disequilibrium in the labour market in the analysis" and also discussed the relationship between inflation and the supply side: "during inflation quite drastic changes in productivity". He also analyzed expectations. In "Final Remarks", Hansen (1951: 246–8) concluded that "price expectations do disturb the analysis in so far as they can render the price-reaction equations unusable ... it is clear that in practical forecasting, price expectations and their changes are a difficulty of the first order, and that a policy which aims to maintain monetary equilibrium is forced to accord a great deal of weight to holding expectations in check".

Thus, orthodoxy continued to allow an important role for expectations. For example, in their seminal extension of Phillips' analysis, Samuelson and Solow (1960: 193, 189) entertained the possibility that a switch in policy regime might alter the shape of the Phillips curve. They also allowed for a vague and loosely defined role for expectations: policies producing "low pressure of demand could so act upon wages and other expectations so as to shift the curve downwards in the long run". Alternatively, this might increase structural unemployment, shifting the menu of choice upwards. The expectation of a continuation of full employment, they believed, might have been responsible for an upward shift in their Phillips curve in the 1940s and 1950s. Samuelson and Solow were not ignorant of inflationary expectations; neither did they believe it was policy invariant. For example, in December 1965, Samuelson acknowledged that targeting a point on a Phillips curve could shift the curve itself: "One ought to admit that the overausterity of the Eisenhower Administration may have done something to give America a better Phillips curve" (cited by Haberler 1966: 130).

Phillips and the Lucas Critique

Robin Court (2000) and Peter Phillips (2000) have highlighted Phillips' analysis of the relationship between policy control and model identification, and the similarity between the equations used by Phillips and Robert Lucas (1976) to derive their conclusions about econometric policy evaluation. Peter Phillips argues that the Phillips Critique implies "that even deep structural parameters may be unrecoverable when the reduced form coefficients are themselves unidentified. One can further speculate on the potential effects of unidentifiable reduced forms on the validity of econometric tests of the Lucas critique ... [this] may yet have an influence on subsequent research, irrespective of the historical issue of his work on this topic predating that of Lucas (1976)."

Two decades before Lucas, Phillips (2000 [1956]: 371) stressed that "There are, therefore, two questions to be asked when judging how effective a certain policy would be in attaining any given equilibrium objectives. First, what dynamic properties and cyclical tendencies will the system as a whole possess *when the policy relationships under consideration themselves form part of the system*? [emphasis added]. Second, when the system has these dynamic properties, will the equilibrium objectives be attained, given the size of the probable disturbances and the permissible limits to movements in employment, foreign reserves, etc. The answer to the first question is important, not only because the reduction of cyclical tendencies is itself a desirable objective, but also because the second question cannot be answered without knowing the answer to the first. And the first question cannot be answered without knowing the magnitudes and time-forms of the main relationships forming the system."

Phillips stressed the importance of Dynamic Analysis and taught a course at LSE called "Dynamic Process Analysis". The Final Report of the Dynamic Process Analysis Project stated that "It can be fairly claimed that the results obtained from [Phillips'] investigations, taken together, constitute a theoretical solution of the central problem which formed the basis of the project. It is believed that they can be applied directly to control problems arising in fields where fairly long time series are available from systems with stationary stochastic disturbances, for example in chemical manufacturing processes. It has to be admitted that direct applicability to control of an economy is limited by shortness of economic time series and the lack of stationarity of the system. However, the results obtained should provide the basis for valid work in this area." Four years later, these 1963 "admitted" doubts matured into the next stage of Phillips' critique of econometric policy evaluation.

Five months before Friedman's famous AEA Presidential Address, a conference was held in London (July 1967) on Mathematical Model Building in Economics and Industry. Both Phillips (2000 [1968]: chapter 50) and Herman Wold (1968) delivered papers that require us to revise the accepted chronology of two seminal ideas in economics – hysteresis and the Lucas Critique. Hysteresis has several applications in economics and Paul Samuelson (February 1968: 12) was thought to have been the first to use the word when writing about economics (Cross and Allan 1988). Wold, however, had used the term much earlier in his discussion of recursive models: time series display "a ubiquitous tendency to persistency and hysteresis" (Wold and Jureen 1953: 14, 52). Wold visited LSE in 1951, and Phillips referenced Wold and Jureen's (1953: 14) recursive system analysis (2000 [1956]: 384, n. 2; [1960]: 410). In his Model Building conference paper, Wold (1968: 156) presented another early application of "hysteresis loops" to economics: "There therefore may not exist a single relationship independent of the direction of movement of the independent variable." Given the importance of reversibility for the Phillips curve trade-off (policy makers were perceived to be able to swing up and down a stable Phillips curve according to political preferences), it is interesting to report that Wold associated Phillips with the "novel . . . question about reversibility in macro-models that are specified in terms of instruments and target variables". Wold demonstrated that economic relationships display asymmetries depending on the policy regime in force, using two physical examples (one from electrical magnetism, the second from the law of thermodynamics developed by the engineer, Sadi Carnot), both of which Phillips with his electrical engineering background would presumably have been familiar with.

The 1967 conference took place shortly before Phillips migrated to Canberra. Richard Stone (1968) also delivered a paper to the conference.

Within months of arriving in Australia, Phillips wrote to James Meade (2000) "asking whether there would be any chance of getting a position in Cambridge to work with Dick Stone and myself on dynamic macro-economics again. It all came to nothing because very soon after he had his stroke ... Perhaps he had some very simple but immensely promising new thoughts on the subject. It is tragic that we will never know." It seems possible that Phillips had given some more thought to his policy evaluation critique, because the only paper that survives from this period (dated July 1972) is the handwritten paper that Robin Court (2000) and Peter Phillips (2000) found to contain a contribution comparable to that later made by Robert Lucas (1976).

Phillips (2000 [1968]: chapter 50) concluded in his Model Building conference paper that "The possibility that operation of the control may prevent re-estimation of the system should lead us to ask whether the decision analysis we have been considering does not have some fundamental deficiency. And indeed it has. The basic defect is simply that in deriving the decision rules no account was taken of the fact that the parameters of the system are not known exactly, and no consideration was given to ways in which we can improve our knowledge of the system while we are controlling it. In my view it cannot be too strongly stated that in attempting to control economic fluctuations we do not have the two separate problems of estimating the system and of controlling it, we have a single problem of jointly controlling and learning about the system, that is, a problem of learning control or adaptive control."

Six years later, Lucas (1973: 333) represented "conventional Phillips curves" as embodying "relatively stable structural features of the economy [which] are thus independent of the nature of the aggregate demand policy pursued." Lucas could have chosen Friedman's (1953: 39, 6) post-war hegemonic methodology of positive economics as the whipping boy for his critique of policy evaluation: "Economics as a positive science is a body of tentatively accepted generalisations about economic phenomena that can be used to predict the consequences of changes in circumstances." Friedman's suggested that empirical evidence could produce "agreement about the economic consequences of ... legislation ... and the effect of counter-cyclical action ... a consensus on 'correct' economic policy depends much less on the progress of normative economics proper than on the progress of a positive economics yielding conclusions that are, and deserve to be, widely accepted". But as Friedman (1956) found Chicago precursors to his restatement of the quantity theory (much to Don Patinkin's annoyance) so Lucas (1976: 20) found Chicago and Carnegie-Mellon precursors to his critique in Friedman (1957), Muth (1961), and Knight (1921). The reason for the urgency behind Lucas' reformulation was to undermine the Phillips curve: "the case for sustained inflation, based entirely on econometric simulations, is attended now with a seriousness it has not commanded for many decades".

Lucas (1976: 19, 22–3) used the Phillips curve to illustrate the proposition that one of the traditions in economics "is fundamentally in error". Lucas complained that econometricians were averse to inspecting data prior to 1947 and rarely used 1929–46 data as a check on post-war fits. This cannot, of course, apply to Phillips' (2000 [1958]: chapter 25) examination of 1861–1957 data since he clearly derived his curve from pre-1914 data and checked the fit on inter-war and post-war data. Neither should Phillips be connected to Lucas' assertion about permanent inflation inducing a "permanent economic high". Lucas refers to the "widespread acceptance of a Phillips 'trade-off' in the absence of *any* [emphasis in text] aggregative theoretical model embodying such a relationship". But this apparently reflects Lucas unfamiliarity with the aggregative theoretical model provided by Phillips (2000 [1954]: chapter 16). The "mysterious transformation" that Lucas described with respect to the Phillips curve was a transformation of perceptions about Phillips' work. That transformation was heavily influenced if not effected by the monetarist and New Classical counter-revolutionaries. The error-ridden tradition unintentionally highlighted by Lucas relates to an a-historical tendency in modern economics.

Like Lucas' mislaid and handwritten April 1973 "Econometric policy evaluation" paper (Sargent 1996: 539, n. 3), Phillips' handwritten 1972 "Phillips Critique" could easily have been lost forever. But it is clear that the Lucas Critique, far from being a critique of Phillips' work, was actually a development of Phillips' research agenda, which, had he not been incapacitated by severe illness, he would presumably have pursued in more detail prior to Lucas (1976). Adding Phillips' name to Lucas' list of precursors to his econometric policy evaluation critique emphasizes that these counter-revolutionaries were elaborating upon expectational themes that were already fairly well developed in the mainstream literature.

Overview and conclusions

Microfoundations and macroapplications

One of the most problematic aspects of the approach to expectations by economists is manifest in their treatment at the hands of those who write the history of economic thought. Two recent examples of this should suffice to make our point. In the third edition of their textbook, *History of Economic Thought*, Landreth and Colander (1994: 481) said "although Muth wrote his article in 1961, the rational expectations assumption did not play an important role in economics until it was adopted by Robert Lucas into macroeconomics". Blaug, in the fifth edition of his book *Economic Theory in Retrospect*, wrote (1997: 683) "the theory of rational expectations made its first appearance in a 1961 article by J.F. Muth on security and commodity markets". As we have shown above, both of these statements are problematic, to say the least. But even those observers who focused on the evolution of rational expectations have overlooked many aspects of its development.

Over the two decades since the initial publication of Sheffrin's survey of the literature on rational expectations (1983), much work has appeared on the topic. We will not even attempt here to provide a comprehensive survey of the literature. Indeed any attempt to give a comprehensive "report of three decades" – to use Lekachman's phrase – of macroapplications of rational and implicit expectations would probably prove futile. Here, we will try to sum up the major issues surrounding the utilization of endogenous expectations of rational and implicit varieties – by economists at the micro and macro levels in both closed and open economy models. Indeed, the application of the implicit expectations approach in the latter case seems to be long overdue, as is the testing of its applicability and comparison to rational expectations results. However, even Sheffrin did not, at the time, recognize the importance of Mills's work on implicit expectations. Indeed, Mills is nowhere to be found in that volume.

But more is at stake than the overlooking of Mills, despite the importance of implicit expectations for macrostabilization policy (Lovell 1986: 114–15). Sheffrin also completely overlooked the important book of Nerlove *et al.* (1979) that introduced the notion of "quasi-rational expectations". Moreover, he did not cite the 1980 special issue of the *Journal of*

Money Credit and Banking, which dealt with the efficacy of the rational expectations approach and included important papers by Cagan among others. In addition, he did not deal with Azariadis's paper on "Self-fulfilling prophecies" (1981), nor the important 1982 paper by Meltzer entitled "Rational expectations, risk, uncertainty, and market responses", and Hart's comment on it. But perhaps the most important omission from Sheffrin's literature survey up to 1983 was Milton Friedman's ongoing treatment of expectations from 1953 onwards. We have dealt with Friedman's macroapplications above. Below, we will briefly discuss his contribution in the context of expectations in the open economy.

Expectations in closed economy micro and macro models

Here we stress the distinction between the theoretician's and econometrician's treatment of endogenous expectations in closed economy micro and macro models. By doing this, we can understand the differences between the *axiomatic* approach of Prescott (1977) and Lucas (1977), among others, the *behavioral* approach as expressed in Sargent's notion of "bounded rationality" (1993), and the *subjectivist* approach, as seen in the work of Cyert and DeGroot (1974) some two decades earlier. Moreover, by doing so we can counterpoint these approaches with econometrician's approaches manifest in Nerlove's "quasi-rational" model (Nerlove *et al.* 1979), and Muth's 1985 "errors-in-variables" model of endogenous expectations formation, encompassing both rational and implicit expectations as "special cases". Because of the importance of the models of Nerlove (Nerlove *et al.* 1979; Nerlove 1983; Nerlove and Bessler 2001) and Muth (1985) as *alternatives* to the conventional rational and implicit expectations approaches, they will be dealt with in detail here.

Since the seminal work of Nerlove *et al.* (1979), *Analysis of Economic Time Series: A Synthesis*, in which "quasi-rational" expectations were introduced, and the publication of Muth's "errors-in-variables" approach (1985), an increasing number of observers have come to advocate not only the testing of rational and implicit expectations but of their alternatives (Lovell 1986: 122). In his 1981 Presidential address to the Econometric Society entitled "Expectations, plans and realizations in theory and practice" published in *Econometerica* (1983: 1254–5), Nerlove wrote:

> Mills introduced the notion of "implicit expectations" and Muth of "rational expectations." The idea of the former is to employ future values as proxies for anticipations of them on the grounds that, on the whole, economic agents forecast successfully and errors are small. Rational expectations are based on a broadly similar hypothesis but one which, especially in recent years, has taken different specific forms. The underlying idea is simply that economic agents behave purposefully in collecting and using information just as they do in other

> activities. In this general form the hypothesis is a compelling one, but in practice this idea is often translated into the requirement that expectations are, in the model at hand, formed in a way that is stochastically consistent with the behavior of the realized values of the variables in question. This is clearly a much stronger hypothesis, which one can reasonably dispute. Clearly, our models of behavior are imperfect and, however attractive consistency may be, it would be unreasonable to insist that expectations and behavior are necessarily generated by the same stochastic approximation, with every restriction pertaining to the one incorporated in the other.

Nerlove went on to say

> A more attractive but weaker form of the rational expectations hypothesis is simply that there is no pattern of systematic error. Purposeful economic agents have incentives to eliminate such errors up to a point justified by the costs of obtaining the information necessary to do so. The most readily available and least costly information about the future value of a variable is its past values. Moreover, in the absence of structural change, the final form of an econometric model leads under fairly general conditions to univariate relations between the current value of a variable and its own past values. Thus one possible approach to modeling expectations formation, consistent with the rational expectations hypothesis, would be to generate MMSE [minimum mean-square error] forecasts (also conditional expectations in the mathematical sense) from empirical time-series models for the variables to be forecast by the economic agents whose behavior we are studying. Elsewhere, I and others [1979] have called such expectations quasi-rational.

An alternative expectations modeling approach to the quasi-rational model of Nerlove was proposed by Muth himself. Muth called it "the errors-in-variables model" (1985: 202–3). This model not only modified his original model, but encompassed "the rational model" and "Mills's implicit model as special cases". Indeed, according to him, this "modification of the rational model is in better, but imperfect, agreement with the facts" (1985: 202).

In his important *AER* paper "Tests of the rational expectations hypothesis", Lovell (1986: 111, n. 2) noted the alternate views held regarding direct empirical testing as against the opposition of theoreticians to tests of rational expectations. But perhaps more significant is the stress he put upon the importance of empirical microfoundations. As he wrote (1986: 111)

> In order to be able to claim that a theory is based on firm microfoundations requires more than the derivation of propositions from the

> assumption that economic agents maximize, however esthetically pleasing such derivations may be; a theory that is said to be based on microfoundations should survive empirical testing at the level of the individual decision making unit. To the extent that the survey evidence supports the hypothesis of rational expectations, results derived under that assumption, policy impossibility theorems, and so forth, will be both more interesting and more demanding of serious attention.

Lovell concluded (1986: 122) "that the weight of empirical evidence is sufficiently strong to compel us to suspend belief in the hypothesis of rational expectations, pending the accumulation of additional empirical evidence". He qualified this, however, by saying that "more attention needs to be given to the empirical testing of the rational expectations hypothesis against its alternatives".

More recently, Nerlove and Bessler (2001) have surveyed alternative models of expectations formation, including experimental studies of expectations, and conclude that "the real issue is not what model to use, but rather how we might best proceed to get answers to the substantive questions with which we are concerned" (2001: 200). The impact of the econometrician's revision of their approach to rational expectations and its limitations, as manifest in the work of Nerlove (Nerlove *et al.* 1979, Nerlove 1983), Nerlove and Bessler (2001), Muth (1985), and Pesaran (1987), among others, has been picked up by the macro theoreticians, and alternate behavioral and systemic models of expectations formation and its impact on macro systems have been proposed; the two most important, in our view being that of Sargent (1993) and Grandmont (1998). Sargent, his book *Bounded Rationality in Macroeconomics* (1993), developed an adaptive behavior model based upon the stochastic approximation approach. Sargent asserted that the intelligent opportunism of the individual economic agents would bring about rational expectations equilibrium via processes of learning and adjustment within a bounded rationality framework. In his 1998 paper in *Econometrica*, entitled "Expectations formation and stability of large socioeconomic systems" – part of which had been presented in his Presidential Address to the Econometric Society in 1990 (1998: 741, n. 1) – Grandmont went even further, and posed a "general '*uncertainty principle*'" regarding "convergence to rational expectations" (1998: 741, 775). He described what he called "complex 'learning equilibria'" and said that they "may be at first sight good candidates to explain why agents keep making significant and recurrent mistakes when trying to predict the fate of the socioeconomic systems in which they participate" (1998: 776). Grandmont concluded by saying that while he was not sure whether a research program studying such "learning equilibria" would "actually generate operational results or is even feasible ... progress on this front, if possible, might provide an interesting alternative to our current paradigms, which rely very heavily on extreme, and often criticized, rationality axioms" (1998: 777).

Open economy models: speculation and expectations

Accounts of how the approach to expectations, and especially rational expectations, developed in open economy models are lacking. Indeed, Sheffrin dealt with this only as a brief "historical note", and even his account is problematic, to say the least. He wrote (1983: 75) "as a historical note, models that combine rational asset markets and nonrational goods markets were first used by Dornbusch (1976c) to discuss issues concerning the behavior of foreign exchange". He went on to very briefly describe Dornbusch's well-known 1976 *JPE* "overshooting" model (1976c), and wrote (1983: 83) "Dornbusch's (1976c) original paper on this topic was motivated by what appeared to be excessive fluctuations in foreign exchange markets. Dornbusch argued that the short-run overshooting of long-run equilibrium that emerged from his model was a possible explanation for the observed volatility of exchange rates".

As early as 1953 however, Friedman had introduced both "foresight" and overshooting phenomenon into his treatment of adjustment of flexible rates and speculation in the foreign exchange market. According to Friedman (1953: 183) "the actual path of adjustment may involve repeated overshooting and undershooting of the final position, giving rise to a series of cycles around it or to other of variety of other patterns". He went on to talk about the implications of "correct" and "imperfect" foresight "on the part of speculators" for stability in the foreign-exchange market, and concluded that "in a free market with correct foresight ... speculation may be stabilizing on balance" (1953: 184–5).

Another significant oversight on the part of Sheffrin was Niehans's (1975) paper, which was actually the basis for Dornbusch's *JPE* paper (1976c), and this according to Dornbusch himself (1976a: 231; 1976c: 1161). In his paper, Niehans introduced "the distinction between the actual exchange rate and what, in analogy to permanent income, may be called the permanent exchange rate" (1975: 276). Niehans went on to assess the relevance for capital flows of this distinction, and linked it both with expectations of appreciation and depreciation of domestic currency, and the stability and instability of such expectations (1975: 277). On this basis, he obtained "the paradox of a possible contractive effect of monetary expansion" under a flexible exchange rate regime, with the limiting case being that "monetary policy loses all its effects on output under flexible rates and there is even an extreme range in which its effect is perverse" (1975: 279–80). He concluded (1975: 280) "in view of the slower adjustment of permanent rates to actual rates ... we may thus live forever in the world of perverse effects. In this case, monetary policy acts itself out in the side show of the foreign-exchange markets, producing large fluctuations in rates, while the effects on real output and employment will remain disappointing". These results called into question those of the Mundell–Fleming model (Dornbusch 1976a: 231). It is not surprising then, that Dornbusch addressed his major papers in the *Journal of International Economics* and the *Journal of Political Economy* in 1976 to the problem raised by Niehans regarding exchange rate expectations, "the trade balance and capital flows" and its implications regarding the efficacy "of monetary policy under flexible exchange rates" (Dornbusch 1976a: 231; 1976c). Isard, in his own "survey" of exchange rate economics (1995), also overlooked the importance of Niehans's 1975 paper in the development of what is now called the "Mundell–Dornbusch model" of exchange rate expectations and dynamics (Dornbusch 1980).

But perhaps the most important development in the treatment of expectations in the open economy case has been the "theories consistent expectations hypothesis (TCEH)" framework suggested by Goldberg and Frydman (1993, 1996). In their pathbreaking work they have introduced a proposed TCEH framework, which encompasses imperfect information states and qualitative knowledge, as against the limitations of the Rational Expectations Hypothesis, which constrains agents to "quantitatively correct forecasts" (1996: 870). The TCEH framework thus enables exploration of the consequences of imperfect knowledge for "exchange rate dynamics" in a way similar to the stress put on imperfect knowledge for understanding "the dynamics in financial markets", as emphasized by Soros (1987, 1995) among others (Goldberg and Frydman 1996: 870, n. 1).

Quo vadis expectations?

The treatment of expectations in economics, and at the hands of economists – theoretical and applied – has undergone a metamorphosis. At the macro level, they have gone from "animal spirits" emanating "outside" the economic model, to become an integral part of the model itself, whether axiomatically predetermined or empirically assessed. At the micro level, the importance of expectations has become paramount, especially in view of their connection with fundamental game-theoretic characteristics. In Weberian terms, as we have shown above, the history of expectations in economics is inherently linked to the predilections of individual economists who have had "patrimonies to defend". A final example should bring home this *central message*.

In 1974, Cyert and DeGroot published their now classic paper "Rational expectations and Bayesian analysis" in the *JPE*. The objective of their paper was "to build on Muth's basic concept by providing some insight into the process by which the rational expectations hypothesis can, in fact, be realized"; this, by means of introducing "the concept of Bayesian learning into expectations" (1974: 521). They approached the issue by describing "the process of generating rational expectations". As they wrote (1974:

522) "it is our view that a process has to be developed if the rational hypothesis is to be a scientific truth rather than a religious belief ... without well-developed process models, the concept of rational expectations is essentially a black box". They concluded by saying that (1974: 535–6) "it is possible to extend the definition of rational expectations to process-oriented model ... Our basic thrust in this paper has been the development of models that describe the process by which rational expectations may be developed within a market ... In particular, the learning process has been ignored and we have attempted to remedy this deficiency by introducing the concept of Bayesian learning". Briefly put, as they asserted, Cyert and DeGroot thought they have provided a "natural setting" for the rational expectations approach "in the Bayesian framework" (1974: 532).

In contrast to this, Lucas wrote (1977: 15) "the general hypothesis that economic agents are Bayesian decision makers has, in many applications, little empirical content: without some way of inferring what an agent's subjective view of the future is, this hypothesis is of no help in understanding his behavior. Even psychotic behavior can be (and today, is) understood as 'rational' given a sufficiently abnormal view of relevant probabilities".

Interestingly enough, neither the Bayesian approach of Cyert and DeGroot, nor the axiomatic approach of Lucas and Prescott (1971) and Lucas (1977), have come to "rule the roost" regarding the treatment of expectations by economists and econometricians, even though both have become the bases for *progressive* research programs. Rather, there has been an ongoing debate between those who advocate the testing of the rational expectations hypothesis and those who consider rational expectations not as a hypothesis to be tested, and possibly rejected, but as an axiom to be accepted and *applied* a priori. In any event, as we have tried to show above, expectations, and the rational and implicit expectations approaches – whether in axiomatic, quasi-rational or other vintages – are the cornerstone of both modern micro- and macroeconomic analysis, and will continue to be in the future.

Bibliography

Adelman, Irma (1992) Letter to authors, 14 January.

Akerlof, G. (1982) "A personal tribute and a few reflections", in G. Feiwel (ed.) *Samuelson and Neoclassical Economics*, Boston: Kluwer.

Arrow, K. (1962) "Economic implications of learning by doing", *Review of Economic Studies* 29: 155–73.

Arrow, K. and Debreu, G. (1954) "Existence of an equilibrium for a competitive economy", *Econometrica* 22: 265–90.

Arrow, K. and Hurwicz, L. (1962) "Competitive stability under weak gross substitutability: nonlinear price adjustment and adaptive expectations", *International Economic Review* 3: 233–55.

Arrow, K. and Nerlove, M. (1958) "A note on expectations and stability", *Econometrica* 26: 297–305.

Azariadis, C. (1981) "Self-fulfilling prophecies", *Journal of Economic Theory* 25: 380–96.

Bailey, M. (1962) *National Income and the Price Level* (1st edn), New York: McGraw-Hill.

—— (1971) *National Income and the Price Level* (2nd edn), New York: McGraw-Hill.

—— (1995) Letter to authors, 30 October.

Barr, N. (2000) "The history of the Phillips machine", in R. Leeson (ed.) *A.W.H. Phillips: Collected Works in Contemporary Perspective*, Cambridge: Cambridge University Press.

Bateman, B. (1987) "Keynes's changing conception of probability", *Economics and Philosophy* 3: 97–120.

—— (1993) "Finding confidence: business expectations, economic policy and *The General Theory*", unpublished manuscript, Grinnell College, Iowa.

Begg, D. (1982) *The Rational Expectations Revolution in Economics: theories and evidence*, Baltimore: Johns Hopkins University Press.

Black, J. (1959) "Inflation and long-run growth", *Economica* May: 145–53.

Blaug, M. (1997) *Economic Theory in Retrospect* (5th edn), Cambridge: Cambridge University Press.

Bossons, J. and Modigliani, F. (1960) "The source of regressiveness in surveys of businessmen's short-run expectations", in *The Quantity and Economic Significance of Anticipations Data,* NBER, Princeton: Princeton University Press.

—— (1966) "Statistical vs. structural explanations of understatement and regressivity in rational expectations", *Econometrica* 34: 347–53.

Boulding, K. (1948) *Economic Analysis*, New York: Harper Brothers.

Bowman, M. (ed.) (1958) *Expectations, Uncertainty, and Business Behavior*, a conference held at Carnegie Institute of Technology, 20–27 October, 1955 under the auspices of the Committee on Business Enterprise Research, New York: Social Science Research Council.

Bradley, P. (ed.) (1959) *The Public Stake in Union Power*, Richmond: University of Virginia Press.

Bronfenbrenner, M. (1992) Letter to authors, 19 August.

Brown, A. (1955) *The Great Inflation*, London: Oxford University Press.

Buchanan, N. (1939) "A reconsideration of the cobweb theorem", *Journal of Political Economy* 47: 67–81.

Burstein, M. (1991) Letter to authors, 26 November.

Bushaw, D. and Clower, R. (1957) *Introduction to Mathematical Economics*, Homewood, IL: Irwin.

Cagan, P. (1956) "The monetary dynamics of hyperinflation", in M. Friedman (ed.) *Studies in the Quantity Theory of Money*, Chicago: University of Chicago Press.

—— (1991) Letter to authors, 28 November.

—— (2000) "Phillips' adaptive expectations formula", in R. Leeson (ed.) *A.W.H. Phillips: Collected Works in Contemporary Perspective*, Cambridge: Cambridge University Press.

Cairncross, A. (1991) "Presidential address to the Royal Economic Society", *Royal Economic Society Newsletter*, January.

Cassidy, J. (1996) "The Decline of Economics", *The New Yorker* 2 December.

Casson, M. (1983) *The Economics of Unemployment*, Cambridge, MA: MIT Press.

Clower, R. (1959a) "Some theory of an ignorant monopolist", *Economic Journal* 69: 705–16.

—— (1959b) "Oligopoly theory: a dynamical approach", *Proceedings of the Thirty-Fourth Annual Conference of the Western Economic Association*, 16–19.

—— (1959c [1960]) "Inductive inference and business behavior", abstract of paper presented at the December 1959 meeting of the Econometric Society, in Report of the Washington Meeting, *Econometrica* 28: 685–6.

—— (1991) Letter to authors, 19 December.

Coase, R. and Fowler, R. (1935a) "Bacon production and the pig cycle in Britain", *Economica* (n.s.) 2: 142–67.

—— (1935b) "The pig-cycle: a rejoinder", *Economica* (n.s.) 2: 423–8.

—— (1937) "The pig-cycle in Great Britain: an explanation", *Economica* (n.s.) 4: 55–82.

Committee for Economic Development (1958) *Problems of United States Economic Development*, New York: Committee for Economic Development.

Cooper, W. (1991) Letter to authors, 5 December.

Cooper, W. and Simon, H. (1955) "Comment on Modigliani and Sauerlender", in *Short-Term Economic Forecasting,* Studies in Income and Wealth, Vol. 17, National Bureau of Economic Research, Princeton: Princeton University Press.

Cottrell, A. (1993) "Keynes's theory of probability and its relevance to his economics", *Economics and Philosophy* 9: 25–51.

Court, R. (2000) "The Lucas critique: did Phillips make a comparable contribution?", in R. Leeson (ed.) *A.W.H. Phillips: Collected Works in Contemporary Perspective*, Cambridge: Cambridge University Press.

Croome, D. and Johnson, H. (eds) (1970) *Money in Britain 1959–1969*, London: Oxford University Press.

Cross, R. (ed.) (1988) *Unemployment, Hysteresis and the Natural Rate Hypothesis*, Oxford: Blackwell.

Cross, R. and Allan, A. (1988) "On the history of hysteresis", in R. Cross (ed.) *Unemployment, Hysteresis and the Natural Rate Hypothesis*, Oxford: Blackwell.

Cyert, R. (1991) Letter to authors, 9 December.

Cyert, R. and DeGroot, M. (1974) "Rational expectations and Bayesian analysis", *Journal of Political Economy* 82: 521–36.

Darity, W. and Young, W. (1995) "IS-LM: an inquest", *History of Political Economy* 27: 1–41.

Debreu, G. (1991) Letter to authors, 22 November.

Dornbusch, R. (1976a) "The theory of flexible exchange rate regimes and macroeconomic policy", *Scandinavian Journal of Economics* 78: 255–75.

—— (1976b) "Exchange rate expectations and monetary policy", *Journal of International Economics* 6: 231–44.

—— (1976c) "Expectations and exchange rate dynamics", *Journal of Political Economy* 84: 1161–76.

—— (1980) *Open Economy Macroeconomics*, New York: Basic Books.

Dorrance, G. (2000) "Early reactions to Mark I and II", in R. Leeson (ed.) *A.W.H. Phillips: Collected Works in Contemporary Perspective*, Cambridge: Cambridge University Press.

Eckaus, R. (1991) Letter to authors, 2 December.

Eisner, R. (1958) "Expectations, plans, and capital expenditures: a synthesis of ex post and ex ante data", in M. Bowman (ed.) (1958) *Expectations, Uncertainty, and Business Behavior*, New York: Social Science Research Council.

Enthoven, A. and Arrow, K. (1956) "A theorem on expectations and the stability of equilibrium", *Econometrica* 24: 288–93.

Evans, G. (1930) *Mathematical Introduction to Economics*, New York: McGraw-Hill.

Ezekiel, M. (1938) "The cobweb theorem", *Quarterly Journal of Economics* 52: 255–80.

Feiwel, G. (ed.) (1982) *Samuelson and Neoclassical Economics*, Boston: Kluwer.

Fellner, W. (1959) "Demand inflation, cost inflation and collective bargaining", in P. Bradley (ed.) (1959) *The Public Stake in Union Power*, Richmond: University of Virginia Press.

Fellner, W., Machlup, F. and Triffin, R. (eds.) (1966) *Maintaining and Restoring Balance in International Payments*, Princeton: Princeton University Press.

Ferber, R. (1953) "Measuring the accuracy and structure of businessmen's expectations", *Journal of the American Statistical Association* 48: 385–413.

—— (1955) "On the stability of consumer expectations", *Review of Economics and Statistics* 37: 256–66.

—— (1958) "The accuracy and structure of industry expectations in relation to those of individual firms", *Journal of the American Statistical Association* 53: 317–36.

Fisher, F. (1991) Letter to authors, 5 December.

Fisher, I. (1896) "Appreciation and interest", *American Economic Association Publications*, Series three, 2: 331–442.

Friedman, M. (1949) "Discussion of Hart and Marschak", *American Economic Review* 39: 196–9.

—— (1950) "Wesley C. Mitchell as an economic theorist", *Journal of Political Economy* 57: 465–93.

—— (1953) *Essays in Positive Economics*, Chicago: University of Chicago Press.

—— (ed.) (1956) *Studies in the Quantity Theory of Money*, Chicago: University of Chicago Press.

—— (1957) *A Theory of the Consumption Function*, Princeton: Princeton University Press.

—— (1958) "The supply of money and changes in prices and output", in J. Lehman (ed.) *The Relationship of Prices to Economic Stability and Growth*, papers submitted before the Joint Economic Committee, Washington: GPO.

—— (1961) Letter to A.W. Phillips, 14 February, Friedman Archives, Hoover Institution, correspondence, A.W. Phillips file.

—— (1962) *Price Theory: A Provisional Text*, Chicago: Aldine.

—— (1966) "What price guideposts?", in G. Schultz and R. Aliber (eds) *Guidelines: Informal Controls and the Market Place*, Chicago: University of Chicago Press.

—— (1968a) "The role of monetary policy", *American Economic Review* 58: 1–17.

—— (1968b) "Factors affecting the level of interest rates", in D. Jacob and R. Pratt (eds) *Savings and Residential Financing*, Chicago: US Savings and Loan League.

—— (1976) *Price Theory*, Chicago: Aldine.

—— (1977) "Inflation and unemployment: Nobel lecture", *Journal of Political Economy* 85: 451–72.

—— (1993) Letter to authors, 25 August.

Friedman, M. and Savage, L. (1952) "The expected utility hypothesis and the measurement of utility", *Journal of Political Economy* 60: 463–74.

Friend, I. and Bronfenbrenner, J. (1950) "Business investment programs and their realization", *Survey of Current Business* 30: 11–22.

—— (1955) "Plant and equipment programs and their realization", in *Short-Term Economic Forecasting*, Studies in Income and Wealth, Vol. 17, National Bureau of Economic Research, Princeton: Princeton University Press.

Frydman, R. (1982) "Towards an understanding of market processes: individual expectations, learning and convergence to rational expectations equilibrium", *American Economic Review* 70: 652–68.

Goldberg, M. and Frydman, R. (1993) "Theories consistent expectations and exchange rate dynamics" in H. Frisch and A. Worgoter (eds) *Open Economy Macroeconomics*, London: Macmillan.

—— (1996) "Imperfect knowledge and behaviour in the foreign exchange market", *Economic Journal* 106: 869–93.

Goodwin, R. (1947) "Dynamical coupling with especial reference to markets having a production lag", *Econometrica* 15: 181–204.

—— (1949) "Discussion of Hart and Marschak", *American Economic Review* 39: 199–201.

Grandmont, J. (1998) "Expectations formation and stability of large socioeconomic systems", *Econometrica* 66: 741–81.

Griliches, Z. (1991) Letter to authors, 4 December.

Grunberg, E. and Modigliani, F. (1954) "The predictability of social events", *Journal of Political Economy* 62: 465–78.

Haberler, G. (1958), "Creeping inflation resulting from wage increases in excess of productivity", in Committee for Economic Development, *Problems of United States Economic Development*, New York: Committee for Economic Development.

—— (1961) *Inflation: Its Causes and Cures*, Washington: American Enterprise Institute.

—— (1966) "Adjustment, Employment and Growth", in W. Fellner, F. Machlup, and R. Triffin (eds) *Maintaining and Restoring Balance in International Payments*, Princeton: Princeton University Press.

Hahn, F. (1952) "Expectations and Equilibrium" *Economic Journal* 62: 802–19.

—— (1991) Letter to authors, 4 December.

Hamouda, O. and Rowley, R. (1988) *Expectations, Equilibrium and Dynamics*, New York: St. Martin's Press.

Hansen, A. (1964) *Business Cycles and National Income*, New York: Norton.

Hansen, B. (1951) *A Study in the Theory of Inflation*, London: Allen and Unwin.

Hart, A. (1936) *Anticipations, Business Planning and the Cycle*, unpublished PhD dissertation, University of Chicago.

—— (1937a) "Anticipations, business planning and the cycle", *Quarterly Journal of Economics*, 51: 273–97.

—— (1937b) "Failure and fulfillment of expectations in business fluctuations", *Review of Economic Statistics* 19: 69–78.

—— (1940a) "Uncertainty and inducements to invest", *Review of Economic Studies* 8: 49–53.

—— (1940b) [1951]) *Anticipations, Uncertainty and Dynamic Planning*, Studies in Business Administration of the University of Chicago, 11.1 [Kelley Reprint].

—— (1942) "Risk, uncertainty and the unprofitability of compounding probabilities", in O. Lange, F. McIntyre, and T. Yntema (eds) *Studies in Mathematical Economics and Econometrics*, Chicago: University of Chicago Press.

—— (1945) "Model building and fiscal policy", *American Economic Review* 35: 531–58.

—— (1948) *Money, Debt and Economic Activity*, New Jersey: Prentice-Hall.

—— (1949) "Assets, Liquidity and Investment", *American Economic Review* 39: 171–81.

—— (1982) "Discussion" in P. Wachtel (ed.) *Crises in the Economic and Financial Structure*, Lexington, MA: Heath.

—— (1991) "Chronological account of Albert G. Hart's role in expectational economics", unpublished manuscript provided to authors by Hart, 6 and 9 September 1991; interview with Hart, 9 September 1991.

Hawtrey, R. (1939a) "Review of Hicks's *Value and Capital*", *Journal of the Royal Statistical Society* 102: 309–12

—— (1939b) "Reply to [Hicks's] notes on the review of 'Value and Capital' ", in Hawtrey Papers, Churchill College, Cambridge, File HTRY 10/54 [handwritten, 10 pages].

Hayek, F. (1928) "Das intertemporale gleichgewichtssystem der preise und die bewegungen des geldwertes", *Weltwirtschaftliches Archiv* 28.

—— (1931) *Prices and Production*, London: Routledge and Kegan Paul.

—— (1933 [1928]) *Monetary Theory and the Trade Cycle* (originally published as *Geldtheorie und Konjunkturtheorie*), translated by N. Kaldor and H. Croome, London: Jonathan Cape.

—— (1935) "Preiserwartungen, monetare storungen und Felhinvestitionen", *Nationalokonomisk Tidskrift* 73.

—— (1937) "Economics and knowledge", *Economica* (n.s.) 4: 33–54.
—— (1958) "Inflation resulting from downward inflexibility of wages", in Committee for Economic Development, *Problems of United States Economic Development*, New York: Committee for Economic Development.
—— (1972 [1960]) *A Tiger by the Tail*, London: Institute for Economic Affairs.
Heady, E. (ed.) (1961) *Agricultural Supply Functions*, Ames: Iowa State University Press.
Hicks, J. (1933 [1980]) "Gleichgewicht und Konjunktur", *Zeitschrift fur Nationalokonomie* 4: 441–55, translated by J. Hicks and B. Schechter, and published as "Equilibrium and the trade cycle", *Economic Inquiry* 18: 523–34; also partially translated by O. Morgenstern (1963).
—— (1939a) *Value and Capital*, Oxford: Clarendon Press.
—— (1939b) Letter to Hawtrey, 15 August; and attached "Notes on Hawtrey's review of 'Value and Capital'", in Hawtrey Papers, Churchill College, Cambridge, File HTRY 10/54 [typewritten, 4 pages].
Hirsch, A. and Lovell, M. (1969) *Sales Anticipations and Inventory Behavior*, Wiley: New York.
Holmes, J. (1995) Letter to authors, 10 November.
Holt, C. (1956) Letter to A.W. Phillips, 6 July, Letter provided by Holt to authors.
—— (2000) "Interactions with a fellow engineer-economist", in R. Leeson (ed.) *A.W.H. Phillips: Collected Works in Contemporary Perspective*, Cambridge: Cambridge University Press.
Holt, C., Modigliani, F., Muth, J., and Simon, H. (1960) *Planning Production, Inventories and Work Force*, Englewood Cliffs: Prentice-Hall.
Holt, C., MacRae, D., Schweitzer, S., and Smith, R. (1971) *The Inflation–Unemployment Dilemma: A Manpower Solution*, New York: Urban Institute.
Hood, W. and Koopmans, T. (eds) (1953) *Studies in Econometric Method*, New York: Wiley.
Hooton, F. (1950) "Risk and the cobweb theorem", *Economic Journal* 61: 69–80.
Hurwicz, L. (1946) "Theory of the firm and of investment", *Econometrica* 14: 109–36.
—— (1950) "Prediction for policy purpose", in T. Koopmans (ed.) *Statistical Inference in Dynamic Economic Models,* New York: Wiley.
—— (1951) "Comment", in *NBER Conference on Business Cycles*, New York: National Bureau for Economic Research.
Isard, P. (1995) *Exchange Rate Economics*, Cambridge: Cambridge University Press.
Jacob, D.P. and Pratt, R.T. (eds) (1968) *Savings and Residential Financing*, Chicago: US Savings and Loan League.
Johnson, H. (1970) "Recent developments in monetary theory – a commentary", in D. Croome and H. Johnson (eds) (1970) *Money in Britain 1959–1969*, London: Oxford University Press.
Jordan, J. and Radner, R. (1982) "Rational expectations in microeconomic models: an overview", *Journal of Economic Theory* 26: 201–23.
Kaldor, N. (1933–34) "A classificatory note on the determinateness of equilibrium", *Review of Economic Studies* 1: 122–36.
Kalecki, M. (1954) *Theory of Economic Dynamics*, London: Allen and Unwin.
Kendall, M. (ed.) (1968) *Mathematical Model Building in Economics and Industry*, London: Griffin.

Keuzenkamp, H. (1989) "The prehistory of rational expectations", Center for Economic Research, Paper No. 8931, Tilburg University, The Netherlands.

—— (1991) "A precursor to Muth: Tinbergen's 1932 model of rational expectations", *Economic Journal* 101: 1245–53.

Keynes, J.M. (1936) *The General Theory of Employment Interest and Money*, London: Macmillan.

—— (1971) *The Collected Writings of John Maynard Keynes*, Vol. 8: *A Treatise on Probability*, New York: St. Martin's Press.

Klamer, A. (1984) *Conversations with Economists*, Totowa, NJ: Rowman and Allanheld.

Klein, L. (1950) *Economic Fluctuations in the US, 1921–41*, New York: Wiley.

Knight, F. (1921) *Risk, Uncertainty and Profit*, Boston: Houghton-Mifflin.

—— (1941 [1963]) "The Business Cycle, Interest and Money: a methodological approach", *Review of Economic Statistics* 23. Reprinted in F. Knight, *On the History and Method of Economics*, Chicago: University of Chicago Press: 202–26.

—— (1951 [1963]) "The Role of Principles in Economics and Politics", *American Economic Review* 41. Reprinted in F. Knight, *On the History and Method of Economics*, Chicago: University of Chicago Press: 251–81.

Laidler, D. (1995) Letter to authors, 2 October.

Landreth, H. and Colander, D. (1994) *History of Economic Thought* (3rd edn), Boston: Houghton-Mifflin.

Lange, O. (1944a) *Price Flexibility and Employment*, Monograph no. 8 of the Cowles Commission, Bloomington: Principia Press.

—— (1944b) *The Stability of Economic Equilibrium*, Cowles Commission Papers, New Series, No. 8, Chicago: University of Chicago Press.

—— (1945 [1978]) *Price Flexibility and Employment*, Westport, CT: reprinted by Greenwood Press.

—— (1961 [1970]) "Forms of Supply Adjustment and Economic Equilibrium", in O. Lange, *Papers in Economics and Sociology: 1930–1960*, trans. P. Knightsfield, Polish Scientific Publishers: Warsaw and Pergamon Press: Oxford: 125–34.

Lebergott, S. (1991) Letter to authors, 2 December.

Leeson, R. (1998 [2003]) "The early Patinkin–Friedman correspondence", *Journal of the History of Economic Thought* 20: 433–48. Reprinted in Leeson (ed.), 2003.

—— (2000a) "Inflation, Disinflation and the Natural Rate of Unemployment: A Dynamic Framework for Policy Analysis", in *The Australian Economy in the 1990s*, Sydney: Reserve Bank of Australia: 2000: 124–75.

—— (ed.) (2000b) *A.W.H. Phillips: Collected Works in Contemporary Perspective*, Cambridge: Cambridge University Press.

—— (2000c) "A remarkable life", in R. Leeson (ed.) *A.W.H. Phillips: Collected Works in Contemporary Perspective*, Cambridge: Cambridge University Press.

—— (2000d) *The Eclipse of Keynesianism: the Political Economy of the Chicago Counter-Revolution*, London: Palgrave.

—— (ed.) (2003a) *Keynes, Chicago and Friedman*, London: Chatto and Pickering

—— (2003b [2000]) "Patinkin, Johnson, and the shadow of Friedman", *History of Political Economy* 32: 733–64. Reprinted in Leeson (ed.), 2003.

—— (forthcoming) *The Political Economy of the Inflation Unemployment Trade-Off*, Cambridge: Cambridge University Press.

Lehman, J. (ed.) (1958) *The Relationship of Prices to Economic Stability and Growth*, papers submitted before the Joint Economic Committee, Washington: GPO.

Leontieff, W. (1991) Letter to authors, 2 December.

LeRoy, S. and Singell, L. (1987) "Knight on risk and uncertainty", *Journal of Political Economy* 95: 394–406.

Lindahl, E. (1939) *Studies in the Theory of Money and Capital*, London: Allen and Unwin.

—— (1957) "Full employment without inflation", *Three Banks Review*, March: 27–40.

Lipsey, R. (1960) "The relation between unemployment and the rate of change of money wage rates in the United Kingdom 1862–1957: a further analysis", *Economica* 27: 456–87.

—— (1981) "The understanding of control of inflation: is there a crisis in macroeconomics?", *Canadian Journal of Economics* 14: 545–76.

—— (1993) Letter to authors, 19 February.

Loasby, B. (1986) "Competition and imperfect knowledge: the contribution of G.B. Richardson", *Scottish Journal of Political Economy* 33: 145–58.

Lovell, M. (1961) "Manufacturer's inventories, sales expectations, and the acceleration principle", *Econometrica* 29: 293–314.

—— (1986) "Tests of the rational expectations hypothesis", *American Economic Review* 76: 110–24.

—— (1991a) Letter to authors, 18 September.

—— (1991b) Letter to authors, 10 December.

Lucas, R. (1973) "Some international evidence on output–inflation trade-offs", *American Economic Review* 63: 326–34.

—— (1976) "Econometric policy evaluation: a critique", in K. Brunner and A. Meltzer (eds) *The Phillips Curve and Labor Markets*, Amsterdam: North Holland.

—— (1977) "Understanding business cycles", in K. Brunner and A. Meltzer (eds) *Stabilization of the Domestic and International Economy*, Carnegie–Rochester Conference Series in Public Policy, Amsterdam: North Holland.

—— (1980) "The Death of Keynesian Economics", *Issues and Ideas* Winter: 18–29.

—— (1981) "Tobin and monetarism: a review article", *Journal of Economic Literature* 19: 558–67.

—— (1984) "Robert E. Lucas, Jr.", in A. Klamer *Conversations with Economists*, Totowa, NJ: Rowman and Allanheld.

—— (1991) Letter to authors, 30 August.

Lucas, R. and Prescott, E. (1971) "Investment under uncertainty", *Econometrica* 39: 659–81.

Lucas, R.E and Rapping, L.A. (1969) "Real wages, employment and inflation", *Journal of Political Economy* 77: 721–54.

Lucas, R.E. and Sargent, T. (1978) "After Keynesian macroeconomics" and "Response to Friedman", *After the Phillips Curve: Persistence of High Inflation and High_Unemployment*, Boston: Federal Reserve Bank of Boston.

—— (eds) (1981) *Rational Expectations and Econometric Practice*, London: Allen and Unwin.

Machlup, F. (1942) "Competition, pliopoly and profit", *Economica* (n.s.) 9: 1–23, 153–75.

—— (1946) "Marginal analysis and empirical research", *American Economic Review* 36: 519–54.

—— (1952) *The Economics of Sellers' Competition,* Baltimore: Johns Hopkins University Press.

—— (1983) "The Rationality of 'Rational Expectations'", *Kredit und Kapital* 16: 172–83.

Malmgren, H. (1961) "Information, expectations and the theory of the firm", *Quarterly Journal of Economics* 75: 399–421.

Marschak, J. (1946) "Von Neumann's and Morgenstern's new approach to static economics", *Journal of Political Economy* 54: 97–115.

—— (1949) "Role of liquidity under complete and incomplete information", *American Economic Review* 39: 182–95.

—— (1950) "Rational behavior, uncertain prospects, and measurable utility", *Econometrica* 18: 111–41.

—— (1953) "Economic measurements for policy and prediction", in W. Hood and T. Koopmans (eds) (1953) *Studies in Econometric Method*, New York: Wiley.

Mason, E. (1952 [1951]) "Prices, costs and profits", in *Money, Trade and Economic Growth: Essays in Honor of John Henry Williams*, New York: Macmillan.

McChesney Martin, W. (1954) Letter to Chairman, Subcommittee on Economic statistics, US House of Representatives, 14 December, in *An Appraisal of Data and Research on Businessmen's Expectations about Outlook and Operating Variables*, Report of Consultant Committee on General Business Expectations, Joint Committee on the Economic Report, September 1955, Washington, DC: Board of Governors, Federal Reserve System.

Meade, J. (2000) "The versatile genius", in R. Leeson (ed.) *A.W.H. Phillips: Collected Works in Contemporary Perspective*, Cambridge: Cambridge University Press.

Meiselman, D. (1962) *The Term Structure of Interest Rates*, New York: Prentice-Hall.

—— (1963) "Bond yields and the price level: the Gibson Paradox Regained", in *Monetary Essays in Communication of the Centennial of the National Banking System*, Board of Governers, Federal Reserve System: Washington, DC.

—— (1995) Letter to authors, 15 November.

Meltzer, A. (1982) "Rational expectations, risk, uncertainty, and market responses" in P. Wachtel (ed.) *Crisis in the Economic and Financial Structure*, Lexington, MA: Heath.

Metzler, L. (1941) "The nature and stability of inventory cycles", *Review of Economic Statistics* 23: 113–29.

Mills, E. (1954–55) "Expectations, uncertainty and inventory fluctuations", *Review of Economic Studies* 22: 15–22.

—— (1957a) "The theory of inventory decisions", *Econometrica* 25: 222–38.

—— (1957b) "Expectations and undesired inventory", *Management Science* 4: 105–9.

—— (1959a) "Uncertainty and price theory", *Quarterly Journal of Economics* 73: 116–30.

—— (1959b) "Expectations, inventories, and the stability of competitive markets", paper presented at Econometric Society Meeting, 30 December 1959.

—— (1961) "The use of adaptive expectations in stability analysis: comment", *Quarterly Journal of Economics* 75: 330–5.

—— (1962) *Price, Output and Inventory Policy: A Study in the Economics of the Firm and Industry*, ORSA Publications No. 7, New York: Wiley.

—— (1971) "Review of *Sales Anticipations and Inventory Behavior* by A. Hirsch and M. Lovell", *Journal of Economic Literature* 9: 107–8.
—— (1991a) Letter to authors, 26 September.
—— (1991b) Letter to authors, 6 November.
—— (1991c) Letter to authors, 27 November.
—— (1995) Interview with Warren Young, 11 January.
Modigliani, F. (1949) "Discussion of Hart and Marschak", *American Economic Review* 39: 201–8.
—— (1991) Letter to authors, 16 September.
—— (1995) "Modigliani", in W. Breit and R. Spencer (eds) *Lives of the Laureates*, Cambridge, MA: MIT Press.
Modigliani, F., Abel, A., and Johnson, S. (eds) (1980) *The Collected Papers of Franco Modigliani*, Cambridge, MA: MIT Press.
Modigliani, F. and Cohen, K. (1958 [1955]) "The significance and uses of ex ante data", in M. Bowman (ed.) *Expectations, Uncertainty, and Business Behavior*, New York: Social Science Research Council.
—— (1961) *The Role of Anticipations and Plans in Economic Behavior and their Use in Economic Analysis and Forecasting*, Studies in Business Expectations and Planning, Urbana: University of Illinois.
Modigliani, F. and Sauerlender, O. (1955) "Economic expectations and plans of firms in relation to short-term forecasting", in *Short-Term Economic Forecasting*, Studies in Income and Wealth, Vol. 17, National Bureau of Economic Research, Princeton: Princeton University Press.
Modigliani, F. and Weingartner, H. (1958) "Forecasting uses of anticipatory data on investment and sales", *Quarterly Journal of Economics* 72: 23–54.
—— (1959) " 'Comment' and 'reply' ", *Quarterly Journal of Economics* 73: 169–72.
Moore, H. (1929) *Synthetic Economics*, New York: Macmillan.
Morgenstern, O. (1928) *Wirtschaftsprognose*, Vienna: Springer.
—— (1935 [1963]) "Perfect foresight and economic equilibrium", translated by author from *Zeitschrift fur Nationalokonomie* 5, Research Memorandum No. 55, Econometric Research Program, 30 April 1963, Princeton University.
Muth, J. (1957) "Special topics in mathematical economics", syllabus for lectures at the University of Chicago, Spring term, in *Milton Friedman Papers*, Hoover Institution, Stanford [Box M (1957)].
—— (1959a) "Rational expectations and the theory of price movements", paper presented at Econometric Society Meeting, 30 December 1959.
—— (1959b) "Rational expectations and the theory of price movements", Carnegie Institute of Technology and ONR Research Memorandum, No. 65.
—— (1960 [1981]) "Estimation of economic relationships containing latent expectations variables", in R. Lucas and T. Sargent (eds) *Rational Expectations and Econometric Practice*, London: Allen and Unwin.
—— (1961) "Rational Expectations and the Theory of Price Movements", *Econometrica* 29: 315–35.
—— (1985) "Properties of some business forecasts", *Eastern Economic Journal* 11: 200–10.
—— (1991a) Letter to authors, 2 August.
—— (1991b) Letter to authors, 5 September.
—— (1991c) Letter to authors, 14 October.
—— (1992a) Letter to authors, 28 February.

—— (1992b) Letter to authors, 14 March.

Nash, J. (1950) "The bargaining problem", *Econometrica* 18: 155–62.

Negishi, T. (1964) "Stability and rationality of extrapolative expectations", *Econometrica* 32: 649–51.

—— (1965) *Kakahu to Haibun no Riron* (*Theory of Price and Allocation*) Tokyo: Toyokeizi.

—— (1991) Letter to authors, 9 December.

Nerlove, M. (1958) "Adaptive expectations and the cobweb phenomena", *Quarterly Journal of Economics* 72: 227–40.

—— (1961a) "Time series analysis of the supply of agricultural products", in E. Heady (ed.) *Agricultural Supply Functions*, papers from the 1960 Conference, Des Moines: Iowa State University Press.

—— (1961b) "Reply to Mills", *Quarterly Journal of Economics* 75: 335–8.

—— (1983) "Expectations, plans, and realizations in theory and practice", *Econometrica* 51: 1251–79.

—— (1991a) Letter to authors, 19 November.

—— (1991b) Letter to authors, 19 December.

—— (1992) Letter to authors, 5 January.

Nerlove, M. and Bessler, D. (2001) "Expectations, information and dynamics" in B. Gardner and G. Rausser (eds) *Handbook of Agricultural Economics*, Vol. I, Amsterdam: Elsevier.

Nerlove, M., Grether, D., and Caravalho, J. (1979) *Analysis of Economic Time Series: A Synthesis*, New York: Academic Press.

Newman, P. (1951) "A note on 'Risk and the cobweb theorem'", *Economic Journal* 61: 334–41.

Niehans, J. (1975) "Some doubts about the efficacy of monetary policy under flexible exchange rates", *Journal of International Economics* 5: 275–82.

—— (1990) *A History of Economic Theory*, Baltimore: Johns Hopkins University Press.

O'Donnell, R. (1989) *Keynes: Philosophy, Economics and Politics*, New York: St. Martin's Press.

Patinkin, D. (1948 [1951]) "Price flexibility and full employment", *American Economic Review* 38, reprinted with corrections in F. Lutz and L. Mints (eds) *Readings in Monetary Theory*, American Economic Association, Homewood: Irwin.

—— (1949 [1981]) "Involuntary unemployment and the Keynesian supply function", *Economic Journal* 59, reprinted in D. Patinkin, *Essays on and in the Chicago Tradition*, Durham: Duke University Press.

—— (1954) "Keynesian economics and the quantity theory", in K. Kurihara (ed.) *Post-Keynesian Economics*, New Brunswick: Rutgers University Press.

—— (1956) *Money, Interest, and Prices: An Integration of Monetary and Value Theory* (1st edn), Evanston: Row Peterson.

—— (1959) "Keynesian economics rehabilitated: a rejoinder to Prof. Hicks", *Economic Journal* 69: 582–7.

—— (1965) *Money, Interest, and Prices: An Integration of Monetary and Value Theory* (2nd edn), New York: Harper and Row.

—— (1973 [1981]) "Frank Knight as Teacher", *American Economic Review* 63, reprinted in D. Patinkin *Essays on and in the Chicago Tradition*, Durham: Duke University Press.

—— (1981) *Essays on and in the Chicago Tradition*, Durham: Duke University Press.

—— (1983) "Multiple discoveries and the central message", *American Journal of Sociology* 89: 306–23.

—— (1989) *Money, Interest, and Prices: An Integration of Monetary and Value Theory* (2nd edn, abridged), New York: Harper and Row.

Pesaran, H. (1987) *The Limits to Rational Expectations*, Oxford: Blackwell.

Phelps, E. (1966) "Optimal employment and inflation over time", *Cowles Paper*, No. 214, Yale University.

—— (1967) "Phillips curves, expectations of inflation and optimal unemployment over time", *Economica* 34: 254–81.

—— (1968) "Money wage dynamics and labor market equilibrium", *Journal of Political Economy,* 76: 678–711.

—— (ed.) (1970) *Microeconomic Foundations of Employment and Inflation*, London: Norton.

—— (1991) Letter to authors, 7 October.

Phelps Brown, E. and Weber, B. (1953) "Accumulation, productivity and distribution in the British economy 1870–1938", *Economic Journal* 63: 263–88.

Phillips, A. (1950) Letter to Dennis Roberston, 19 September, Robertson papers, Trinity College, Cambridge.

—— (1955) Letter to Milton Friedman, 22 January, Friedman Archives, Hoover Institution, correspondence, A.W. Phillip file.

—— (1956) Letter to Charles Holt, 15 October, Letter provided by Holt to authors.

—— (1957) "Stability of 'self-correcting' systems", paper presented at Robbins Seminar, LSE, 21 May, Phillips Archives, London School of Economics.

—— (1958) "The relationship between unemployment and the rate of change of money wages in the United Kingdom, 1861–1957", *Economica* 25: 283–99, reprinted in Leeson (ed.), 2000b.

—— (1961) Letter to Milton Friedman, 25 January, Friedman Archives, Hoover Institution, correspondence, A.W. Phillip file.

Phillips, P. (2000) "The Bill Phillips legacy of continuous time modeling and econometric model design", in R. Leeson (ed.) *A.W.H. Phillips: Collected Works in Contemporary Perspective*, Cambridge: Cambridge University Press.

Pigou, A. (1912) *Wealth and Welfare*, London: Macmillan.

—— (1927) *Industrial Fluctuations*, London: Macmillan.

—— (1933) *Theory of Unemployment*, London: Macmillan.

Prescott, E. (1977) "Should control theory be used for economic stabilization", in K. Brunner and A. Meltzer (eds) *Optimal Policies, Control Theory and Technology Exports*, Carnegie–Rochester Series on Public Policy, Amsterdam: North Holland.

—— (1991) Letter to authors, 30 September.

Radner, R. (1967) "Equilibre des marches a terme et au comptant en cas d"incertitude", *Cahiers d"Econometrie* (CNRS, Paris) 4: 35–52.

—— (1968) "Competitive Equilibrium under Uncertainty", *Econometrica* 36: 31–58.

—— (1991) "Intertemporal General Equilibrium" in L. McKenzie and S. Zamagni (eds) *Value and Capital Fifty Years Later*, proceedings of an IEA Conference, London: Macmillan.

—— (1992) Letter to authors, 5 February.

Ramsey, F. (1931) *The Foundations of Mathematics*, London: Routledge and Kegan Paul.

Redman, D. (1992) *A Readers Guide to Rational Expectations*, Aldershot: Elgar.

Rees, A. (1970) "The Phillips curve as a menu of policy choice", *Economica* 37: 223–38.

Report of the Washington Meeting, 28–30 December, 1959 (1960), *Econometrica* 28: 670–708.

Richardson, G. (1953) "Imperfect knowledge and economic efficiency", *Oxford Economic Papers* 5: 136–56.

—— (1956) "Demand and supply reconsidered", *Oxford Economic Papers* 8: 113–26.

—— (1959) "Equilibrium, expectations and information", *Economic Journal* 69: 223–37.

—— (1960) *Information and Investment,* London: Oxford University Press.

—— (1964) *Economic Theory*, London: Hutchinson.

—— (1990) *Information and Investment* (2nd edn), London: Oxford University Press.

—— (1993) Interview with Warren Young, 25 January.

Robbins, L. (1952) Letter to Milton Friedman, 4 March, Friedman Archives, Hoover Institution, correspondence, L. Robbins file.

—— (1976) *Political Economy: Past and Present: A Review of Leading Theories of Economic Policy*, London: Macmillan.

Robertson, D. (1950) Letter to James Meade, 27 August, Robertson papers, Trinity College, Cambridge.

Rosenstein-Rodan, P. (1930) "Das zeitmoment in der mathematischen theorie des wirstschaflichen gleichgewichtes", *Zeitschrift fur Nationalokonomie* 1: 129–42.

—— (1934) "The role of time in economic theory", *Economica* (n.s.) 2: 77–97.

—— (1936) "The coordination of the general theories of money and price", *Economica* (n.s.) 3: 257–80.

Rousseas, S. (ed.) (1968) *Inflation: Its Causes, Consequences and Control*, Wilton, CT: Kazanjian Economics Foundation.

Samuelson, P. (1941) "The stability of equilibrium: comparative statics and dynamics", *Econometrica* 9: 97–120.

—— (1957) "Intertemporal price equilibrium: a prologue to the theory of speculation", *Weltwirtschaftliches Archiv* 79: 181–221.

—— (1965) "Proof that properly anticipated prices fluctuate randomly", *Industrial Management Review* 6: 41–9.

—— (1968) "What classical and neoclassical monetary theory really was", *Canadian Journal of Economics* 1: 1–15.

Samuelson, P. and Solow, R. (1960) "Analytical aspects of anti-inflation policy", *American Economic Review* 50: 177–204.

Sargent, T. (1991) Letter to authors, 17 September.

—— (1993) *Bounded Rationality in Macroeconomics*, Oxford: Oxford University Press.

—— (1996) "Expectations and the non-neutrality of Lucas", *Journal of Monetary Economics* 37: 553–48.

Sargent, T. and Wallace, N. (1976) "Rational expectations and the theory of economic policy", *Journal of Monetary Economics* 2: 169–83.

Saulnier, R. (1963) *The Strategy of Economic Policy*, New York: Fordham University Press.

Schmidt, C. (2002) "Hayek, Morgenstern and game theory", in J. Birner, P. Garrouste, and T. Aimar (eds) *F.A. Hayek as a Political Economist*, London: Routledge.

Schotter, A. (1992) "Oskar Morgenstern's contribution to the development of the theory of games", in E.R. Weintraub (ed.) *Toward a History of Game Theory*, annual supplement to *History of Political Economy* 24, Durham: Duke University Press.

Schuh, G. (1991) Letter to authors, 3 December.

Schultz, G. and Aliber, R. (eds) (1966) *Guidelines: Informal Controls and the Market Place*, Chicago: University of Chicago Press.

Sent, E. (2002) "How (not) to influence people: the contrary tale of J.F. Muth", *History of Political Economy* 34: 291–319.

Shackle, G. (1940a) "Nature of inducement to invest", *Review of Economic Studies* 8: 44–8.

—— (1940b) "Reply to Hart", *Review of Economic Studies* 8: 54–7.

Sheffrin, S. (1983) *Rational Expectations* (Cambridge Surveys of Economic Literature), Cambridge: Cambridge University Press.

Simon, H. (1945) "Review of Von Neumann and Morgenstern's *Theory of Games and Economic Behavior*", *American Journal of Sociology* 50: 558–60.

—— (1954) "Bandwagon and underdog effects and the possibility of election predictions", *Public Opinion Quarterly* 18: 245–53.

—— (1955) "A behavioral model of rational choice", *Quarterly Journal of Economics* 69: 99–118.

—— (1957) *Models of Man*, New York: Wiley.

—— (1958 [1955]) "The role of expectations in an adaptive or behavioristic model", in M. Bowman (ed.) *Expectations, Uncertainty and Business Behavior*, a conference held at Carnegie Institute of Technology, 20–27 October 1955 under the auspices of the Committee on Business Enterprise Research, New York: Social Science Research Council.

—— (1959) "Theories of decision-making in economics and behavioral science", *American Economic Review* 49: 253–83.

—— (1976) "From substantive to procedural rationality", in S. Latsis (ed.) *Method and Appraisal in Economics*, Cambridge: Cambridge University Press.

—— (1978a) "Rationality as process and as product of thought" [Ely lecture], *American Economic Review* 68: 1–16.

—— (1978b) "On how to decide what to do", *Bell Journal of Economics* 9: 494–507.

—— (1979) "Rational decision making in business organizations" [Nobel lecture], *American Economic Review* 69: 493–513.

—— (1982) *Models of Bounded Rationality: Economic Analysis and Public Policy*, Vol. 1, Cambridge, MA: MIT Press [Collected works – *CW*].

—— (1991a) *Models of My Life*, New York: Basic Books.

—— (1991b) Letter to authors, 2 December.

Smith, V., Suchanek, G. and Williams, A. (1991 [1988]) "Bubbles, crashes, and endogenous expectations in experimental spot asset markets", in V. Smith (ed.) *Papers in Experimental Economics*, Cambridge: Cambridge University Press [originally published in *Econometrica* (1988)].

Solberg, W. and Tomilson, R. (1997) "Academic McCarthyism and Keynesian economics: the Bowen controversy at the University of Illinois", *History of Political Economy* 29: 55–81.

Solow, R. (1968) "Recent controversy on the theory of inflation: an eclectic view", in S. Rousseas (ed.) *Inflation: Its Causes, Consequences and Control*, Wilton, CT: Kazanjian Economics Foundation.

—— (1978) "Summary and Evaluation", in *After the Phillips Curve: Persistence of High Inflation and High Unemployment*, Boston: Federal Reserve Bank of Boston.

—— (1991) Letter to authors, 2 December.

Soros, G. (1987) *The Alchemy of Finance*, New York: Simon and Schuster.

—— (1995) *Soros on Soros: Staying Ahead of the Curve*, New York: Wiley.

Stone, J. (1968) "Economic and social modeling", in M. Kendall (ed.) *Mathematical Model Building in Economics and Industry*, London: Griffin.

Stigler, G. (1941) "Review of Hart's *Anticipations, Uncertainty and Dynamic Planning*", *American Economic Review* 31: 358–9.

—— (1942) *The Theory of Competitive Price*, New York: Macmillan.

—— (1946) *The Theory of Price* (1st edn), New York: Macmillan.

—— (1952) *The Theory of Price* (2nd edn), New York: Macmillan.

—— (1961) "The economics of information", *Journal of Political Economy* 69: 213–51.

—— (1966) *The Theory of Price* (3rd edn), New York: Macmillan.

—— (1987) *The Theory of Price* (4th edn), New York: Macmillan.

Swade, D. (2000) "The Phillips machine and the history of computing", in R. Leeson (ed.) *A.W.H. Phillips: Collected Works in Contemporary Perspective*, Cambridge: Cambridge University Press.

Tinbergen, J. (1930) "Bestimmung und deutung von angebotskurven: ein beispiel", *Zeitschrift fur Nationalokonomie* 1: 669–79.

—— (1932) "Ein problem der dynamik", *Zeitschrift fur Nationalokonomie* 3: 169–84.

—— (1933) "The notion of horizon and expectancy in dynamic economics", *Econometrica* 1: 247–64.

—— (1934) "Annual survey of significant developments in general economic theory", *Econometrica* 2: 13–36.

—— (1937) *An Econometric Approach to Business Cycle Problems*, Paris: Hermann and Co.

—— (1956) *Economic Policy: Principles and Design*, Amsterdam: North Holland.

Tobin, J. (1949) "Discussion of Hart and Marschak", *American Economic Review* 39: 208–10.

—— (1968) "Discussion", in S. Rousseas (ed.) *Inflation: Its Causes, Consequences and Control*, Wilton, CT: Kazanjian Economics Foundation.

—— (1972) "Inflation and unemployment", *American Economic Review* 62: 1–18.

Vines, D. (2000) "The Phillips machine as a progressive model", in R. Leeson (ed.) *A.W.H. Phillips: Collected Works in Contemporary Perspective*, Cambridge: Cambridge University Press.

Von Mises, L. (1974 [1958]) *Planning for Freedom*, Chicago: Libertarian Press.

Von Neumann, J. (1928) "On the theory of games of strategy", translated from German, *Mathematische Annalen* 100.

Von Neumann, J. and Morgenstern, O. (1944) *The Theory of Games and Economic Behavior*, Princeton: Princeton University Press.

—— (1947) *The Theory of Games and Economic Behavior* (2nd edn), Princeton: Princeton University Press.

Watts, H. (1991) Letter to authors, 10 December.

Wold, H. (1968) "Model building and scientific method: a graphical introduction", in M. Kendall (ed.) (1968) *Mathematical Model Building in Economics and Industry*, London: Griffin.

Wold, H. and Jureen, L. (1953) *Demand Analysis*, John Wiley: New York.

Yamey, B. (2000) "The famous Phillips curve article: a note on its publication", in R. Leeson (ed.) *A.W.H. Phillips: Collected Works in Contemporary Perspective*, Cambridge: Cambridge University Press.

Young, W. (1987) *Interpreting Mr Keynes: The IS-LM Enigma*, Oxford and Boulder: Blackwell-Polity and Westview Press.

—— (1989) *Harrod and his Trade Cycle Group: The Origins and Development of the Growth Research Program*, London and New York: Macmillan and New York University Press.

—— (1991) "The early reactions to *Value and Capital*", *Review of Political Economy* 3: 289–308.

Young, W. and Darity, W. (2000) "Reply to Ahiakpor", *History of Political Economy* 32: 915–18.

—— (2001) "The early history of rational and implicit expectations", *History of Political Economy* 33: 773–813.

Young, W. and Lee, F. (1993) *Oxford Economics and Oxford Economists*, London: Macmillan.

Zellner, A. (ed.) (1968) *Readings in Economic Statistics and Econometrics*, Boston: Little, Brown and Co.

—— (1991) Letter to authors, 30 December.

Index

For Product Safety Concerns and Information please contact our EU
representative GPSR@taylorandfrancis.com
Taylor & Francis Verlag GmbH, Kaufingerstraße 24, 80331 München, Germany

www.ingramcontent.com/pod-product-compliance
Ingram Content Group UK Ltd.
Pitfield, Milton Keynes, MK11 3LW, UK
UKHW011017180926
475701UK00004B/784
* 9 7 8 0 4 1 5 6 4 7 3 2 8 *